The

MARRIAGE
FIRST AID KIT

The
MARRIAGE
FIRST AID KIT

Bryce Kaye PhD

Bascom Hill Books
Minneapolis, Minnesota

Bascom Hill Books
212 3rd Avenue North, Suite 290
Minneapolis, MN 55401
612.455.2293
www.bascomhillpublishing.com

ISBN - 978-0-9820938-8-7
ISBN - 0-9820938-8-8
LCCN - 2009925537

Order Fulfilment Center:
Blu Sky Media Group, Inc.
P.O. Box 10069
Murfreesboro, TN 37129
Toll Free: 1.888.448.BSMG (2764)
Phone: 615.995.7072
Fax: 615.217.3088 E-Mail: info@bluskymediagroup.com

Illustrations by: Bob Ostrom, Richard Carbajal and Bryce Kaye

Final editing by Dr. Ruth Russell-Stern

Cover Design by Alan Pranke
Typeset by Kristeen Wegner

Printed in the United States of America

BASCOM
HILL BOOKS

This book is dedicated to my wife Helen

who has been my best teacher about intimacy

And also to Ernest, Joe, Hobart, Nicholas

and all the other boys who grew up enough to pass it on.

Contents

Preface

Let me start by saying that I've had this bug, even as a child. I remember reading a personal biography that I wrote for a sixth grade homework assignment. There it was, plain as day. I wanted to be a psychologist! In my high school science fair, I won runner-up for my sensory deprivation experiments using an isolation chamber that my father helped me build. Even to this day, my former classmates remember me as the weird kid who ran the strange experiments on other students down in my "dungeon." Before I graduated, I was mentored by a prominent scientist, Dr. Jay Shirley, who pioneered research in the field of sensory deprivation. When I was 17, I spent one incredible summer floating in his sensory deprivation tanks and watching the brain waves of his sleeping subjects. The bug bit me hard and early. Of course, I'm referring to my intense desire to explore the depths of our human mind and our human experience.

In 1977, I completed my graduate program in personality at the University of Illinois at Champaign-Urbana. At that time, personality was viewed as consisting of the sum of relatively consistent traits. Since that time, my odyssey through various fields of study has given me a more complex and dynamic picture. I gradually came to view people as being a mosaic composition of sometimes conflicting self-parts. There were several experiences that promoted this evolution. My training in EMDR (Eye Movement Desensitization and Reprocessing) psychotherapy taught me about different types of memory and different types of learning. My training in the treatment of dissociative disorders increased my understanding of how personality is composed of an internal family of self-parts. For a number of years I independently studied both recent brain imaging works and decades of old Soviet research in reflexology and psychophysiology. I successfully used this information to evolve some of my techniques for treating trauma and dissociation. The Soviet research by Evgenii Nikolaevich Sokolov was an important early influence. Later influences include Hobart Mowrer's work on socialization, Michael Posner's work on attention, Michael Apter's Reversal Theory, and especially C. Robert Cloninger's work on personality and levels of consciousness.

All the while I studied personality, reflexes, and emotion, I also worked with couples and read the usual literature about relationships. Since emotions are reflexes, my background served me well by enabling me to see the underlying reasons why many couples develop emotional difficulties. I was also struck by how so much was missing from the literature about relationships. Few authors write about how people can train their emotions over time. Most self-help authors recommend fast food strategies that purport quick and easy solutions. One popular author exhorted his readers to exorcise their "bad spirits" by choosing to just give them up. Very few of the authors are willing to say that some relationship problems can only be fixed with repetitive training. Other relationship problems require the more arduous task of integrating personality. Knowledge and will power alone are inadequate for many problems. However, that kind of honesty usually doesn't sell many books.

I've come to believe that people can understand shame, inhibition and reactive defenses without referring to them as "bad spirits." There are better methods than willful exorcism for working with emotion. But how would I convey these dynamics and methods to readers such as you? That was my challenge in writing this book. I decided to adopt a vernacular style of writing, complete with slang, contractions, and self-disclosure. I even consciously violate some grammatical rules similar to the way I normally speak. My intent is to make you more comfortable to face some of the challenging insights that you might find a bit unsettling. I also hope that the cartoons, illustrations, stories and out-takes will provide you with some periodic relief from what is an inherently complex topic. We're not going to take the fast food approach. Even though the title of this book uses a first aid metaphor, we're going to be honest. Many problems can be helped quickly, but others require protracted care.

I should mention something about the therapy cases in this book. For obvious reasons, I couldn't reveal any identifying information about my clients. I also couldn't risk their emotional injury if they were to specifically identify themselves in the text. For these reasons, no case story is real in the sense that it depicts a specific case. Most are "Frankensteined" together from several cases as well as my own personal material. The case material has been sufficiently mixed and shuffled so that my clients are well protected. However, the case stories in this book are *psychologically true* in that they closely resemble the stories and dynamics that I see in many couples.

I hope you find the book helpful and enjoyable.

- *Bryce Kaye, October 2008*

Chapter One

The Great No-No

If you picked up this book because of difficulties in your own relationship, then your simple act indicates two important things about you. First, it signifies that you're feeling some pain. I'm not talking about the obviously physical, just-cut-your-finger kind of pain. I'm talking about the kind of pain that hurts somewhere in your spirit. But even though your pain is spiritual, it can still be described in physical terms. If your relationship is in acute crisis, then the pain may feel sharp and piercing. Or if your frustration is chronic, then the pain may feel like a dull ache or perhaps an empty, hungry kind of sensation. Another possibility is a stifling, suffocating kind of feeling. You may associate it with your chest, your heart, the pit of your stomach, the back of your neck or even your head. But wherever you feel it, whether it's subtle or intense, you're still feeling some form of pain. You may also have the disturbing sense that your life wasn't supposed to turn out this way. You started this marriage with dreams that you hoped your relationship would fulfill. You wanted love, respect, and a soul-mate with whom you could share life's experiences. You not only wanted to be nurtured, but you wanted to be appreciated for being the loving person you always knew you could be. You wanted the opportunity to let your love unfold, and now you fear that the opportunity is passing you by.

The second thing indicated by your picking up this book is that you still harbor hope. Maybe it's not a lot of hope. Perhaps it's just the tiniest fraction of hope. However, it's still hope. After all, this isn't a book about divorce. And you're probably also hoping that this book will offer you tools that are effective. You want this help to be practical because you're concerned about results. You're probably tired of skimming the plethora of self-help books that speak of the eight principles of this and the six rules of that and yet still leave you with unsettling questions of how to get from here to there. Questions like: "HOW can we work on emotional intimacy when all we do is fight?" or "HOW can we rebuild this relationship when all I ever get from my partner is the feeling that *I'm never enough?!*" You want practical interventions for these kinds of problems.

This book will be practical. You can expect to learn the following:

- Strategies to build love and affection in your relationship

- Exercises to bring you and your partner into closer intimacy

- The <u>real</u> hidden dangers to your relationship that most people don't know

- Common myths that hinder your relationship

- Destructive relationship patterns such as enmeshment, conflict avoidance and the delinquent helper syndrome

- Six types of conflict including three that can actually help your relationship

- Strategies to manage conflict more effectively

- A strategy for structuring finances in a way that reduces conflict

- Methods to keep your relationship in balance in order to maintain passion

- Exercises to strengthen the healthy parts of your personality that support your relationship

In this book you can thoroughly learn all of these things. Your perspective and understanding may become crystal clear. And even if your vision does become clear, and even if you do see your past mistakes as well as a new and better path, even if all this happens and you rely on this knowledge, but only on this knowledge to help you, then you will probably fail. That's right. I said "Fail." Not that I want you to fail. In fact I'm going to do my very best to help you succeed. But if you rely only on your insight and knowledge to help you, then you will probably fail because the biggest obstacle we all face in emotional intimacy isn't our ignorance. It's our fear. And we usually fear ourselves most of all.

> The biggest obstacle we all face in emotional intimacy isn't our ignorance. It's our fear. And we usually fear ourselves most of all.

If you're going to successfully improve your marriage, then you will need more than insight and knowledge. You will need both courage and faith to help you face whatever it is that you fear most about yourself. In addition to teaching you new behavioral strategies, this book will help prepare you for the emotional challenge ahead. Most self-help relationship books shy away from this topic. A few exhort you to get your external life in order and focus on your interests or behavior. That's OK advice, but I'm more concerned that you get your internal life in order. Strategies for changing a relationship usually fail a person who is emotionally unprepared. In fact, most surveys of couples in marriage counseling indicate that only one-third of them report significant improvement. My interpretation of this disappointing percentage is that most people unknowingly sabotage their attempts at marital improvement because of emotions they don't understand or even recognize. The reason why these emotions are so enigmatic is because we don't want to talk about them. We're afraid of them. We collectively keep each other in the dark because we all act as if these emotions don't exist. The emotions to which I'm referring are shame and the fear of shame. And an interesting thing about shame is that, like mold, it grows in the dark.

If there were ever such a thing as a worldwide conspiracy it would be this: that no one wants to admit that we are all influenced by fear throughout our everyday existence; that along with the more positive emotions of love, curiosity, sensuality, and the desire for pride and self-actualization, we are similarly motivated by the fear of shame that both nips at our heels and narrows our vision of opportunity. But a conspiracy involves people getting together to covertly communicate. What do we call it when people are secretive about something and they covertly _discourage_ communication? An "un-conspiracy" or a "reverse conspiracy"? Somehow, those don't quite work. For want of a better name, I've resigned myself to calling it "The Great No-No."

At this point, let me invite you to get a more personal feel for this subject. The following self-exam lists personal challenges that we all experience. The items are framed in the first- person plural, "we" instead of "you," because I don't want you to feel individually targeted as if the rest of the human race doesn't struggle along with you. If you're feeling especially adventurous you might ask your partner to take the exam too and then compare your answers.

The "No-No" Self-Exam

Instructions:

Make a copy of this self-exam so you can write on it. For each item, write in a "0", "1", or "2" to indicate how frequently or how relevant each item pertains to you. Do not leave any fields blank and use the following key:

0 = Never or irrelevant   1 = Occasionally   2 = Frequently or very relevant

_____   We don't try something new because it might feel "silly."

_____   We keep focusing on responsibilities because they seem all important.

_____   We don't take time out to wonder and explore.

_____   We consider fun to be unimportant.

_____   We hesitate to pursue our heart's desire because of other people's opinions.

_____   We don't request a "favor" from our partner because it might be turned down..

_____ We accuse our partner of being selfish or insensitive so that we don't have to make a request.

_____ We only comply with our partner's expectations and don't initiate our own plans.

_____ We don't take time in our day to daydream about possibilities.

_____ We raise our voice while arguing.

_____ We focus on how to change our partner instead of how we want to be.

_____ We try to show how independent and strong we can be.

_____ We focus on our partner's forgiveness instead of devising a plan for correction.

_____ We refuse to acknowledge a mistake even though we're aware of it.

_____ We wake up in the morning and initially feel uneasy and anxious for no reason.

_____ We make pride the most important thing in our lives.

_____ We insist that our partner must change before we do.

_____ We don't tell our partner when we're angry because it wouldn't be nice.

_____ We try to make our partner love us by sacrificing what is important to us.

_____ We make approval more important than truth.

_____ We let obligations control our time and we don't schedule any time for enjoyment.

_____   We use sarcasm against our partner.

_____   We dredge up old resentments as weapons.

_____   We invade or refuse our partner's privacy.

_____   We fail to establish our own privacy.

_____   We hold onto unrealistic hope in a truly abusive
relationship.

_____   We hide lying or dishonest behavior.

_____   Total (Sum up the column when finished)

The purpose of this exercise is to let you confront some of your own defenses, not for you to obtain a score. However, I know that some of us have a proclivity towards measuring things. Therefore, let me interpret the following. If you score 5 or less then you are exceptionally free from shame. If your score is above 40 then you're experiencing a lot of defensive inefficiency. Your life may be disrupted in a number of spheres. Most people score between 10 and 40.

All of the items in the preceding self-exam involve our fear of shame. We fear and try to avoid the shameful sense that we're unimportant and undeserving. Shame takes different forms, but in this context shame is the pain of feeling that we're somehow _less_ than we're supposed to be. While guilt is a negative feeling about what we do, shame is a devaluation of who we are. It's about whether we perceive our very existence as being important. And this fear of shame plays out on a totally symbolic level. In our civilization we no longer fear cave bears and saber-toothed tigers. Instead, we fear a loss of stature in our own self-evaluation. Because this self-evaluation isn't about physical reality, what we're really afraid of is something symbolic. We fear the symbolic meaning of a mistake or a poor performance. We're afraid of the negativity in a disapproving glare, a sarcastic comment, a forgotten date, a raised eyebrow, or a bored sigh. We're vulnerable to the personal devaluation inherent in a raised voice, an irrelevant interruption in the middle of our talking, inequity in our relationships, having another person tell us how we feel, the lack of pursuit by people who say they still love us, and especially, the experience of not being asked about what we want or how we feel.

Most of us don't fully appreciate how much the fear of shame operates in our lives. One reason is that we don't like to admit to others anything about ourselves that doesn't enhance our popularity. Neither fear nor shame is a hot commodity in the interpersonal status market. We want others to view us as always being motivated by positive emotions. Nobody wants to talk about or acknowledge the negative feelings. And when we adopt a distorted popular image of what being human *should* be, we often fool ourselves about how we really are. We want to fit in. We want to be *normal*. We don't like to admit, even to ourselves, that we have feelings of vulnerability. The irony in this situation is a truth that sounds like a weird distortion of Roosevelt's famous admonition about fear. Only this one goes: "We're afraid of our shame and ashamed of our fear."

We're afraid of our shame and ashamed of our fear.

Another reason why we're unaware of this fear is that the feeling can be very subtle. It's usually not the experience of strong terror. It's more often a subtle anxiety that leads us to react quickly before we even become consciously aware of its presence. Think about whether you've ever experienced the following:

- You didn't apply for a position or opportunity because you thought you might fail even though there was a possibility for success. (Probable dynamic: You were afraid that failure would give you the shameful feeling that you didn't deserve what you wanted.)

- Another person directly expressed their deep affection to you. You became uneasy and changed the subject. (Probable dynamic: You were afraid that you wouldn't be able to say or do *the right thing* in return. You were afraid of feeling the shame of an inadequate emotional performance.)

- You didn't pursue a private interest of yours because your partner wanted you to stay home. You really didn't want to stay home, but you didn't want to cause any friction. (Probable dynamic: You were afraid of your partner's wrath and/or accusations of your "selfishness." More importantly, you were afraid of having to use your anger in a conflict. You were afraid that your own anger would make you appear "ugly," "selfish," or "unloving.")

- At the end of the day, you think about taking your coffee cup to a private place to relax and think. However, you quickly change your mind because you have more important things to do. (Probable dynamic: If this happens only occasionally, you may just have pressing responsibilities. If it happens more frequently, you're probably afraid of letting go of responsibilities because they're your defense. Your activity helps you to avoid feeling shame. Although you tell yourself that relaxing would be too indulgent, you're actually afraid to stop depending on the pride of your accomplishments to prop up your self esteem. You feel driven to accomplish things because you're afraid of otherwise feeling unimportant or inadequate. Many people start feeling depressed and unimportant if they stop frenetic activity.)

- When you sometimes get up in the middle of the night, you think about how quickly time is passing in your life. You feel some of your losses more acutely. You fear your eventual death and you wonder about the overall meaning of your life. However, you never get around to sharing these thoughts and feelings with your partner. (Probable dynamic: You're afraid of talking about these feelings and sounding silly or weird. You're afraid of your partner's possible reaction if you do share them. You're afraid that they might confirm that you're abnormal or perhaps intellectually inadequate for attempting such a weighty discussion.)

- You're feeling taken for granted in your relationship. You indict your partner for a long list of past wrongs. You demand that they change instead of requesting that they sit down with you for some planning sessions. (Probable dynamic: You covertly fear that you're too dependent. You're afraid that being too dependent makes you weak and defective. Therefore, you don't want to appear weak by making a request. By making demands, you get to view yourself as strong. By indicting your partner for past transgressions, you feel superior as well. More importantly, you protect yourself from having to experience your personal request being ignored or refused. Demands don't hurt as much if they're rejected. A request that is ignored, forgotten, or refused is more likely to stir up the sense that you expected too much for yourself. After all, it seems that if you were truly important to your partner, he/she would have been more responsive.)

• You indict your partner for not being sufficiently available to the children. You omit the fact that you especially want your partner to be available for you. (Probable dynamic: You're ashamed of your dependence again. You're afraid of a more obvious and therefore more painful rejection compared to the subtle one you're already experiencing. While it's true that you're concerned about your children's welfare, it's also true that the children are to some extent being used as surrogates for your own needs. You're afraid of feeling ashamed if those needs were to be exposed and somehow ridiculed.)

• You want your partner to "help" with the household responsibilities. You're critical of him/her not helping enough. (Probable dynamic: It doesn't occur to you that you're holding onto authority by delegating tasks. You're unaware that you're treating your partner as a subordinate. You resist the loss of authority that would come if you and your partner were to negotiate task ownership as equals. After all, it seems that the household *should* be your domain. There's a subtle threat of covert shame if you were to give away some of your control. Your partner's different performance standards might negatively reflect on you. Besides, you don't like giving up your pride in organizing all aspects of your household.)

All of these situations involve the fear of shame. It's subtle and usually operates well beneath our awareness. What's more relevant to the current discussion is that our fear of shame inhibits our ability to change our behavior or negotiate changes from our partner. If our relationship were a car, then our fear of shame would be the emergency brake stuck on hold. We might move forward, but slowly and with great resistance.

> **If our relationship were a car, then our fear of shame would be the emergency brake stuck on hold.**

In the following vignette, these dynamics are revealed in a case example that happened to coincide with my writing on this topic. It's a good illustration of how the fear of shame can influence our interactions far beyond our awareness. Read about Jim and Marie's argument and see if you can recognize any of yourself in their story.

Anatomy of a Quarrel

Jim and Marie came for marriage counseling to increase communication and to help Jim with his anger management. Jim acknowledged that he had a short fuse and that his raging was sometimes excessive. This was probably accentuated by his tall imposing physique. He was able to keep his anger in check for his upper management position but didn't do nearly so well at home. In contrast, Marie was a rather quiet and petite school teacher. She had emotionally distanced herself from Jim for the past several years. The couple had been married twenty-two years and had three children, two of whom were still living at home. There had been no separations, no violence, and no history of affairs. After a half-dozen counseling sessions, the couple reported their relationship and communication had improved.

During one of the later counseling sessions, Marie reported a recent quarrel. The whole family, except for the oldest son, had been together for their big Sunday dinner. Jim and Marie were both upset about having recently discovered that their oldest son had lied to them. Their son had taken a loan from them under false pretenses. He did not have a job as he had previously led them to believe. During dinner, Jim ranted and raved about the situation. Although Marie was similarly upset about the news, she was also concerned that their other two children were present. For her, Jim's angry venting was spoiling a ritual for family cohesion. Having already learned a new tool from counseling, she asked Jim to come with her into a different room so they could speak privately. Marie then told Jim that his anger was excessive and that it was spoiling the dinner. Jim protested that he was entitled to his feelings and she shouldn't demand that he give them up. Marie persisted in telling him that she wanted the family to enjoy their dinner without further turmoil. When they returned to dinner, Jim was quiet for a while but eventually lapsed back into his angry venting. After dinner, Jim and Marie continued to quarrel. However, there was now a new dimension. Marie tried to escape Jim's anger by retreating to another room, but Jim followed her and kept up his diatribe. Marie then tried to escape to yet another room, but again, Jim followed her and kept on ranting. Even though Jim was criticizing their oldest son, and not Marie, she had had enough and didn't want to hear any more. The quarrel ended only because Marie had to leave the house to drive one of the children to an event.

During the counseling session when Marie and Jim were describing their recent quarrel, I made some interesting observations. One was that Jim didn't want to talk about the issue of Marie's right to retreat from his anger. When I kept raising the issue, Jim's facial expression was that of bored disgust. He frequently diverted attention back to the subject of his son's deceit. This was a seemingly unintelligent response from a man who works in the field of human relations. I wondered what was really going on with him. Marie then brought up the fact that Thanksgiving dinner was coming up soon, and she didn't want a repeat performance of Jim's anger at the table. I invited Marie to work that out with Jim right there in the session. She then turned to Jim and bluntly stated that she didn't want the issue of the oldest son raised at all during Thanksgiving dinner. She then turned back to me as if she had finished what I had asked her to do. At that point something became clear to me; I asked her about how she had negotiated for Jim's cessation of ranting during the initial dinner incident. When she had him off privately in the side room, did she actually ask him for a *commitment*? Marie's first response was one of confusion. After a bit more discussion, she finally admitted that, "No," she had not asked Jim for a commitment. I then asked Marie to turn toward Jim and actually *ask* if he would agree to refrain from angry expressions during Thanksgiving dinner. Marie halted and turned back with a bewildered look on her face. The ensuing dialogue went something like this:

"This is hard. I'm afraid I'm going to be hurt if he actually says he's going to do something and then he doesn't. That would be really painful."

I replied "Yes, I imagine that might be true. And you don't feel as vulnerable if you merely state your expectations or throw them at him, do you? You feel a lot more vulnerable asking him for something when there is the possibility that you might be rejected. I would guess that if he rejects your request outright, you'd take it like a personal rejection — or am I wrong about that? Tell me if I'm wrong."

"No, you're right. That's how I would feel."

I continued: "That's really a kind of fear. It's subliminal, but your reaction just now indicates that you don't ask for a commitment because you're afraid. Do you think that the same fear was operating that night after the dinner incident? I mean you didn't actually ask for a commitment then either, did you?"

Marie leapfrogged ahead a giant step at this point. We had had previous discussions about the possible influence of her uninvolved parents when she was a child.

"You know it makes sense, but I guess I really didn't realize it at the time. Remember we talked before about how, when I was growing up, my parents really ignored me. I didn't ask for anything back then either. I couldn't. There was no use."

I tried to give her support. "And it helped you to survive. It really fit back then. It helped you survive it without getting overwhelmed with pain. For a little child, feeling rejected is almost like feeling annihilated. But that was then and this is now. Go ahead and *ask* Jim this time. Ask him about Thanksgiving dinner. Give him an opportunity to get involved with you."

Marie proceeded to do a commendable job of asking for a commitment. Of course by this time Jim was really primed. He even articulated back to her his detailed commitment to avoid expressing anger during Thanksgiving dinner. Marie was pleased.

The next part of the session focused on how Marie had previously complicated the original argument by confronting Jim about his anger's intensity. I pointed out to Marie that Jim's poor timing in ranting during dinner was a valid issue. However, why was she evaluating its intensity? I confronted Marie and told her that Jim had been correct in one respect. He accurately perceived that she was trying to invalidate his feelings. When she did that, she ruined her chances for successfully confronting him about his timing. Marie was perplexed. She asked if it really was all right for him to get so angry and loud.

"Did he attack you at all? Did he hit you or threaten you? Did he use sarcasm on you?" I asked.

"No," Marie replied.

"Well, if the two of you had been alone and he wasn't intruding on your privacy and there was no dinner to be disrupted, then would you have been OK with his intense anger? You know, if the two of you were just privately discussing your son?"

She replied, "I really don't know, probably not. I don't think I'll ever feel comfortable when he gets like that. Is it really OK for him to get like that? I really don't know. I'm not sure I really know what is normal or what I really should expect."

Marie's comment about not knowing normalcy was a surefire indicator that she was struggling with her past. We talked about her family background: that her parents yelled and sometimes got violent, that her mother often hit her, and the near absence of loving attention from either of her parents. Marie agreed that she associated Jim's intense anger and loud expression with the lack of safety she experienced as a child. We discussed how some people are relatively comfortable around their partner's intense anger because they've never experienced violence. She eventually accepted the interpretation that her parents' violence had left her over-reactive to her husband's non-violent anger. Marie and I discussed how she would need to accept her husband's anger. She would also need to learn how to retreat from Jim in situations where she felt too uncomfortable.

The remaining piece of the puzzle was Jim's tendency to follow and intrude on Marie's privacy whenever she wanted and needed to retreat. Even if Marie could accept that Jim had "a right to his feelings" (as he termed it), Jim was still programmed to block Marie's right to retreat in future conflicts. At this point, I figured that Marie's preceding disclosures might have made Jim less defensive. I decided to try a new tack.

"Jim, what's the story on your following Marie when she's trying to calm herself down?"

Jim thought for a moment before replying. "I just didn't want to leave it before she could understand. I could tell from what she was saying that she didn't understand the situation. I didn't want to end our discussion with a lack of understanding."

"But Jim, at that point she was no longer listening. She was hearing your anger and reacting to that instead of your ideas. You would never have gotten her to understand by continuing with your ranting, especially by violating her privacy."

"I know, I know. But you asked me what was going on back then and I told you. I had this very strong frustration that I wasn't being understood. I just couldn't leave it like that."

I took a chance. "So you couldn't leave it because that's a very painful feeling, an almost unbearable feeling for you …. not to be understood about something you feel strongly about….and then to be left, maybe that plays in there too. How about it, Jim? How about the possibility that you've felt that before?" I watched Jim closely because something about his demeanor indicated we were onto something important. I continued pressing. "Where does that come from? Who used to do that?" Jim's sudden stillness and inward gaze confirmed my hunch. "Who was it, Jim….who was it?" I waited and was determined to say nothing until Jim answered me.

In the tension of the moment, Marie's patience abandoned her first. She blurted out the answer for her partner, as is all too common among couples in counseling: "It's his dad! He used to tell me his dad would yell and scream and then leave home for days at a time."

By now, Jim was beginning to mobilize. He also probably didn't want his wife to continue talking authoritatively about his most vulnerable subject. He echoed Marie:

"It was my father. He was a bad drunk and he'd just take off for days, usually after he got real mad about something." He nodded while saying this, then became silent and continued with an inward expression with his eyes not focusing on anything around him. He remained still while I picked up the conversation.

"Let me guess at something, Jim. Back then, could you talk to him at all? Could you ever get him to understand you?

Jim's facial expression was saying a lot. In addition to the change in his facial color, the telltale glint of welling tears was beginning to show along his lower eye lids. By now his voice had become more "breathy" from painful emotion and the tightening in his diaphragm.

"No… I never could get him to listen…especially when he was angry. Everything came down from him but nothing could go back the other way. I didn't dare….not when he was angry. He was a real rage-aholic. An alcoholic and rage-aholic, too.

"So Dad would rant and rage and he would act in such a way that you never felt understood by him….and then he'd up and leave you. Is that how it was? Did I get that right?"

Jim didn't answer. He just sat there, teary-eyed, looking miserable.

I continued. "It's a heck of a coincidence, but you know it's really not a coincidence, don't you? I mean, you can't stand for Marie to leave you without your being understood. It has both elements there. You can't stand it when you're not understood, and you can't stand to be left. So you try to avoid that old awful feeling that you are worthless, unimportant, like a nothing, but you avoid it in a desperate kind of way. You continue raging and you don't allow Marie to have her privacy to collect herself. Tell me if I'm off-base."

Jim replied very solemnly: "No. You're not off-base. In fact, I think you're hitting the nail right on the head. I just never looked at it like that before. He continued to reflect. After a while he concluded, "I've got a lot to think about."

The rest of the session flowed with understanding and cooperation. We all now had a common model for what had really transpired during the day of the infamous dinner quarrel. The blaming had stopped and both Jim and Marie were now more receptive to each other. It was obvious that we had opened up issues for each that they would be examining for a long time to come. Before they left, I gave each of them an assignment to practice certain self-suggestions. I wanted them to consolidate their gains. A lot of additional work would be required, but we had established a good start.

The reason why I present this little vignette is to further clarify the biggest obstacles people face when attempting to change their own emotionally-rooted behavior. There's a good metaphor to help you with your understanding. Imagine that most of your relationship behaviors are like plants that have roots extending way down into deep emotions. You can't see all the roots but they're vitally important to what happens up above on the surface. In Jim and Marie's case, what can we conclude about some of their obstacles? Let's take that same question from a different angle. Let's suppose both Jim and Marie were not in counseling and were trying to improve their communication on their own. The central questions would then be the following:

1. What feelings would Marie have to endure if she were to start *asking* Jim to commit to suppressing his anger in certain situations?

2. What feelings would Marie have to endure if she were to start accepting that it's often OK for Jim to express his intense anger?

3. What feelings would Jim have to endure if he were to start accepting that it's OK for Marie to disagree and "not understand" his position?

4. What feelings would Jim have to endure if he were to start accepting Marie's retreat from his anger and her withdrawal to her privacy?

Taking it from the top, this is how I would answer the questions.

For #1 (Marie's asking Jim to commit to suppressing his anger in certain situations): Marie would have to wade through her fear that Jim would either refuse her request or possibly even ignore it. But it wouldn't be the actual refusal that she would fear. She would be afraid of triggering her old shame of feeling unimportant and worthless. She had originally felt that way about herself when her parents were self-absorbed and oblivious to her need for attention. She had worked many years to become a worthwhile and important human being. She didn't want her worst fears confirmed: that she's still the same little girl who isn't worth being noticed. It's important to note that even with full knowledge of her fear's origin, she will still have that fear. That's because insight and awareness don't prevent the triggering of painful shame in a person's memory. The latter is a neurological event. Insight can help modulate the feeling, but it doesn't prevent it. So, the simple version of my explanation is that Marie would have to endure the discomfort of subtle fear. The technical term is "anxiety," but it's still a type of fear.

For #2 (Marie's accepting that it's often OK for Jim to express his intense anger): Marie would have to endure fear from two sources. One is that she would fear the re-emergence of her feeling inadequate and defective as she had when her mother became violent. As a child, she made heroic efforts but could never be good enough to prevent the violence. By the same childish logic, she was never good enough to stop her parent's destructive fighting. For Marie to begin to accept Jim's intense anger, she might start feeling the same old shame that she is inadequate to bring about love and harmony in her family. Even with new conscious knowledge that anger has a valid place, Marie would have to endure discomfort. She would still be afraid that her feelings of defectiveness might re-emerge.

For #3 (Jim's accepting that it's OK for Marie to disagree and "not understand" his position): Jim would have to endure the fear that he's not sufficiently important to be noticed. He would have to endure the covert fear that he's once again letting himself be treated as an insignificant victim. As a child, he had to hide his thoughts and opinions. He couldn't afford triggering his father's rage and disappearance from the family. During these early years of hiding his symbolic self, Jim accumulated a great sense of weakness and unimportance. Now as an adult, he unconsciously fears the re-emergence of those old feelings. To start accepting Marie's disagreement would stir up the fear that she's ignoring him just like his father had. And that would stir up the fear that he's still weak and unimportant.

For #4 (Jim's accepting Marie's retreat from his anger and her withdrawal to her privacy): By now you can probably infer the answer from our past examples. Marie's withdrawal serves to stir up old emotions from when Jim's father disappeared for days. For Jim to start accepting Marie's privacy, he would have to covertly be afraid of feeling worthless and powerless. As a child, he felt worthless and powerless to prevent his father from abandoning the family for long stretches of time. It's not surprising that Marie's withdrawal into privacy threatens to trigger Jim's old shame. Jim is afraid of feeling that old pain. Again, it's probably not a conscious and obvious fear. It's probably a vague kind of anxiety. For Jim to be more accepting of Marie's privacy he would have to wade through that anxiety.

Now let's bring all of our discussion and all of these dynamics down to a simple conclusion. For Jim and Marie to successfully change their conflict behavior, they'll each have to endure fear and anxiety. It's like the popular adage: "No pain, No gain." As Jim and Marie change their behavior, each will be afraid of being overtaken by parts of themselves they're trying to leave behind. Knowledge, insight, and effort won't be enough. They'll also need courage and faith. The rest of us are no different in that regard.

At this point you may be thinking something like "Wait a minute. I didn't get beaten, I didn't have parents who raged, and I didn't have a parent who left for days at a time. My parents loved me and treated me well. All of this fear and shame stuff really doesn't apply to me." If this is what you're thinking, then you're only partially correct. You're probably not as encumbered with old traumas as many of the people who show up for counseling. But you're only partially correct because it's only a matter of degree. All of us (except the purest of psychopaths) pick up shame along the way.

I presented Jim and Marie's case here only because their dynamics were so simple and obvious. For many of us, the origins of our shame are subtle. We may have had the most perfect parents, yet we were still exposed to smaller traumas. We may have been exposed to the teasing of playmates, the occasions when our parents were too depressed or emotionally depleted to notice us, and times when we failed miserably to meet the expectations of our family and friends. We may also have unconsciously adopted the shame of our parents. Our parents may have been so ashamed of certain emotions that they never risked expressing them. For example, they may have been so afraid of anger that they never disagreed, argued, or forcefully negotiated among themselves. Perhaps they were loving parents, but they never touched or verbally expressed their affection. They may have felt so undeserving that they never took off time from work and responsibility to have fun. Throughout childhood we can't avoid vicariously picking up some of our parents' shame. The other way we pick up shame is from the history of our own relationships. Over time, spousal looks of disapproval, eye-rolls, criticisms, interruption of our sentences, and other minor intrusions can build up accumulated shame in our system. This relationship shame can trigger and combine with core shame from our childhood. The process can be gradual and very subtle, but powerful. In fact, it's powerful enough to knock our relationships out of balance.

The concept of balance is crucial if you're going to understand how to maintain a thriving relationship. This book will teach you how to keep such a balance. It will also teach you some of the things that you can do to successfully counter its greatest saboteurs: your own inhibition and fear of shame.

Chapter Two

The Structure of Vital Relationships

Maintaining a passionate, committed relationship is an extremely difficult challenge that most of us underestimate. If you look at it realistically you should really appreciate two things. First, you should realize that you're really trying to do something that isn't "normal." Although this statement sounds strange, consider that nearly one out of two marriages today will end in divorce. This means that nearly half of us are either getting divorced or are on the edge of a divorce, hiding our quiet frustration and discomfort from view. That's normal. What you should strive for is to have a better than normal relationship — a truly extraordinary relationship. If you merely want a normal relationship, why are you setting your sights so low? Try to appreciate that what you really want to have is a superior relationship that will demand extraordinary skill to accomplish.

The second thing you should realize is that you're expecting more emotional perks than previous generations have expected. For most of history, marriages have been more survival oriented. Even through the eighteenth century, emotional fulfillment in a marriage was not paramount. If none your children died and you got your crops in before winter, that was considered a pretty good year! You focused on helping each other survive. You went to church, feared God, and expected the big pay off after you died. You didn't have the luxury of worrying about spiritual fulfillment from your marriage. This latter expectation is a recent historical development. Having much higher marital expectations can create additional obstacles. If your relationship isn't going well, you now feel more shame. You can develop a sense of failure that you haven't been able to maintain an intoxicating, in-love state and where there's such shame, there's always the temptation to blame.

> **If you want to try for the brass ring of an enduring passionate relationship, you will need to learn how to cultivate and influence emotions over time.**

If you want to try for the brass ring of an enduring passionate relationship you will need to learn how to cultivate and influence emotions over time. These are not emotions that you directly control with your intellect. Emotions are actually reflexes and obey a different set of rules than voluntary behavior. You will need to learn these rules with a full appreciation that mere intellect is insufficient. Anyone who has struggled with a diet has experienced how emotion can defy intellectual control. You will need to learn the art of influence instead. Exercising influence means that you must be patient and smart. Instead of taking a bull-headed approach, you need to repetitively do things that gradually shift your emotions in a certain direction. It's like growing a plant. You don't just grab it and yank the plant up to its desired height. You supply sunlight, fertilizer, and water and protect the seedling from danger. Then you have to accept that the other processes that affect the plant are beyond your personal control. Growing love and affection is like this. You have to create the appropriate conditions for love and affection and be patient while other processes take over. If you can't ease your grip on control, then you are doomed. You will need to learn how to maintain a delicate balance, and you will also need to learn the fundamental components that must be maintained.

To grow a really great relationship, you need to jettison a very popular but destructive myth. Everyone will tell you that the very foundation of your relationship is love for each other. Are you ready to hear that it's not? Believing that this kind of love is your foundation can cause problems because it can lead to unrealistic expectations. There are things that are far more fundamental. Personal integrity and respect are more precious and elemental. To say that mutual love is the foundation of a great relationship is like saying that a roof is a good foundation for a house. It's the end stage and not the foundation. If you think mutual love is your foundation then you will expect it as your due. When your partner doesn't supply the love, you will be righteously indignant. You will perceive that they're betraying their responsibility to support the relationship with the "right" feelings. Then the blaming can and will start. Bad stuff! The truth is that love will repeatedly come and go over time.

I frequently see couples where the wife bitterly complains that her husband doesn't show affection. She shares her own frustration and indignation quite freely. Meanwhile, I can see the poor guy sulking in his chair as if his emotional impotence is revealed to the world. This angry focus on emotional production is really counter-productive. One metaphor would be that the wife might as well berate the husband for "not getting it hard enough!" The anxiety that the wife is generating by her emphasis on control will make the husband's emotional approach nearly impossible.

A number of years ago I experienced a humorous incident. I conceived what I thought was a clever metaphor to promote an "easy does it" attitude in some of my couples. I planned that at the end of a session I might give them a "gift" of a Chinese finger trap. These are the little straw tubes that are sometimes given as party favors. They trap your pinkies and winch down harder if you try to forcefully pull your hands apart. The trick is to relax and use minute movements to loosen its grip. I figured that this metaphor would amuse the couples and demonstrate how they were trying to force affection. I felt just a little proud at this uniquely clever intervention. However, when I went down to the local magic shop to buy a few dozen, the store owner informed me that they were all gone. He said, "Yeah, some lady came down here yesterday and bought a couple hundred. She said she was a marriage counselor or something like that." Now it could be interpreted that this was a divine lesson for my humility. However, the more relevant interpretation is that other therapists recognize the same problem when couples try to directly control emotional production. You need to be able to grow emotions patiently, like vegetables in a field. There's a science and a method to it. You need to learn it.

The Love-Based Relationship Model

To have a decent relationship, you need to get your priorities straight. If you don't, you will sink and drown. We're going to use this metaphor for several reasons, one of which is that your experience will be viscerally similar to drowning if you mismanage things. I have seen too many couples where one or both partners express a suffocating or choking feeling in their relationship. There's a physiological explanation to this that I'll explain later. For now, let's use an analogy.

When I was seven years old, my family would vacation each summer in the Catskill Mountains in New York. The resort we stayed at had a swimming pool where we would swim each afternoon. I was still not a proficient swimmer but could just keep my head above water if I used my swim fins and dog-paddled. I was just approaching the confidence level that I could do this without swim fins. One day, my brother asked if he could use my fins and I agreed, thinking that I would just swim around holding onto the edge of the pool. I did this for a while and started feeling more confident. I started believing that I had reached the stage when I could really swim. My brother was swimming down at the deep end of the pool and I made my way down to him. However, I made the mistake of getting too far from the edge and suddenly started taking in water and choking. I panicked. At this point, my brother ceased being my brother to me! He became a mere object that I could climb upon to get my next breath. It didn't matter that I loved him dearly. In fact, I no longer was aware of him as a person. I shoved him under while I clambered up on him to get higher. The only thing that mattered was my next breath. Fortunately, some nearby grown-ups noticed our predicament and pulled us both from the pool.

I often think of the above incident when I meet with couples who are tearing into each other. What exactly is happening with them? Both spouses usually seem like reasonable people until they get into their "STUFF." Then they start behaving like two drowning cats in the center of a pool, both clawing at each other to seek purchase. If we stay within the metaphor, it's apparent that their love for each other can't keep its head above water. That's the problem with a love-based relationship model. It puts emphasis on a feeling that you can only partially influence. The model doesn't point out other more functional priorities that can get your system re-stabilized when it's in trouble. If the love is temporarily removed, then you will have no way to keep your oxygen supply. It's as if you can't swim. Everything depends on having the love.

**Mr. and Mrs. Bartlett review the status
of their monthly household budget.**

To assist with our future discussion, let's switch to a new metaphor. Drowning is a good metaphor for how "The Great No-No" of shame and inhibition can destabilize relationship partners. The unconscious can slowly accumulate inhibition over the years and gradually suffocate our identity. Alternatively, it can paralyze us within seconds if we have to face our partner's intense disapproval. Either way, drowning or asphyxiation is a close metaphor. However, it's not a good metaphor for how we develop a vital relationship. We need a better metaphor that implies the appropriate sequencing of priorities. For this, we're better off visualizing our relationship like a house.

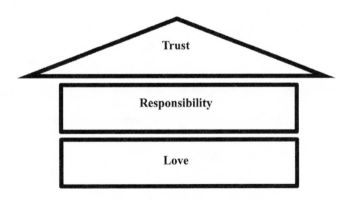

A love-based relationship model

In the house metaphor, the foundation is the basic material we lay down first. The picture of this model illustrates the commonly held view that the foundation of this relationship house should be passionate love. Many people hold a view similar to the lyric from an old disco song: "I want a love that's hot enough to last!" This hot passion is expected to motivate the other partner to remain responsible. Then trust is supposedly guaranteed. The conclusion from this belief is that you can trust passion. What a prescription for disaster! One reason why this belief is dangerous is because the "hottest" passion derives very easily from a process called "projective identification." Projective identification is produced mostly by your unconscious, magical expectations about being personally completed rather than any sober assessment of reality. There are some 12-step programs full of people trying to "kick the habit" of pursuing projective identification. They have well-established histories of repeatedly falling in love and producing dysfunctional relationships.

The Integrity-Based Relationship

Instead of a love-based relationship, let's consider an integrity-based relationship. When we base our relationship on integrity, it doesn't mean we give up love. It just means that passionate love isn't the constant basis for keeping a relationship stable. It's the final prize, but not the foundation. Picture the foundation of a healthy relationship as being like two strong pillars. Each pillar represents one partner's identity. You want each pillar to be strong and resilient. You certainly don't want any cracks. You want each pillar to have its own integrity. Each has to be able to stand on its own if necessary and have its own autonomous strength. If a sailing ship were to be constructed with strong cross-timbers, good caulking, good righting moment, and other features that ensure she won't break apart and sink, one could say she has good integrity. We could say the same of a house with a good foundation, strong main beams, and other features giving it sturdy resilience. In the present case we're not referring to high moral standards. We're referring to the strength of character that allows a person to adaptively use their own wisdom instead of raging, freezing, or avoiding issues altogether.

A simplified integrity-based relationship model

I should now confess that I've been purposely holding back from telling you something. I've been trying to prevent your possible confusion if I were to introduce a certain truth too early. This truth has to do with the real nature of integrity. Ordinarily, when we hear the word "love," we think of directing love towards another person. That's the same kind of love to which we were referring when we discussed love-based relationships. However, the truth is that integrity involves love as well. It's just a different kind of love. Integrity involves love being directed inward instead of outward. It's a more sophisticated form of loving. Some people call it spiritual love but it can also be called "heterocentric" love. It requires a higher level of consciousness than merely wanting to connect to a person. Because most people are so inclined to think of love as only directed outward, I thought it better to use the expression "integrity based" to name this relationship model. I wanted to help you to clearly distinguish it as being different from conventional love.

Integrity involves love being directed inward instead of outward.

Strong integrity is based on loving spiritual principles such as truth, responsibility, contribution, and creation, among many others. This framework is woven into a person's implicit world view even on an unconscious level. When facing an emotional challenge such as when our partner is becoming furious, it's our attachment to this heterocentric integrity that allows us to be psychologically autonomous and reasonable. Some people might refer to it as "maturity." Others might use the term "character." If we don't have it, we'll lose our autonomy and be knocked off balance into rage or emotional paralysis. Most people don't realize that strong integrity doesn't just regulate moral behavior; it also helps keep us safe! It gives us a type of *internal protection* against the bruising and shaming that can take place in a relationship. Our own internal attachments to the spiritual parts of self can literally block the drowning and suffocating feeling of shame. I'm not referring to a theological event. I'm talking straight neurology. (We're going to avoid a boring technical discussion here.) Just realize that when our integrity blocks shame, we're capable of thinking more maturely. We can then be more careful and respectful with our partner.

It makes sense that we prioritize safety next, even above affection. If we don't feel safe with our partner, then it's going to be very difficult to feel love. We might have a regressive or abusive dependence on them, but not a very high quality love. We need to know that we won't be abused or hurt, and our partner needs to feel the same way. Then we can grow affection on top of our mutual safety. If our historical behavior trains our partner to fear us, then their affection will be squashed by their instinctive concern for safety.

When we feel relatively safe with each other, we can then focus on cultivating the sweet stuff. This upper-most level of bonding depends on all the lower components in our house model. Integrity allows safety. Safety then allows us to build affection. It works in that order. However, it's still not enough to merely have integrity and safety. There are certain things you have to *do* in order to grow affection. These are various bonding behaviors that train the emotion of affection. Of course we're not referring to the in-love phenomenon that nature throws at us without any up-front costs. We're referring to the sentimental love that we have to earn through nurturing treatment of each other. If we have the integrity to keep the relationship safe and we keep nurturing each other in skilled and creative ways, then the resulting sentimental love can last a lifetime.

Components of Integrity

Integrity is one of the most complex subjects of this book. We'll be discussing how it's critical for maintaining the vitality of a relationship. It has 3 major dimensions which can be summarized as follows.

Emotional Resources: Emotional resources are personal memories or memory-held templates of other people that we find positive and empowering. There's evidence to suggest that positive memories, when activated, can trigger major dopamine circuits in such a way that we think and behave more maturely. These dopamine circuits project from the brain stem to the upper anterior cingulate, a part of the brain that mediates flexible and creative thinking.

Integration: Integration refers to the different parts of the brain and memory system working together with good coordination. Merely having good emotional resources doesn't mean that they'll be active when they're needed. Integration refers to the brain's ability to activate whatever useful parts of the memory system that are needed for a particular situation.

Maintenance of Autonomy: Maintenance of autonomy refers to certain actions a person must perform in order to keep his or her own separate identity alive and robust in a relationship. If a person doesn't perform these actions, then they'll gradually lose their sense of identity.

I sometimes give couples a personal example of when my own **emotional resources** once protected me from becoming emotionally overwhelmed. There have been other times when my integrity has failed, but on this one occasion it came through like a champ. It occurred during an incident involving my father while my wife and I were in the process of adopting a second child. My father was undoubtedly the most nurturing influence in my life. During my childhood he was very loving. He played with me, taught me to dance, and shared wonder with me to such an extent that I believe he gave me my greatest gifts in life. Yet everyone sometimes reaches their limitations. When I phoned him to tell him that we wouldn't be having our own biological child, it must have come as quite a shock. He had no doubt been hoping for a biological grandchild. I explained to him that my wife and I had gone through a number of medical procedures but our own biological child was just not going to be in the cards. He may have absorbed this OK, but he obviously wasn't prepared for what came next. I explained that we were adopting a 4-month-old little girl from Korea and that her name was Soh In Kim. At that point, he was facing the additional shock that not only would his grandchild be biologically unrelated, she wouldn't even be his own race. What I heard over the phone sounded like an angry snarl: "Why don't you just go ahead and adopt a black child!" This racial slur came from a man who had never before seemed preoccupied with racial issues. However, it was my own reaction that surprised me the most. Instead of becoming defensive or enraged, I felt sad. It wasn't so much a conscious deliberation but rather an implicit understanding that my father could not immediately appreciate what was most important.

If my internal frame of meaning could have talked at that moment it would have said the following:

1. The most important thing is to be creative with my life and to contribute the best way I can.

2. This promotion of another life (my new daughter) is a truly beautiful creation.

3. My father is overwhelmed about his own mortality and finiteness.

4. He just doesn't have the emotional resources to extend his loving this far beyond his own struggle.

5. It's sad that I have to grow beyond him here.

It's important to note that these were not explicit thoughts at the time but were all a part of an intuitive view of what was going on. This view allowed me to feel compassion for him, a sadness that he could not share our current joy, and a calm appreciation that I was connected to what was most important. If the same incident had occurred earlier in my development, I'm sure that I would have become enraged.

Although this story doesn't involve warring spouses, it's a clear example of how one's psychological connection to one's own emotional resources can stabilize a person to avoid over-reaction. More evidence for this dynamic comes from the results of doing therapy. There's a type of therapy I perform that I call conflict inoculation training (CIT). In CIT, clients are taught to practice accessing their emotional resources when threatened with shame. As a result of their practice, these clients have often been able to stop raging toward their spouses. Others have been able to stop freezing with emotional paralysis when facing disapproval.

Integration is the second essential component of personal integrity. Many people don't realize that all of our wisdom and information isn't "on-line" at any given time. Physicians will sometimes claim that they forget medication dosage levels when they're vacationing at the beach. Once they arrive at the hospital, see the white uniforms and smell the hospital antiseptic odors, their memory of dosages is much easier to recall. In a troubled relationship, partners may agonize with the knowledge that their raging behavior is sinking their marriage. It may grieve them terribly. However, in the heat of an argument they may no longer remember or care. Once the fight is over, they may grieve again. In more extreme cases, the person may have little or no memory of what he or she did while enraged. I had occasion to see this dynamic in a surprising way with one of my patients. She was a petite, middle-aged lady who was very polite and demure. One day I said something that very much riled her up. "You fucking son of a bitch!" was just one of a string of expletives she railed at me. I was surprised when she showed up at the following session. In this next session we talked for a while and it became apparent she wasn't going to bring up her rage in the previous session. I asked her, "By the way, what do you remember about our last session?" She casually replied, "Oh, nothing unusual…just one of our usual sessions, really." She had no recall of her previous rage. Further discussion did nothing to trigger more recall. It was apparent that the memory of what had happened was locked in a part of her memory that wasn't integrated with her usually-polite personality.

This is an example of dissociation, which is the opposite of integration. Dissociation means that we can't activate the parts of our memory that would otherwise help us out with the challenge at hand. We may have the resources, but we just can't get to them. When dissociation occurs, the brain isn't working efficiently. In extreme cases new personal identities may be associated with different emotional states. This was once called multiple personality disorder but has now been renamed Dissociative Identity Disorder (DID). While DID is infrequent, we all have some degree of dissociation. Integration helps us to act more rationally in a relationship. If we have the knowledge about how to behave constructively, then integration lets us retain the knowledge in awareness when we need it.

The third component of personal integrity is the **maintenance of autonomy**. We're really referring to psychological autonomy here. It doesn't mean adolescent defiance or proving that you can be physically apart from another. Psychological autonomy means the ability to have your own views about what's important. It also means that the ability to initiate your own behavior is based upon your own true desires and not how you will be evaluated by another. When individuals lose their autonomy in a relationship, they conform their behavior to what they think their partner expects and they lose touch with what they want themselves. If they carry this to the extreme, they may even claim that "they don't know who they are anymore." It's as if they start to feel like a footnote on somebody else's life. This is a kind of slow numbing of the soul that frequently kills relationships. It's the result of our natural inhibitory system that unconsciously prevents us from violating social norms. This system operates "under the radar" and has a known reflex in the brain that turns off other dopaminergic reflexes. However, when our inhibitory system repeatedly turns off our expression of positive desire for too long, we then lose a sense of who we are. This is the painful sense of losing ourselves that we call "depersonalization." A thirty-year career of counseling couples has convinced me that this kind of subtle depersonalization is the number one reason why many people have affairs. It's an easy way to escape feeling so numb by bringing back the sense of being alive. Clients will talk about how dreary they felt before they started their affairs. When I ask them about their conflict style, the majority give a picture that they are the more passive partner. It's rare when I find a person having an affair who has been assertively negotiating for what they want.

A person may start a relationship with insufficient autonomy from the beginning. For example, they may leap into a marriage directly from their dysfunctional family of origin. These marriages that involve rescuing an insecure person will often develop serious problems down the road. Even if the relationship start-up is more equal, a partner's autonomy can be gradually lost over time if one doesn't take precautions. The gradual accumulation of shame and inhibition can do this. If a person doesn't service his autonomy to prevent this corrosion, then he'll probably experience the suffocating or drowning feeling of depersonalization.

Let us recap this part of our discussion. The foundation of an integrity-based relationship is comprised of two individuals having their own solid integrity. This integrity is best defined as having emotional resources, the integration to activate those resources when needed, and the autonomy to keep exercising and protecting their emotional system from debilitating shame. There is a parallel between my emphasis on integrity as a foundation for relationships and the structure of 12-step programs such as Alcoholics Anonymous (AA). The twelve steps were developed as a spiritual program that strengthens moral and ethical resources within a person. As a result of doing "step work," participants in AA find increased ability to operate out of the higher-functioning, non-addictive parts of their personalities. In other words, they become more able to act autonomously from their drug. The spiritual integrity helps them to better "down-regulate" their emotional compulsion to drink. Similarly, a strong connection to one's own integrity can inoculate against the emotional challenges inherent in a long-term relationship. If we can connect to our higher consciousness, then we're less likely to fracture in the face of our partner's disapproval. If we can maintain this type of autonomy, then we don't have to react aggressively. We can behave respectfully.

Components of Safety

Once we feel safe and stable in our own integrity, then we're able to provide the safety our partner wants and needs. This safety consists of the two main components of respect and responsibility.

Respect is the appreciation that people have a right to be different from us. Even though they're different, respect means they are accorded deference without the assumption of their being inferior or invalid. The ability to respect is dependent upon one having sufficient integrity and autonomy within oneself. If a person is desperate to avoid shame and fails at his own autonomy, then respect will be an early casualty. Blaming starts at this level. Couples get into shame fights like tossing a hot potato back and forth. When this happens, both parties have failed the autonomy test. Each is unconsciously trying to avoid the shame of blame by putting the other down.

Respect is a fundamental resource that is most undervalued in relationships. It's much more valuable than passion. Passion is relatively cheap and can come without much work. Many people can form passion on a first date. There are others who are addicted infatuation junkies and hook up with new lovers every few weeks. In contrast to easy passion, respect is like platinum. In our metaphorical house of an integrity-based relationship, respect forms an important part of the relationship's safety. It doesn't mean submission or putting someone up on a pedestal. It really means that you're willing to value someone's differences. It's this fundamental appreciation of differences, the healthy humility of losing egocentrism, that is the precious respect that stabilizes good relationships. It also requires a maturity of character that many of us have failed to achieve. A partner who bullies or intentionally inflicts pain is depriving the relationship of a foundation of safety. As a result, affection will be nearly impossible.

Responsibility is the next part of the safety platform for a good relationship. It means that we keep agreements, tell the truth, keep the relationship safe from internal and external dangers, and carry out tasks that help the relationship survive and thrive. Actually, respect is a fundamental type of responsibility to the relationship. Because it involves providing safety from each other's aggression, it's even more basic than other forms of responsibility. It makes sense that you need to first guarantee that your partner is safe with you before you guarantee to protect the relationship from other outside dangers. However, there's a very good reason to view the responsibility dimension somewhat separately from respect. There are many respectful and "nice" people who repeatedly and passively expose their partners to dangers. Instead of being personally aggressive, they are loving and deferential. Meanwhile, they're failing to make mortgage payments, failing to get a job, and failing to ward off other dangers that can eviscerate a family's financial safety. They may also have affairs. What's tragic is that these people are hard to spot. People initially see that this kind of partner has respect and passion. They don't see the danger from <u>incapacity</u> until it's too late. They don't see it coming because they're looking for more aggressive disrespect. For this reason, we're going to stipulate that personal respect should be considered first, but that responsibility needs to be separately considered.

Bonding

When safety can be maintained, then our relationship is ready for the fun stuff. The process of bonding is in one way similar to farming. When someone farms, there's a period for planting and then there's a period for harvesting. The benefits don't all come right away. When we engage in nurturing attachment behavior, we're satisfying each other's need to feel connected and close. This involves many different ways to help our partner feel important to us, from saying "I love you," to offering touch, to asking about the meaning of their experiences, to delighting them with symbols of affectionate thoughtfulness. We'll be discussing the many creative things that couples can do to build affection. However, these behaviors should not be confused with the actual feelings of affection. Affection may not be immediate and may lag behind attachment behavior for a variety of reasons, especially when a couple is overcoming a painful history. The danger of lumping affection with attachment behavior is that it can lead to damaging expectations. When a person expects their partner to express a high level affection but it doesn't get expressed, then the expectations can backfire and cause anxiety.

Gabe and Shirley were a middle-aged couple who had been married twenty years. They had been very sexually active in the early years of their marriage. Prior to marrying, Shirley had also been very promiscuous with many men. She had a long history of prescription drug abuse that continued on into the marriage for many years. The couple's marital problems began to develop shortly after Shirley attained sobriety, started attending a 12-step group, and started individual therapy with another therapist. Her individual therapy sessions had uncovered that Shirley had suffered traumatic sexual abuse as a child. She had been clean from drugs and working on that trauma for about a year when I first saw them. What was initially presented by both of them was that Gabe was preoccupied with sex. I initially thought that the problem might be that Gabe had a sexual addiction. However, a number of exploratory sessions revealed a different picture. It was true that Gabe wanted sex with Shirley. He had been angrily complaining to Shirley that her sexual interest had shut down. But it was also true that he was not pervasively interested in porn or sex with other partners, as is the case with many sex addicts. What seemed to be happening in this situation is that Shirley had allowed herself to be sexually used for many years before marriage. She had been using sex to barter for attention and she had been using alcohol to sedate her anxiety. In other words, her sexual activity was actually pre-sexual. It had not involved her own sensual enjoyment; rather, it had been more of a tool to meet a pre-sexual need for approval.

To her credit, Shirley was struggling to graduate to a higher level of consciousness. She had attained sobriety. She was addressing her sexual trauma but had not yet developed the ownership of her own sensual sexuality. Gabe had unfortunately bought into her polarized view of him that he was depraved for wanting "too much sex." Actually, his problem was that he was just a bit concrete in the manner in which he wanted affection. He lamented to me not just about the absence of sex, but about the absence of affection in general. What made problems worse was that every now and then, he would erupt in frustration to Shirley about her lack of affection. Shirley then took these eruptions as confirmation that Gabe merely wanted to use her like all the previous men in her life. This dynamic became a recursive dance in their relationship. She polarized further and further into a defensive posture providing no real attachment. He polarized into angry frustration with occasional outbursts that confirmed that she wasn't safe. The more he tugged at her affection, the more she backed away and labeled him as abusive. This is an all-too-common dynamic in many relationships. I call it the "pursuer-evader syndrome." It's a dance that takes two. One way the pursuer-evader syndrome can start is when one partner unrealistically expects that the other can voluntarily produce affection.

> **One way the pursuer – evader syndrome can start is when one partner unrealistically expects that the other can voluntarily produce affection.**

Affection, like sexual desire, does not thrive well under command. Affectionate feelings are not voluntary. You can't consciously choose to feel affection any more than you can choose to produce erotic arousal. You need to create enough safety in your relationship so that conditions are conducive for both affection and sexual desire to emerge naturally at their own pace.

The final product of an integrity-based relationship is the affection itself. Like flame from a fire, it will wax and wane depending on the care shown for its basic requirements. It should be noted that this sentimental affection isn't the same as in-love infatuation that is alternatively based on unconscious projection. Unlike in-love infatuation, sentimental affection can be rekindled and maintained over many decades if handled with skill.

Putting the House Together

The following figure shows the integrity-based relationship model in more detail. Notice how it's hierarchical. In some ways it parallels Maslow's description of a hierarchy of needs. It makes sense that your oxygen supply over the next five minutes is a more basic and demanding need than getting food and shelter. Similarly, it makes intuitive sense that maintaining one's individual identity (through integrity operations) is more fundamental than enjoying affection. It also makes sense that experiencing safety (through mutual respect and responsibility) is a more fundamental need than affection. You can also see the hierarchical nature of this model by observing what happens when more basic levels are disrupted. For example, poor integration due to dissociating childhood trauma will often lead to disruption of respectful behavior in relationships. Similarly, poor emotional resources due to under-socialization will frequently lead to poor responsibility in adulthood. The safety operations in a relationship are naturally dependent upon an individual's integrity. Nurturing attachment behaviors won't build sentimental affection when safety operations are inadequate and leave a partner frightened and resentful. So, the rule of thumb needs to be: First things first!

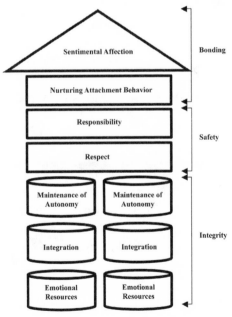

An integrity-based relationship model

35

Now that we've reviewed the integrity-based relationship model, please take a few minutes to complete the following quiz about your own intuitive model of relationships. The results of the quiz will help you to examine some of your own expectations. It might even help you pinpoint where you may want to make some revisions.

Your Own Relationship Beliefs: A Short Quiz

Answer *true* or *false* to each of the following. It's best if you give your initial quick response because that will more accurately reflect your behavior in your relationship.

1. _____ When my partner and I are in conflict, we're both obligated to work it out then and there.
2. _____ If my partner insults me, then he/she is to blame if I attack in retaliation.
3. _____ My own needs are minimal, and it is more important to meet my partner's needs.
4. _____ It's a duty in my relationship to avoid conflict whenever I can.
5. _____ It's a responsibility to love my partner.

6. _____ We should resolve arguments before going to bed.

7. _____ It's OK to lie to keep the peace if I know my partner will otherwise get very angry.
8. _____ I should be generous by deferring to my partner whenever we have conflicting needs.
9. _____ I feel selfish if I ask for what I want in a relationship.

10. _____ If my partner yells at me first, then it's good to yell back to show that he/she not the boss.
11. _____ I'm more comfortable doing chores and fulfilling responsibilities for my relationship than indulging in "fun."
12. _____ It's my partner's obligation not to leave me alone when I'm upset.

13. _____ One should provide sex to one's partner because it's a marital responsibility.

14. _____ If we're doing all the right things, then we should remain in-love forever.

15. _____ It's my obligation not to leave my partner alone if he/she's upset.

16. _____ All my sacrifices for my partner build upon my entitlement to be loved.

17. _____ Working together through all of life's problems is a great way to grow love and affection.

Now total up all the items for which you answered *true*. This total score indicates the degree to which your intuitive beliefs deviate from an integrity-based relationship model. Let's revisit each of the questions along with a brief explanation about what each answer actually reveals.

1. **When my partner and I are in conflict, we're both obligated to work it out then and there.** There's no such obligation, and this belief will actually prevent you from postponing a conflict until you both are more stable. When emotions are running too high, it's important to temporarily stop the argument and stabilize yourselves.

2. **If my partner insults me, then he/she is to blame if I attack in retaliation.** If you attack in retaliation, then you're starting to fight in order to avoid shame. The problem is that your partner will probably feel the same defensive need to counter your attack. Then you both are locked into a rigid blaming dance.

3. **My own needs are minimal. It's more important to meet my partner's needs.** One responsibility in a relationship is to keep a good, equitable balance of meeting both of your needs. Habitual self-sacrificing isn't responsible to either yourself or the relationship. Your relationship doesn't need you to covertly resent inequity or possibly even lose your sense of self.

4. **It's my duty in my relationship to avoid conflict whenever I can.** It's your responsibility to avoid unnecessary and unproductive conflict such as fighting to establish dominance. It's also your

responsibility to risk certain conflicts in order to rebalance your relationship.

5. **It's my responsibility to love my partner.** It's your responsibility to contribute to a safe environment that will allow affection to grow. It's not your responsibility to try to "squeeze" out emotions that you can't directly control. If you make love a responsibility, you will contaminate your love with guilt. It's a bad mix that can lead to emotional impotence. Don't do it.

6. **We should have arguments resolved before going to bed.** What a popular and destructive myth. (See the explanation for #1.)

7. **It's OK to lie to keep the peace if I know my partner will otherwise get very angry.** This behavior is very destructive. You will hurt your own integrity and accumulate shame. Over time, this will cause you to emotionally withdraw from the relationship. You will also destroy your partner's trust.

8. **I should be generous by deferring to my partner whenever we have conflicting needs.** It's a good idea to be generous and deferential to your partner much of the time. However, sometimes you need to hang tough for a need that's very important to you. It's your responsibility to weigh both your partner's need and your own from a heterocentric perspective. A heterocentric view considers the relative balance of both of your needs together.

9. **I feel selfish if I ask for what I want in a relationship.** This indicates the presence of core shame. If you feel selfish when you advocate for your own desires, then you have a serious threat to your relationship. Your relationship will fall out of balance when you gradually lose your sense of autonomy and identity. Your expression of self interest is necessary if you want to maintain your attraction to your partner.

10. **If my partner yells at me first, then it's good to yell back to show that he/she isn't the boss.** If you yell back, then you're not focusing on managing your own emotions. You've lost your autonomy by trying to prove that you're not the victim. By trying to

avoid shame you will only provoke damaging escalation in the fight.

11. **I'm more comfortable doing chores and fulfilling responsibilities for my relationship than indulging in "fun."** Keeping your "fun" self alive in the relationship is a responsibility of keeping the relationship balanced. If you turn into a depressive drone, then you won't be able to keep your passion alive, and you won't be attractive to your partner.

12. **It's my partner's obligation not to leave me alone when I'm upset.** No, no, no! It's your own responsibility to self-comfort. It's one of the basic ingredients of autonomy. It's nice if your partner can soothe you but sometimes he/she may feel too angry or hurt. Nurturing you when you're upset needs to be a completely voluntary and elective act by your partner.

13. **One should provide sex to one's partner because it's a marital responsibility.** The operative words here are "provide" and "responsibility." The implication is that it's not really for ourselves. We're now doing it as a chore and using it as a tool to achieve another goal to avoid the shame of otherwise being an inadequate spouse or incurring the wrath of the partner. In this way, the provision of sex as a responsibility is motivated by fear. It's a contamination of emotional reflexes that's damaging over time.

14. **If we're doing all the right things, then we should remain in love forever.** It's well known that the titanic "in-love" feelings originate more from projection and anticipation than reality. Within two to three years of living with each other, frustrating each other, stepping on each other's toes, and bruising each other, most couples are no longer "in-love." It's a nice condiment to be enjoyed while it lasts. However, the main fare is sentimental loving that must be earned through mutual respect and skilled relationship craft.

15. **It's my obligation not to leave my partner alone if he/she's upset.** (See # 12)

16. **All my sacrifices for my partner build upon my entitlement to be loved.** You are deserving of love, but you are not "entitled" to

demand love from anyone. If you feel entitled to be loved, you will be set up to feel rage whenever your expectations aren't met. Love isn't a bartered commodity. It's a feeling that needs to be freed from fear and shame. All your work in a relationship is to create conducive conditions for love to blossom on its own. If you miss one of the necessary conditions (e.g. respect for your partner's autonomy), love may not bloom. Even if you meet all of the conditions, your partner may still have limitations and be incapable of love.

17. **Working together through all of life's problems is a great way to build love and affection.** Actually, it's a relatively poor way to grow love and affection. Slaving away together is often necessary for survival. However, our emotional state during work makes it difficult to grow much affection. Affection is more easily grown in the free states of wonder, curiosity, and play.

I hope that this short self-examination has helped you to examine some of your intuitively-based assumptions about how relationships "should" run. Unfortunately, many people have impaired relationships because they expect constant love. Their relationships aren't integrity-based. In the next chapter, we'll be examining a relationship truth that is counterintuitive.

> **A vital relationship is one in which we take responsibility for keeping ourselves emotionally stable and don't look to our partner to guarantee he/she will feel constant love.**

In conclusion, a vital relationship is one in which we take responsibility for keeping ourselves emotionally stable and don't look to our partner to guarantee he/she will feel constant love. We accept that human nature is variable and that our partner is limited and imperfect. He or she won't constantly love us unconditionally. We are therefore prepared to "run off our own battery" when our partner shows disapproval and doesn't have the feelings we want. When we "run off the battery" of our integrity, we rely on these internal resources to help us behave respectfully and responsibly. This provides safety in the relationship. Because our resources are internal, we can behave this way even when our partner doesn't. In essence, we behave respectfully and responsibly because we love these values, and not because we love our partner. We also assume responsibility for nurturing mutual affection by initiating shared attachment experiences. We strive to gradually "grow" affection by positively influencing our relationship, not by exerting coercive control.

Chapter Three

Balance and Paradox

The fertile conditions for maintaining passion require that you and your partner satisfy two core human needs for each other. These needs are part of a profound human paradox. We all want to belong, to be connected, to be nurtured, and to be held in high regard in the mind of our partner. We want to be attached. On the other hand, we also want our privacy, to stand on our own two feet, to make our own choices, to be our own person, and to be autonomous and independent. Attached versus independent: they're opposites! We have opposing needs. In fact, we have a number of opposing needs. We want to relax, but we also want excitement. We want to cooperate with others, but we also want to compete. We want to build for the future, yet we want to be able to enjoy the moment. We carry all of these paradoxes together within our natural genetic endowment. All of these needs are important, but when it comes to maintaining passion in a relationship, none are as important as attachment and autonomy. If you learn only one thing from this book it should be this: your relationship requires a balancing act between the two opposing needs of attachment and autonomy, not mere "closeness." In fact, enmeshing attachment without a counter-balancing sense of autonomy is a sure-fire way to kill your attraction to your partner.

> **Your relationship requires a balancing act between the two opposing needs of attachment and autonomy, not mere "closeness."**

If you want to maintain a strong relationship, you must service the needs for both attachment and autonomy without ignoring either one. This may seem counterintuitive, but think of it this way: How long can you feel attracted to someone whom you don't respect? And how long can you respect someone who is too afraid of your disapproval to speak his own mind? Or how long can you feel attracted to someone whose disapproval you fear so much that you always cave to his desires and let his preferences eclipse your will? If you do the latter, then you're well on the way to joining the legions of numbed-out depersonalized zombies whose frequent refrain is "I don't know who I am anymore." The sad fact is that total self-sacrifice kills relationships just as effectively as narcissistic selfishness. The trick is to maintain balance and that's not easy.

The Myth of a Homogenous Self

It will be a very useful aid for balancing your relationship if you can adopt a radically new and different view of yourself than what most people perceive. Paradigm shifts are not uncommon in science. For example, the paradigm shifts from Newton to Einstein to quantum views of the universe were all counterintuitive radical changes. Neuroscience has similarly shifted our understanding about what constitutes the "self." The conventional view is that the self is like an onion. But in reality, it's more like a potato.

> **The conventional view is that the self is like an onion. But in reality, it's more like a potato.**

Potatoes are tubers that are connected but also somewhat separated in their structure. They are interconnected by their root structure under ground. In a similar way, our brains have neurological clusters of memories, emotions, and attitudes bundled into different self parts. At any given time, one self part is usually more dominant than the others. These parts will communicate with each other most of the time, but not always. We can see this most clearly when our memories don't transfer from one part to another.

However, it's not just memory that may not make the jump between parts. Neurohormonal resources also may not make the jump. I sometimes ask my clients, "How sexy do you feel three minutes after completing your annual taxes?" Some things may not work for quite a while after.

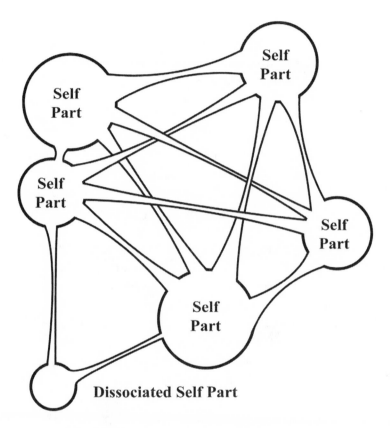

A simplified model of personality self parts

I have a personal story that illustrates how separated self parts can disrupt memory transfer. However, I need to risk disclosing a painful episode in my own history so that you can understand the story's context. When I was twenty one years old, I made the mistake of marrying a girl when my own identity and maturity had not yet consolidated. What followed was eight years of a tumultuous relationship. We loved each other, but that still didn't prevent her from violating our marital boundaries in some very serious ways. I finally reached the point where I decided to end the relationship rather than risk having children with a woman whom I doubted could ever become trustworthy. Out of courtesy, let's refer to her using the alias name "Janie ."

Twelve years after our divorce I paid a visit to my parents at their lake house where I had spent much time while starting my relationship with my first wife. My brother was also visiting so our complete original family was gathered together, much like the old days. It was a rare event. After standing in the main living room and talking with them for several minutes, I noticed that my parents were grinning and my brother was laughing. "What's going on? What's so funny?" I asked. My brother then explained: "Do you realize that for the past five minutes you've been referring to Janie as if she's your wife? You've mentioned her three or four times." I was stunned. I had been divorced from Janie for twelve years. I'd been happily married to Helen for the previous eight years. This wasn't a case of early Alzheimer's. It was a case of one of my younger self parts being evoked by all the contextual cues around me at the time: the old lake house associated with my younger self and all the old family members similarly associated. I unconsciously responded to all these old cues by reactivating an implicit memory set that was consistent. "Janie" was the name of my primary attachment in that memory set and I was in a younger self part.

For years now, my clinical practice has routinely involved accessing people's different self parts by using hypnosis and trance. I've learned that having differing self parts is the norm and not the exception. What really varies is the degree of separation between parts. This is called dissociation. We all have these separations to some degree. When one self part is dominant, certain reflexes will work. If another self part is dominant, they won't. You can see this most visibly with sexual arousal. If either of you are in work mode, forget it! If you're both in play mode, then you will probably have more luck. When you're really smart about managing your self parts, you can begin to predict under what circumstances the most appropriate self part will be more easily available to you. This can be *very* beneficial to the intimate side of your relationship.

Experience-Focused Versus Goal-Focused States

Understanding your different self parts can help you to manage them more intelligently. If you're oblivious to the fact that you have different parts, then you won't see certain dangers. Many marriages are lost this way. The most common example is when a couple trades all of their romantic privacy for round-the-clock parenting. In the parenting role, affection usually won't build. It tends to wither. Couples who intelligently manage their mental states make sure that they routinely share private time away from their children. Similarly, smart couples will schedule work and play so that the two opposing states are safely compartmentalized from each other.

British psychologist Michael Apter has studied and researched opposing states for over forty years. He summarizes several dimensions of Reversal Theory in his book *Motivational Styles in Everyday Life.* His Reversal Theory has stimulated the publication of over 800 papers and accounts for extensive research in over fifty universities. Its core premise is that we humans aren't comprised of static traits because we often reverse or switch states of mind. The theory proposes that four motivational dimensions account for most state reversals in our everyday life. We'll only concern ourselves with one dimension because it has the most profound effect on marital satisfaction. It pertains to reversals between "telic" and "paratelic" states.

Apter explains that we're in a telic state when we're focused on achieving some goal. This is how we are when we're thinking about a responsibility. We're trying to get from here to there. Being in the moment isn't as important as maintaining order while we try to reach the desired goal. In a telic state, the more we're aroused, the more we'll feel stressed. It's my own belief that this stress occurs because there's a heavy lacing of fear while we're trying to avoid disorder. It evokes what neuroscientists refer to as the "fight/flight" system. So when we talk about work or try to achieve some goal, fear is usually in the background. We covertly fear that we'll make a mistake and fail to reach our goal. Most of us don't recognize this as fear; we think of it as healthy caution. But caution involves a subtle fear.

An experience-focused paratelic state is quite different. Instead of trying to accomplish some goal, we're focused on savoring experience. It's the taste of the food. It's the feelings that we have during lusty sex. It's the wonder of exploration and learning. It's the aesthetic appreciation we feel when we view a beautiful painting. Our arousal feels positive when we're in this state. We experience it as joy and excitement.

You can greatly improve your relationship if you become savvy about these different goal-focused and experience-focused states. The following lists should help but there's a caveat I first need to give you. Telic and paratelic states are mental and not behavioral. You can ride your bicycle to work merely to get there, or you can ride your bicycle so you can enjoy the scenery and the sensations. The former involves a goal-focused telic state.

The latter is paratelic. In a similar vein, you can experience sex as a paratelic joy or you can put up with it as a telic chore. You might even reverse states in the middle of an activity. It's all a matter of where your attention is focused. So when you review the following lists, be aware that they describe behaviors in which the average person will be in a particular state <u>most of the time</u>. Here are the lists.

Goal-focused (Telic) State

- Supervising a child to look out for its safety
- Balancing a checkbook
- Cleaning the house
- Mowing the lawn
- Folding laundry
- Going to the doctor for a physical
- Negotiating with a spouse about buying a new car
- Replacing a light bulb
- Cooking dinner
- Driving to work
- Shopping for groceries
- Voting for your favorite candidate
- Bringing the car in for inspection
- Having sex with one's husband in order to pacify him

"Having sex with one's husband to pacify him?" What kind of item is that? Well, if truth be told it involves a goal-focused state. Notice that there's a subtle fear involved. The focus is on achieving the goal of safety instead of enjoying the experience. We'll discuss this kind of perversion later in our chapter about sex. Now, let's review a list of activities that usually involve more focus on experience.

Experience-Focused (Paratelic) State

- Having lusty sex with a partner and enjoying both the emotional closeness and the sensations
- Exploring a new museum with a sense of wonder
- Dancing with your child to a lively tune
- Riding the Ferris Wheel at the state fair

- Enjoying the taste of a candy apple
- Bathing among the breaking waves at the beach
- Enjoying a back rub from your partner
- Reading a good novel or magazine
- Listening to a concert
- Enjoying the company and story telling of some good friends
- Browsing in some gift shops just to explore
- Taking a vacation cruise
- Embracing a partner and feeling close
- Listening with curiosity to a partner tell about her day

It's important to maintain a balance over time between goal-focused and experience-focused states. If we only indulge in the pleasures of experience-focused states, then we won't be disciplined and toughened for life's challenges. This kind of damage is similar to when a young man lives in his original home and is over-nurtured by his mother through his twenties. She takes care of his every need. Such coddling can leave a man woefully dependent upon females and unprepared to face life's challenges. It's also like someone lying in bed for six months after an operation instead of following the doctor's orders for exercise and physical therapy. The absence of any challenge will stunt a person and make him weak.

While it's damaging to continually stay in an experience-focused paratelic state, it's also destructive to remain in a telic goal-focused state. Unfortunately, the latter occurs frequently in modern life. People often work two jobs, lug their laptops home, stay plugged into work when they're at home, think about work, talk about work or, in a similar manner, talk all the time about their children. Like work, parenting most often involves a goal-focused responsibility state. When we're parenting, we're usually focused on the safety and the welfare of our children. We're thinking about how to responsibly raise them and very often we're not as free as we'd like to be. If you have children, just think about how nonsexual you feel when you're supervising them. The reason is because parenting most often involves a responsibility-focused telic state.

The propensity to remain in a telic state doesn't just come from the outside. It can also come from our own internal mandate. Some of us may carry so much unconscious inhibition that we can feel that it's wrong to relax. We may feel that without hard toil we're undeserving and "not enough." It's as if we're wasting time when we're not working. Our unconscious might constantly search for things to be done, while relaxation, fun, exploration, and all the unnecessary stuff is put off for when there's time left over. But somehow there's never enough time left over because the unconscious is always slating us up with more commitments. This is how many of us hide from the shame of enjoyment. That sounds strange doesn't it? "The shame of enjoyment." It's a very real phenomenon. It often results from the person's disturbed relationship with his or her parents during childhood. These first relationships have a profound effect on how well a person can relax and play in later adult life. It also affects their adult relationships with his spouse and children. Inhibiting shame can become trans-generational when it's transmitted to children and even through children to grandchildren.

> # The shame of enjoyment is a very real phenomenon.

The balance between goal-focused and experience-focused states is critical because affection is grown mostly while we're in an experience-focused state. We usually don't feel very close when we share responsibilities. This conclusion doesn't come from Apter's research, but from my own work with thousands of couples. Although this rule of thumb is practical because it's generally true, there are a few exceptions. When shared responsibilities hold a tremendous personal value for a person, that person may grow affection despite being in a telic state. For example, soldiers in wartime will develop strong affectionate bonds with each other while trying to protect each other's lives. Sensitive partners may grow affection if they perceive that their spouse's help with chores is a tremendous, love-motivated sacrifice. Patients who fight a serious illness may develop strong affection for their doctors. However, these exceptions aren't usually present in everyday marital life. We usually don't perceive that sharing responsibilities will save us from imminent death. Responsibilities and chores are usually ineffective symbols for communicating love. Therefore, it's best that we keep the rule simple. Affection can build in a paratelic, experience-focused state but usually not in a goal-focused state.

> ## The balance between goal-focused and experience-focused states is critical because affection is created mostly while we're in an experience-focused state.

One of the questions I like to ask couples is "How many minutes do you spend alone together each week, not solving any problem but just talking for the fun of it?" I then ask, "How many minutes each week do you spend exploring something new or doing something fun away from the kids?" Most often the husband and wife will give each other a bewildered look until one of them will turn and blurt out the answer with some exasperation. Their answer is usually somewhere between zero and twenty minutes per week. Of course my practice has a self-selecting population with relationship problems. The general population may fare somewhat better, but perhaps not much.

My wife Helen and I had a relevant experience when we adopted our daughter. At the time, I was working hard to establish a new practice, while Helen was doing her best to mother a difficult, screaming infant. After several months of this ordeal, our bickering and fights had increased to toxic levels. Helen, brilliant lady that she is, was the first to take corrective action. One day she confronted me so directly that it felt as if she were grasping my lapels in her hands. It went something like this:

> "All we do is work, work, work. All I am is a nanny and a diaper changer. Your head is always at work even when you're with me. We're just like two ships passing each other in the night. This isn't what I signed up for. When was the last time we really connected? When have we had time for just the two of us? What are we going to do about this?"

I had to agree with her. The balance between our work and play selves had gone "out of whack." We discussed how we would deal with the problem methodically. We finally decided to create a routine that would guarantee that we'd spare time for each other. Every Thursday evening we would have a babysitter arrive at 6:00 PM. We would leave and have dinner at a cozy local restaurant. After dinner, we had several hours with no other

51

agenda than to reconnect by talking and listening to each other. We brought various self-help books solely for the exercises that we used to help jump-start the process. We eventually found we didn't need them. We learned to avoid talking about any responsibilities or problems. We trained ourselves to jointly slip into an experience-focused state by sharing curiosity. Then a funny thing happened. The fighting and bickering stopped almost completely. Things started going really well between us.

In certain fields of research this is called a "time series" study. You plot a symptom for a while to get its pre-treatment level. Then you introduce a treatment intervention to see if the symptom level changes over time. Ours did! In fact, it did several times because we got complacent after a while. When the babysitter moved out of town, we let our routine slip. Things were going so well we didn't make an effort to replace the babysitter. We let things slide. The result should be obvious. Our fights and bickering went back up. We eventually went through three cycles of this fiasco before I finally woke up. I figured that if I can change the oil in my car every 3,000 miles to avoid engine burnout then I can also make sure my marriage has regular connection time. Over the years, this awareness has served us well. It's also served others well because there have been many couples who have replicated our experience. These couples have been able to dramatically increase their mutual affection by regularly scheduling experience-focused time together. These same couples have usually experienced a reduction in their destructive fighting.

John Gottman is a therapist and prolific author who has conducted extensive research on the behavioral dynamics in couples. One behavioral dimension has to do with "repair techniques." A repair technique is when one partner uses good tact to help the other partner emotionally recover from feeling hurt during a conflict. Gottman found that some small gesture of good will can often prevent a small conflict from sinking into a toxic fight. However, he also found that even excellent repair techniques don't work very well if the quality of the friendship is poor. Good tact alone isn't enough. It needs to be accompanied by a recent history of emotional connection in the relationship. Gottman's conclusion is consistent with what I've observed. The frequency of toxic fighting will often go up when goal-focused and experience-focused states are so out of balance that there's no emotional connection. I interpret this as built-up shame in each partner's unconscious: "I'm not feeling loved or important in my marriage. It must be my partner's fault!" When couples share experience-focused paratelic states with each other, they enable the strengthening of their friendship. Consistent with

Gottman's findings, this improved bond makes couples more resilient to little triggers and annoyances. Repair techniques can then nip potential fights in the bud before they gain momentum.

Attachment and Autonomy

Maintaining balance is dynamic. An acrobat on a high-wire is constantly moving, making small, counter-balancing adjustments to maintain his center of gravity. If he were to freeze in a stationary position, he would fall. This is why I prefer the verb "balancing" instead of the noun "balance." Balancing a relationship isn't static. Not everything has to be 50-50 at any given point in time. We need both air and water to survive, but we satisfy each of these needs at different times. Our needs for autonomy and attachment are similarly satisfied at different times. We alternate between these two states in a vital relationship. Sometimes we enjoy closeness. At other times we enjoy privacy. Sometimes we enjoy sacrificing in order to nurture our partner. At other times, we need to confront our partner about an issue in order to protect ourselves. Sometimes we want our partner to lead us. At other times we want to take the lead ourselves. Back and forth, back and forth. A good relationship keeps moving in a kind of resonance where both partners do a coordinated dance. And when this dance results in our attachment and autonomy needs both being satisfied over time, then passion will flourish. When our fear of shame interferes with this dance, our passion then becomes comatose.

> **A good relationship keeps moving in a kind of resonance where both partners do a coordinated dance.**

So what exactly are these two essential determinants of passion? What is the true nature of attachment and what exactly does autonomy mean? Each of these topics is worthy of a book in its own right. In fact, many books have already been written about attachment. Since the mid 1980s, researchers and authors have written extensive treatises about it. Attachment is a need that starts shortly after birth and initially involves the child observing his or her caregiver's nonverbal behaviors to determine whether the caregiver is emotionally attuned. The child learns to search out the caregiver's eyes, facial muscles, and tone of voice for signs of attention and emotion. When the child observes positive attention and the caregiver's contingent response to the child's own behavior, then attunement has occurred. This attuning process initially involves the right hemisphere of the child's brain, even before the child organizes language centers in the left hemisphere. As the parent and child go through repetitive cycles of attachment, attachment break, and then attachment repair, an important process takes place in which the child is trained for emotional stability. Through this cyclical process the mind of the parent actually helps organize the child's prefrontal cortex. This is how we learn to regulate shame and other emotions.

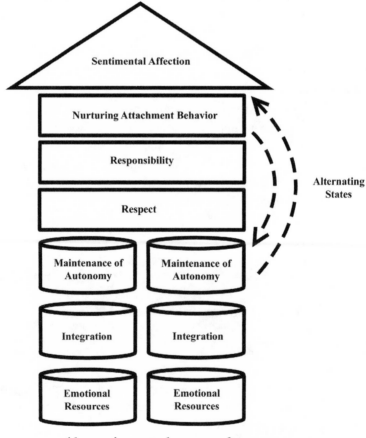

Alternating attachment and autonomy

Touch also serves an extremely important role in developing attachment. In fact, it's so crucial that a newborn infant will usually die without it. In the beginning of the 1900s many institutions were giving orphaned infants good food and medical care. However, it was not known that human touch was essential for infant survival. In one early study, it was discovered that the majority of orphaned infants who were never touched would actually die. That's right. We die if we're not touched during infancy and now we know why. Without human touch in early infancy, our stress system secretes cortisol which in turn switches off the immune system. Opportunistic infections can then settle in. In addition, human touch mediates the activation of genes that produce orthinine decarboxylase which in turn mediates protein production. Without human touch stimulating orthinine decarboxylase release, infants are much more likely to experience failure to thrive. The important truth to be drawn here is that attachment is a critical psychobiological need and not merely a lifestyle luxury.

In adulthood, we still desire touch, the loving tone of voice, and the facial displays that indicate positive attunement and approval. Our attachment mechanisms and our attachment needs still endure. However, as adults we have elaborated our identities beyond our physical beings to include many facets of mind. Our memories, fantasies, experiences, and especially our desires and our loves become the essence of what we want our partner to notice. So instead of looking for attunement to our physical presence alone, we even more strongly crave attunement to our minds. When we observe our partner's facial expression light up with the discovery of what we value and when we notice their curious excitement when they seek to know more about how we feel, then our adult attachment needs are being satisfied. When this experience happens repetitively, then it conditions into us a feeling of affection that we call love. This is the essence of healthy adult attachment: the pursuit and appreciation of mind, mirrored back mostly by nonverbal displays of positive emotion. It is essential if you're going to keep passion alive in your relationship. We're simplifying some things in this explanation. It's true that there are other forms of attachment besides the healthy adult variant. However, since we're shooting for health, we'll save our discussion of destructive attachments for later.

This is the essence of healthy adult attachment: the pursuit of mind mirrored back mostly by nonverbal displays of positive emotion.

Autonomy is the other essential ingredient for preserving passion. It is a concept that is less commonly defined than attachment. Earlier in our discussion, we said that autonomy involves being motivated by one's own views and desires instead of other people's evaluations. However, we'll also give it a more general definition so that it can be a handy construct in your relationship work. First, let's dispel a common but potentially misleading definition of autonomy. It's not proving to yourself that you can't be controlled by your partner. People who seek to prove their autonomy are operating at an adolescent level and may in fact wind up negatively enmeshing with their partner. When we say a person is enmeshed, we mean that he's overly focused on his partner's desires and emotions. So if Peter focuses on proving that he's not ruled by Jane's insistence that he shouldn't meet his friends at the pub, he would still be controlled by her opinion, but in the opposite direction. If Peter were to defocus off of Jane's mind and instead let his actions be guided by a matrix of considerations, including self-maintenance, his partner's needs, prior commitments, and other ethical considerations, then his decision making would be truly autonomous. So our operational definition of autonomy is this: we are autonomous when we are motivated by our own self-generated frame of meaning. By "self-generated" I'm referring to positive desires, values, and principles that we've chosen for our own. When we're solely focused on satisfying the expectations we think are held in other people's minds and we don't consider our own perspective, autonomy is lost. So, in essence, autonomy is really something that is determined by what happens inside us. It can't be determined by merely looking at our external behavior. It's the emotional stability that we generate within ourselves based on what we love and find valuable in our lives.

When we talk about the balance between autonomy and attachment, we're really talking about how we flow back and forth between these two states. It's not a static proposition of merely dividing the distance between the two. At one time we allow ourselves to be nurtured and to enjoy feeling important in the other person's mind as we perceive it. We like the feeling we get of being important to our partner and, in that sense, we're momentarily like a baby being cradled in the mesh of our partner's frame of meaning. But if we stay there permanently, something damaging begins to happen. If all we do is allow ourselves to be loved, we'll eventually lose a sense of who we are independent of our partner... and that's going to start to feel very painful. So, maintaining balance means that we sometimes push off of our partner's mind, hang onto our own frame of meaning, and make choices for ourselves. For example, suppose tonight our partner wants to eat Italian, but we want our turn and instead press for Thai. They want to take a vacation at the shore, but we may press our point that we've conceded to go to the shore for the past two summers. We now want our turn in the mountains. These are the risks that we take in stating our preference. They're vitally important to maintaining the balance between feeling connected to our partner versus feeling connected to our self. And that's the balancing we really need to do. Connection to other versus connection to self is primarily a question about to whom we are attaching in the moment.

> **We'll lose our own emotional integrity if we don't exercise our choice-making and tend to our needs.**

It's critical to service autonomy in a relationship. If we don't, then the very foundation of our relationship begins to crack. We'll lose our own emotional integrity if we don't exercise our choice-making and tend to our needs. As implied by our house metaphor, affection will suffer if the foundation of personal integrity isn't maintained. Exercising autonomy is one major way that we maintain our personal integrity foundation. Self-sacrificing to placate a partner is paradoxically one way we can kill a relationship. It's like acid on the beams of a house. It won't cave immediately but the long-term effects are predictable.

> **Self-sacrificing to placate a partner is paradoxically one way we can kill a relationship.**

I remember one couple where the husband's self-sacrificing behavior was most visibly killing their relationship. Rodney and Paula were a couple in their late thirties with sexual difficulties. Rodney had lost all attraction despite professing that he still loved and cared about Paula. Paula had been struggling with a depression that had episodically reoccurred throughout her life. She had come from a dysfunctional family background and had an older brother who had sexually assaulted her repeatedly during childhood. Paula responded well to a combination of anti-depressant medication as well as EMDR psychotherapy. However, Rodney didn't correspondingly regain sexual interest despite Paula's improved mood. There was another more subtle dynamic at play. One clue to its nature was Rodney's guilt. He was exquisitely sensitive to Paula's every need. While she was depressed and inactive, Rodney wouldn't consider doing anything without her. He would tell me that he'd feel too guilty leaving her at home. Initially, his rationale was that he didn't want to exacerbate her depression. However, as Paula's depression improved, Rodney still showed a reluctance to pursue separate interests. He still complained that he would just feel too guilty if he did so. I strongly suspected that Rodney had lost so much autonomy that his emotional integrity was compromised. He and Paula were an intelligent couple so I was able to explain to them the suspected dynamic of enmeshment. I also outlined how we would go on a campaign for Rodney and Paula to exercise autonomous pursuit of interests. Paula was even able to advocate for Rodney to leave her at times in place of the hovering behavior to which they both had become accustomed. The couple's emotions didn't immediately change but did gradually shift over several months. With this shift, Rodney reported that he felt much less guilt. At the same time, Rodney's sexual interest resurrected. They both started jumping each other's bones with relish. So here's a case of a phenomenon that's rarely discussed: that sexual interest can be squashed by too much of the wrong type of "closeness." When partners enmesh by taking too much responsibility for each other's feelings, the loss of autonomy will often suppress their sex life. It's a frequent phenomenon.

> **You can starve a relationship by not feeding it enough attachment. You can also smother a relationship with too much guilt-riddled responsibility.**

Imbalance in a relationship can take place in either direction. You can starve a relationship by not feeding it enough attachment. You can also smother a relationship with too much guilt-riddled responsibility. It's like over-feeding or under-feeding. Either can kill. The enlightened view is more heterocentric. Your responsibility needs to be that you keep a balance in ALL the parts of a relationship. This includes servicing both attachment and autonomy. You make sure that you and your partner have enough free paratelic time together to enjoy a sense of connection. You must also make sure that you service your autonomy—your need to be a separate human being. Your respect for your partner allows him to do the same, despite your differences. Your responsibility in keeping commitments builds a sense of safety and trust. All of these "moving parts" need to be functional to provide the fertile conditions for affection to grow.

Assessing Your Own Balance

Here's a little quiz to help you evaluate the balance of your own lifestyle. Answer T (True), F (False), or NR (Not Relevant) to each of the following.

Part I -

1. _____ I usually know the times in my day in which I look forward to relaxing and "letting down."
2. _____ I usually know when my partner and I will have our next "get-away" for just the two of us.
3. _____ My partner and I frequently schedule times dedicated to just "tuning in" to each other.
4. _____ I occasionally enjoy a lazy afternoon reading a good book or doing something else just for fun.
5. _____ We do everything together as a family, children included.
6. _____ I can't ever take time for myself because there's always too much to do.
7. _____ I sometimes come up with ideas of things to do that my partner and I can explore for fun.
8. _____ My partner and I usually look forward to talking during meal time.

9. _____ My partner and I usually make an effort to share some talk or touch at bedtime.

10. _____ I feel silly or guilty if I'm not doing something productive.

Part II -

11. _____ I usually treat other people's needs as more important than my own.

12. _____ I usually give in rather than see my partner disappointed.

13. _____ I feel guilty when I tell my partner what I really want.

14. _____ I sometimes tell small lies to avoid my partner's disapproval.

15. _____ I'm a good negotiator for what I want, but I try to be fair.

16. _____ I can usually confront my partner in the moment when I think he's doing something unfair.

17. _____ I usually freeze up in conflict and can't think very well.

18. _____ I usually wait for my partner to tell me what she wants without expressing my own ideas.

19. _____ I prefer to deal with problems when they arise. I don't hold my resentments for later.

20. _____ I avoid conflict at all costs. I harbor resentments and sometimes blow up at a later time.

Now let's revisit each of the items from the first part of the quiz along with a brief explanation about what each item actually reveals. This first part may reveal whether or not you have a free paratelic state deficiency (i.e., living your life predominantly in a constant telic state).

1. **I usually know the times in my day in which I look forward to relaxing and "letting down."** If you carry no shame about giving yourself pleasure, then you will integrate it into your day. You will have routine times when you know you will enjoy that quiet moment to relax with a cup of coffee while you read the paper or listen to a song on the radio. You will have a few of these sprinkled throughout each day like little oases in the desert where you can refresh. If you answered "False" here, take a look at your inhibition about giving yourself pleasure.

2. **I usually know when my partner and I'll have our next "get-away" for just the two of us.** This item is similar to #1 except on a different time scale. If you answered "False" to this item then you're not being very proactive in giving yourselves free time together. You're also missing out on a great method to help you both feel emotionally closer. Shared anticipation is a powerful way to feel connected, even before you have your "get-away."

3. **My partner and I frequently schedule times dedicated to just "tuning in" to each other.** If you answered "True" to this item, then you're probably feeding the relationship great attachment through emotional intimacy. If you are not really "tuning in" to each other and you interpreted this expression as watching TV or a movie together, then you're missing the boat.

4. **I occasionally enjoy a lazy afternoon reading a good book or doing something else just for fun.** If you answered "True," then you're probably fairly uninhibited about giving yourself free paratelic time. However, you also want to arrange leisure time to share with your partner.

5. **We do everything together as a family, children included.** This is a classic mistake. Almost all of your parenting time puts you in a telic state because you're responsible for setting limits, scanning for safety, etc. If you answered "True" to this item, you will be one of the majority with children who lose satisfaction with their marriage. You and your partner need some free time to be alone with each other.

6. **I can't ever take time for myself because there's always too much to do.** If you answered "True" then you may be fooling yourself into thinking that the problem is all situational. All of us sometimes feel overwhelmed with responsibilities. But if you have a long history of near constant crises, consider the possibility that you may unconsciously seek them out. You might be unconsciously avoiding the anxiety you would otherwise feel in a free paratelic state.

7. **I sometimes come up with ideas of things to do that my partner and I can explore for fun.** Great stuff! This is high-level functioning if you answered "True."

8. **My partner and I usually look forward to talking during meal time.** Meal time is a paratelic ritual for many people. If you're looking forward to it, then you're doing a good job of keeping it free and enjoyable.

9. **My partner and I usually make an effort to share some talk or touch at bedtime.** Here's another routine paratelic moment that's great for building affection. Even if you're tired and brain-dead from a stressful day, low intensity stroking or massage can go a long way.

10. **I feel silly or guilty if I'm not doing something productive.** If you answered "True" to this, then you're probably inhibited about giving yourself paratelic experiences. This unconscious shame will block you from creating shared free time with your partner.

Now let's revisit each of the items from the second part of the quiz along with a brief explanation about what each item shows. This second part reveals the ease with which you express your autonomy.

11. **I usually treat other people's needs as being more important than my own.** A "True" answer here indicates that you will probably be self-sacrificing in your relationships. This can result in the gradual build up of shame and/or depersonalization. You ideally want to feel as lovable and as deserving as anyone else.

12. **I usually give in rather than see my partner disappointed.** If your needs are as important as everyone else's and if you're doing your job in protecting your autonomy then you will be a good negotiator. This means you will ask your partner to yield to your wishes about half the time when you're negotiating. Your partner's disappointment shouldn't be your only criterion. If it is, then you will sacrifice yourself and the relationship will eventually suffer. Answering "True" to this item suggests you may gradually build up resentment or shame.

13. **I usually feel guilty when I tell my partner what I really want.** Answering "True" to this question indicates that you probably have core shame that's inhibiting you from expressing your desires. It can

also pull down your self-esteem to the point that it will be hard for you to get close to your partner.

14. **I sometimes tell small lies to avoid my partner's disapproval.** If you answered "True", this is an indicator of an extremely serious problem. It means you don't think you have the internal resources to defend yourself against your partner's disapproval. If you're not a psychopath and you don't think that lying is OK, then you're engaging in a compulsive behavior. Compulsive behaviors generate shame and will make you fearful of getting close. Your deceit is also ruining the foundation of trust in your relationship.

15. **I'm a good negotiator for what I want, but I try to be fair.** Good for you if you answered "True." This is the heterocentric perspective that involves considering both of you at the same time.

16. **I can usually confront my partner in the moment when I think he's doing something unfair.** The key phrase here is "in the moment." Many people are too afraid to speak up in the moment and stew about it instead. They may confront their partner later when it's 90 % forgotten. When you have good autonomy skills, you're able to efficiently deal with problems in real-time.

17. **I usually freeze up in a conflict and can't think very well.** A "True" to this one usually indicates that your autonomy is momentarily lapsing. There's a neurological basis for this parasympathetic shut-down which we will discuss later.

18. **I usually wait for my partner to tell me what he/she wants without expressing my own desires.** A "True" here is deadly to your relationship. If you let your partner's will completely eclipse your own then you're on your way to "losing yourself" in the relationship. When this happens, you lose attraction to your partner and you start feeling that "you don't know who you are anymore." It's no fun being a footnote to someone else's life.

19. **I prefer to deal with problems when they arise.** I don't hold my resentments for later. You earn a gold star if you said "True" to this one. (See #16.)

20. **I avoid conflict at all costs.** I harbor resentments and sometimes blow at a later time. If you avoid conflict at all costs, then it may cost you your relationship. There's a common pattern that occurs for people with poorly integrated anger: hold back, hold back, hold back, hold back, BLOW! Afterwards, you feel terribly ashamed about your blow out. The natural consequence is that you accumulate even more shame about your un-integrated anger. Healthy conflict is a good rebalancing tool in a relationship. If you don't use it, you will use less beneficial defenses like self-sacrifice and avoidance.

Now that you've evaluated your own degree of balance, it's a good idea to get your partner to take the same quiz. It'll be interesting to compare answers and discuss their implications. However, it's best to hold off from planning any interventions until you've read the rest of this book.

Where we place our focus determines the direction in which we're going to grow.

A final point is relevant to our discussion about balancing states. That fact is that we grow ourselves by what we do every moment we're alive. Where we place our focus determines the direction in which we're going to grow. If we maintain an existential diet that's loaded only with the work or responsible telic state, then we're going to be focused primarily on maintaining order, and we're going to increasingly discount the importance of other kinds of fun experiences. I've seen clients who have focused for decades on achievement and who have let the more sensitive, emotional sides of their personality atrophy. These clients are less capable of a healthy intimate relationship now then they were when they were more balanced earlier in their lives. The issue of attaining and maintaining balance doesn't just pertain to our current relationship. It's also relevant to how we develop as a person. If we want to limit our growth, then all we need to do is keep focusing and striving in one quadrant of our emotional experience. We'll consequently be sure to develop limitations in our other dimensions. Conversely, if we keep challenging ourselves to welcome experiences in different states that require different mindsets, then we'll grow our capacities in complex and ultimately more adaptive ways.

Chapter Four

Nurturing Healthy Attachment

In 1984, I established a counseling practice in Cary, North Carolina. Several years before I arrived, an incident occurred in the next building. I was told about it from neighboring tenants in the building. A lady was visiting with her attorney to prepare for a divorce from her husband. While they were meeting, her husband unexpectedly showed up wrapped in dynamite, all wired up and holding a contact switch. The attorney dove out of the office while the husband wrapped his wife in one last embrace. He then blew both of them up along with a large section of the side of the building. He was very attached to his wife. I tell the preceding story to provoke some thought. Not all forms of love or attachment are constructive and beneficial. The man in this unfortunate story obviously had an intense attachment to his wife. Unfortunately for her, it wasn't one of the better types.

> ## We rarely ask the question, "What part of us is being loved?"

Most of us have heard and read about different types of love. We usually ask the question, "What does it mean when someone loves us?" Then we try to answer the question by categorizing different types of love according to different roles that we see, such as brotherly love, parental love, romantic love, and loving friendship. However, there's another radical angle from which we can try to view love. We rarely ask the question, "What part of us is being loved?" We probably don't ask this because most of us subscribe to the myth of having a homogeneous self. It seems obvious. You might say something like, "There's only one **me** and I'm so-and-so. I'm a kind, generous, and competent person. When someone loves me they must appreciate all that." But consider the following ways that another person can be attached to you:

> **You have some trait that your partner disowns from his/ her experience (e.g. aggressiveness). You "complete" your partner.**

> **You enhance your partner's social status. You look good as a husband or a wife.**

> **You're the mother/father of your partner's children. You preserve and complete the family.**

> **You do a lot of things that make your partner's life comfortable. You keep things clean and orderly.**

> **You supply your partner with sex.**

> **You keep your partner from feeling anxious by supplying a warm body that makes him/her feel safe and not lonely.**

> **You give your partner financial security.**

Yuk! It's pretty vapid stuff and not very satisfying in the long-run. Yet these are some types of the attachments that many people really form. They're all examples of love from an egocentric level of consciousness: "I love you because you meet a need that I have." What's missing from these examples of primitive love is the core of what constitutes you. What's being loved is some service you're performing for the other person. You perform this operation for them and they're going to appreciate you for it. That's what makes these examples of low consciousness. They're examples of commodity transactions.

Heterocentric loving involves a lot more than merely considering your own needs. It involves your empathically appreciating what your partner feels and experiences in his or her own world. It's an appreciation of the partner's separate mind and at the center of the mind of what he or she wants and loves. In all of my decades as a therapist, I've never found anything more at the core of self-esteem than what a person wants and loves. We previously discussed how the organization of the self is more like a potato and less like an onion. That was referring to how our memory and states are organized. However, for visualizing domains of self-esteem, it's better to use the conventional onion metaphor.

The onion metaphor of core self and levels of self-esteem

Self-esteem is a useful construct for tagging which level of self is being loved. Think of self-esteem as organized into three levels. The most peripheral sense of self occurs on the external, behavioral, and exhibitory level. This level of self yields very little steady satisfaction. You may get some temporary highs, but this level alone will also yield long periods of depressing inadequacy. I've observed a frequent example of this among some extraordinarily beautiful women. These women had initially relied on their beauty to attract attention from others. However, many of them eventually came to resent their physical beauty because they feared it symbolized their superficial and insubstantial character. Clearly, their beauty wasn't doing the job of making them feel very adequate. Similarly, some very prosperous men have shown a parallel phenomenon. One of the wealthiest clients I've seen used to privately complain, "I'm garbage at my core!" I feared for his life because he was so miserable. It didn't matter that he was a CEO of a large, successful corporation that he had built from scratch.

Arctic Hare

I like to use the following metaphor to illustrate a statement about human nature. It relates to what part of our self we value and seek to have loved. When I was in graduate school, I would often tire of my studies and go exploring other parts of the library. One day I happened upon a book on wilderness survival. In the book I found many interesting tips for how to survive in the wild, such as eating beaver tail for nutrition and instructions for building dead fall traps. What I found particularly interesting was a story pertaining to fur trappers who would trap beaver in Canada during the 1700s. In the spring, the trappers would head up the rivers into the wilderness. After they did their trapping in the fall, they would have to be careful to get down the rivers and back to civilization before the freeze. Sometimes they wouldn't make it in time and they'd be locked in by ice and snow for a long, hard winter. After eating up their food stores, they'd have to live off of the land by hunting and trapping. This was very difficult. However, there was always a certain animal that was easier to hunt than any other. It was the prolific arctic hare. It's a snow-shoed relative of the rabbit that turns pure white during winter and is able to run over the top of the ice crust without breaking through.

The story goes that these now trapped trappers would go out and kill arctic hare to bring back to their shelter. They would skin them, prepare them, and roast them up for sustenance. The meat was quite palatable. They would continue eating hare, but noticed that they were starting to lose weight. So, they would stuff themselves with more arctic hare in an effort to rebuild their own body fat. It wouldn't work. The more they ate, the more they would waste away. Finally, they would die stuffed with the delicious arctic hare. Because no matter how delectable it tastes, no matter how filling and satisfying it seems, arctic hare doesn't provide some of the necessary amino acid complex when it's digested in the human body. This phenomenon became known as "hare starvation."

I like to tell this story to clients who try to build their self-esteem by feeling proud of their achievements. The story is also a metaphor for the paltry sharing of peripheral self with which some of us try to nurture attachment in our relationships.

Our Experiential Core

What correlates with self-esteem is a person's appreciation of their emotional experience and especially of what they love and want. People who openly express what they love and want are usually people who feel more substantial. I never hear these people say, "I don't know who I am." Our attachments lie at the core of who we are. They define us more than anything we do or show. When I use the term "attachments," I'm using it in a very liberal way. I'm not just referring to external attachments such as things or people. I'm referring to internal constructs. These include the hopes and dreams we have for the future, the values and principles by which we want to live and the meaning of our past experiences. As we develop maturity and a level of consciousness beyond childhood, our attachment systems become more sophisticated and abstract. When we start life, we initially want to attach to that big Mommy thing in front of our eyes. In mid-life, we may want attachment to the meaning we find in promoting our children. At the end of our lives, we may want attachment to the larger spiritual realm that transcends space and time: truth, integrity, honor, contribution, creation, service. These can all be attachments if we incorporate them into our field of meaning. They can become part of our core.

So the relevant question is, "Are you and your partner attaching to each other's core selves?" If your partner is asking you about what you want and prefer, what you love, what you hope and dream about, what you remember and the meaning you place on those memories, and if your partner also shows excited delight in her face and eyes as she hears what you say and asks questions so that she can receive even more…then it's a good bet you will feel loved. It won't take much of that kind of experience to feel loved unless you're one of the poor unfortunates who have been shamed to the core by early trauma. If not, then your partner's delight in exploring these attachments in your mind is probably the most profound way you can feel connected. Physical sex can momentarily drop more opiates into the reward centers of your brain, but intimate reception is a more enduring way to sustain the sense that you're truly loved.

NURTURING HEALTHY ATTACHMENT

> ## Adult loving has more to do
> ## with receiving than giving.

Nearly thirty years ago, my own therapist mentioned that adult loving has more to do with receiving than giving. Since then, I have learned what he meant. It's the curious pursuit to receive our partner's experiential core that is the most powerful way to nurture the sense that we're close. That's the essence of intimacy: to communicate by our pursuit of our partner's experiential core that we really value his or her essence.

> ## Autonomous attachment means you don't have to
> ## rely on your partner to define or complete you.

Intimacy isn't easy. Many people just plain lack the emotional capacity for it. In order to sustain intimacy, you will need to be highly receptive and comfortable with yourself. Dan Siegel has written prolifically about the neuroscience of the mind. His term "autonomous attachment" refers to the capacity to attach while simultaneously maintaining a separate self. Autonomous attachment means you don't have to rely on your partner to define or complete you. Instead, you run off your own battery pack. If you have to define yourself by attaching to your partner, then you will probably wind up fighting about how he's doing such a poor job. Conversely, having your own personal autonomy gives you the internal security so that you can respect your partner. It allows you to let go enough to love. Sound familiar?

Modalities of Attachment

Intimacy isn't the only way to nurture attachment. Even though it's the most powerful way for conditioning affection, there are other modalities that shouldn't be overlooked. Touch, sex, symbolism, anticipation, and affiliation are all useful ways to nurture attachment. We spend more time affiliating than we do in all of the other attachment modalities combined.

> **When we're intimate, we're facing each other and looking into each other's minds.**

There's a big difference between affiliation and intimate communication. When we're intimate, we're facing each other and looking into each other's minds. Our main focus is our partner's mind. When we affiliate, we're side by side, looking out on the world and comparing notes. The main focus is the outer world. If we're smart enough to sometimes do this in a free paratelic state, then we'll gradually condition some affection into our relationship. If we affiliate in a responsible telic state, it doesn't count because affection can't build. Unfortunately, this happens to be most of the time with nearly all couples. The dictates of life require that we tend to survival first. We may affiliate cooking dinner, paying bills, working on the house, doing laundry, minding the children, and working on the computer. However, affection doesn't build nearly as much in these responsibilities as when you go out together to share a picnic, enjoy some dancing, explore a new restaurant, or party with some friends. When you compare notes with each other during these free paratelic activities, you're likely to build some emotional connection. You're doing some head connecting when you share the experience. But remember, your eyes are directed out there on the world most of the time. You're only occasionally connecting heads to compare your experiences. This means that, relative to intimacy, free paratelic affiliation is only thin gruel. It doesn't stick to your ribs as well. I like the following metaphor: one minute of intimacy equals one hundred minutes of affiliation.

> **One minute of intimacy equals one hundred minutes of affiliation.**

Most of us feed attachment into our relationships through a mix of affiliation, intimacy, sex, touch, anticipation, and symbolism. When we start our relationships, we use a tremendous amount of all six. Intimate communication is frequent. But over time, the rigors of living together make things more difficult. We take shortcuts to get things done. We step on each other's toes and our emotions begin to bruise. As our covert inhibition and shame accumulate, there's a tendency for intimacy to wane. Our unconscious knows that it's safer that way. We're not as likely to get bruised. When the children come, there's usually a larger quantum drop in affection because all modalities of attachment take a hit. Energy levels become tapped and opportunities for spontaneous sex get squashed. The magic of anticipation, which so powerfully fuels early in-love feelings, becomes supplanted with routine and fatigue. Affiliation time dries up when the black hole of child care sucks down all discretionary time.

Rick and Sylvia were a British couple who had originally been quite content. They both came from wealthy families and were quite comfortable financially. In the early years of their marriage they would go skiing in Norway, sailing in the Caribbean, and traipsing all over the globe. They felt affection for each other with all of this fun affiliation time being spent together. Their problems started when children first came on the scene. The couple settled down, and Sylvia became a full-time mother. Rick became the CEO of a US company and was soon preoccupied with all the corporate intrigue. All of their leisure time was gone, and their affiliation time was now all responsible telic. When they finally came to me, their relationship was a basket case.

Rick and Sylvia are typical of many marriages. Early years of affection can be sustained on affiliation, but relationships deteriorate when free paratelic affiliation time disappears after couples have children. For this reason, I like to tell couples that they need to switch to a higher octane than mere affiliation. Remember? One minute of intimacy equals a hundred minutes of affiliation. When you no longer have much free paratelic time, you need to make it count. That's why planning for intimacy is efficient and smart when life gets complicated.

When life gets complicated, planning for intimacy is efficient and smart.

Planning for intimacy? Does that sound like sacrilege? Many people think that intimacy should be spontaneous. After all, you don't want to make it a routine chore. This is where some people get confused. Of course you don't want to make it a chore. But there's nothing wrong with setting up routines that promote intimacy. Then, when you're in the zone, you can be your own free agent. Think of your intimacy time like a free paratelic bubble in time. You can be very methodical in setting it up. When you're both finally in the bubble, you can both temporarily forget about the chores and focus on each other. Getting to this state will probably require a weekly schedule involving babysitters or grandparents. However, having it as a weekly default makes all the difference. If you have children and you don't have weekly routines for intimate connection, then there's close to zero chance that it'll happen. The law of inertia will usually hold.

What you want is a mix of all the attachment modalities in your schedule. On a daily basis, there are usually two main connection points in people's schedules. Dinner time is one of the few times for free paratelic affiliation after everyone sits down to eat. If there aren't any children, then the time can be more intimate. With children present, the experience is usually more affiliative. Even so, it still helps. Bed time is the other main connection point in daily schedules. This is a good time for touch, especially if both parties are too brain-dead to talk. Hugging, stroking, massage, and back-scratching are all great nonverbal ways of nurturing attachment. Bed time is obviously a good time for sex as well. But while sex can be nurturing, it's not necessarily so in every case. The psychology of intimate sex will be discussed later in this book.

On a time-scale longer than a daily or weekly cycle, it's smart to have some get-away planned in your more distant future for a couple of reasons. First, your initiation of a get-away plan is a powerful symbol of your pursuit. It's not just that you spend time together. It's also the fact that you *thought* up the idea which indicates that close attachment to your partner has some priority in your mind. The second reason it's a good idea is that it pays emotional dividends over time. Many people don't realize the power of anticipation. It's the gift that keeps on giving. If you suggest going out together at the last minute, it doesn't give the same sense of importance as something you set in motion a week before. If you let your partner know that the getaway is for intimacy and not just affiliation, then the benefit will be even greater. If your partner has agreed on a getaway two weeks in advance, then he or she has two weeks of awareness that you will be connecting. That knowledge itself, even if it's just operating in the unconscious, will nurture some sense of attachment. Remember that attachment is experienced in the mind. Anticipation can provide that. This is also an important message for divorced dads to hear. Telling their children of specific plans a week ahead of their scheduled visitation can help them to feel psychologically connected. Children get to feel more attachment over the preceding week, knowing that Dad is looking forward to those plans with them.

Symbolism is the remaining modality for nurturing attachment. Here we might source up romantic images of dressing up, flowers, jewelry, chocolate, Hallmark cards, saying the *right* words for the occasion, etc. On second thought, let's not. Let's junk the term instead! I personally hate the word "romantic." I see the concept hurt many relationships by discouraging creativity. Romance is a concept that is heavily merchandized by the media and an alliance of various industries: the jewelry trade, candy corporations, chain restaurants, and greeting card companies. They all have a stake in limiting your vision. Most people approach romance from the disempowered position of compliance and not authority. The media tells you how to be romantic. Think about it. How long has it been since you've sent a blank greeting card with only original sentiments that you personally wrote? On Valentine's Day, how many of us creatively deviate from doing our compulsory duty. Romance is so heavily indoctrinated into our minds that we've lost the essence of it. I recommend throwing out the concept. "Creative sentiment" is a better term. It's much more empowering, although I'll admit it doesn't have a convenient ring.

> **The more external justification you have for expressing sentiment, the less it will mean to your partner.**

Here's a question for you. When's the best time to send flowers? Consider this: the more external justification you have for expressing sentiment, the less it will mean to your partner. This doesn't necessarily translate to forgetting your anniversary. That would become a different kind of symbol, and one you won't likely live down for a long time. But it's still true that sentimental symbols that aren't provoked by the situation will generally nurture more attachment. So, that means that the best time to send flowers is when absolutely nothing is happening. No Valentine's Day, no post-argument make-up, no anniversary. Nothing. The same reasoning holds for expressing the words, "I love you." If you say those words in response to some sentiment that your partner has expressed, it won't mean as much to them. That's because we all attribute motives to people's behavior. We intuitively know that there's a difference between creatively expressing affection from a passionate motive versus expressing sentiment to meet expectations. The latter is really being done out of compliance and fear. We're trying to do what we *should* do and we're in a more child-like emotional state trying to put authority outside of ourselves. It's really a very young state in which we put authority outside of ourselves.

"Authority" is an interesting word and one that's relevant to our discussion. Most people think of authority as pertaining to social status and power. The authorities have determined this or the authorities have legislated that. Through its common usage, we've associated it with power and status. But think of what it means to author something. An author writes a book. It's a creation. Authorship in its essence is really more about creativity. When we author a symbol of affection for our partner, it carries an extremely powerful message. The authorship of meaning is what it's really all about.

> **When we author a symbol of affection for our partner, it carries an extremely powerful message.**

One of the most enjoyable experiences in my own marriage occurred the evening before we were about to fly to our twentieth anniversary getaway in the Bahamas. I took my wife Helen out to dinner the evening before we were scheduled to leave. While having desert and coffee, I presented her with a jewelry box bearing the trademark of a local jeweler. It was the size and shape for a necklace or bracelet but it contained neither. The box was actually a diversion. I had gone to the jewelry store to get the jewelry box merely to enhance the surprise. It worked! Instead of jewelry, the box contained two tickets to swim with dolphins which had been a long held wish that Helen had hoped to fulfill sometime in her lifetime. The memory of that experience *and the fact that I had understood and remembered her secret desire* remains one of the highpoints in our common story.

So what's the point? The point is that creative sentiment may not be romantic in the classic sense but it's even more intimate. When you symbolically celebrate the meaning in your partner's mind, it generates a powerful sense of connection. It's the unnecessary sentimental symbol that nurtures your partner most.

Guidelines for Intimacy Exercises

While other modalities of attachment can help supplement the experiential diet of your relationship, there's no more effective modality for nurturing attachment than intimacy. For this reason, I've included some intimacy exercises in this book to help "prime the pump." These exercises are designed to merely get you started. They're not meant to keep you regimented in any ongoing mechanical solution. The reason they're so highly structured is that they're designed to help you get past your own inhibition. It can be safely assumed that anyone reading this book has some internal fear and resistance to intimacy. Some will have so much inhibition that the exercises won't work. They may feel too alien, too silly, too anxiety provoking. "The Great No-No" may be too powerful an influence so that curiosity in your partner can't ignite. But what the hey! Let's give it a shot anyway!

In order to do emotional intimacy well, you both need to be in "the mood." This means being in a free paratelic state without guilt or anxiety about what tasks you're leaving undone. For this reason, it's important to get out of the house, without children, and be away from all those responsibility cues. Try to find a quiet little coffee house or perhaps a restaurant that's slow enough to let you sit for several hours. It's best if you sit across from each other so you can look at each other. If you're dining out, don't start your intimacy exercise until you've finished eating. Coffee or tea is OK. You need to be alcohol free so that all your frontal lobes are on-line. You want at least an hour without distractions for each exercise.

Just before starting your exercise, make an agreement that you will both avoid discussing any problems or responsibilities. The Big Five are especially taboo:

1. Work
2. Children
3. Money
4. Any problem-solving whatsoever
5. The relationship

Many people are surprised about the fifth taboo topic—the relationship. It's a common mistake to think that analyzing and discussing your relationship brings you closer. It might if your relationship is something you can both truly celebrate. If not, then discussing your relationship will bring on defensiveness and problem solving rather quickly. Save this type of discussion for one of your business meetings, not when you're trying to build affection.

> **It's a common mistake to think that analyzing and discussing your relationship brings you closer.**

You can add any other topics that you think might get you into conflict. If you've had conflicts about sex, put that on the list. In my own community we have many residents who have migrated from the Far East. Having come from a much more extended family culture, these clients are noticeably more conflicted about their in-laws. For them, in-laws are #6. You may know of other conflict-generating topics specific to your relationship. The reason you're avoiding these topics is that they'll quickly lead you into a responsible telic state and problem solving. Actually, your unconscious may try to steer you into a responsible telic state because it may actually feel less vulnerable than a state of intimacy as if your unconscious wants you to hide in these familiar topics rather than risk shame in a free paratelic state.

The state you're trying to create consists of curiosity and wonder. This is a very fragile state that is necessary for intimacy. It's quickly snuffed out by any anxiety from conflict or even just from focusing on responsibilities. The following exercises are designed to nudge you past your unconscious inhibitions and ignite your curiosity about each other. They both use a 10-minute preparation period to help you transition to a more receptive state. However, these exercises are not fail-safe. If either of you have very strong core shame from early childhood relationship trauma, you may still feel too anxious to be curious. It's best to do the exercises a couple of times before you decide if this is the case.

Q & A Intimacy Exercise

After you've finished your meal and you have at least a full hour with no distractions, proceed with the following steps:

1. **Preparing your Q & A list.** Each of you should start with a pencil and a piece of paper in front of you. For 10 minutes you will list questions that you can use to quiz your partner. You're going to ask your partner to guess the answers. The questions are about what's in **YOUR** mind and memory, usually involving preferences, fantasies, and the meaning of your memories. Here are some examples:

- What's my favorite color?

- What's my favorite food?

- What's my favorite song?

- What's my favorite book?

- Where would I most like to go for a vacation if I could go anywhere in the world?

- What do I most want to accomplish before I die?

- What was my most embarrassing moment?

- What regret would I most want to reverse if I could?

- What was the happiest moment in my life?

- What achievement in my life brings me the most pride?

- What was my biggest loss?

As you compose your list, you will be disinhibiting yourself. You may notice that your questions become less concrete as you get yourself into the zone. It's important to use the full 10 minutes to write. It's not just the written product that's important. It's also the neuro-hormonal state that you're creating in your body and your brain while you write.

2. **Flip a coin to choose who starts first.** One partner does NOT volunteer the other to go first!

3. **The first partner asks the second to guess the answer.** The second partner gets up to three guesses. Usually the partner won't be successful, so expectations need to be kept low. There should be no recriminations and no criticism about not knowing the right answer.

4. **The first partner elaborates on his or her answer.** Whether or not the second partner guesses the correct answer, the first partner elaborates on the answer. It's OK for this to take a long time, especially because the first partner is allowed to ask expanding questions. These are questions that help the first partner to share more details about the answer. However, the second partner should not venture any opinions or criticisms or talk about his/her own reactions. Here's an example of my own elaboration about my favorite color:

"Green is my favorite color and I know why. When I was a small child I always looked up to my brother. He was six years older and I always wanted to be 'cool' like him. He was popular, good looking, and of course much stronger. When he reached high school he became a letterman for wrestling. The school color was green, so he used to wear his neat green letterman's jacket with the high collar flipped up in the back. He also used to wear a lot of green in his outfits to match. Even before I reached high school, my brother taught me to wrestle. He trained me so well that I became a letterman and even won some wrestling tournaments in my freshman year. So I got to wear the cool green jackets like him.

Starting in college, I wanted to cultivate a relationship with my father. I knew he wouldn't be around forever. So, we used to hunt together each fall. Hunting was his big passion. We used to hunt in the forests of Maine and Canada. He was an artist and often pointed out the beautiful colors and textures in the forests—the evergreen forests. So, green has been closely associated with these two relationships. It's something I associate with all this male bonding I was fortunate to have. I associate it with love."

Notice how my elaboration isn't just about concrete events. It also involves my interpretation of my own personal meaning. Shared meaning is the essence of intimacy. It's hard to risk exposing this stuff because you can be so easily hurt if it gets criticized or ridiculed.

5. **The second partner asks the <u>same question</u> of the first partner.** That's right. Each question goes in both directions. In the example above, then it would be my turn to venture three guesses about my partner's favorite color. It's important that the second partner actually verbalizes the same question even though both of you know what it's going to be. It's also important that all of your questions be gender neutral. You shouldn't use questions like "Who's my favorite quarterback?" or "What's my favorite perfume?"

6. **The second partner elaborates on his/her answer.** This is just like step #4 but now with the other partner.

7. **The second partner chooses a new question from his or her list.** You've finally squeezed all the juice out of the first question by elaborating its answer in both directions. It's time to get a new question to start the process again. This time, the second partner starts it.

8. **Steps 3 through 6 are repeated.**

Repeat the Q & A exercise for at least a full hour. An hour and a half is better still. It's highly structured and may seem hokey because it's so unnatural. However, its structure is designed to keep you from defeating yourselves by unconsciously hiding in a responsible telic state. The task of requiring three guesses is designed to stimulate curiosity by manipulating a psycho-physiological variable known as "significance." This variable has the potential of turning on curiosity, if you're not too anxious.

You may want to do this Q & A exercise several times before moving on to the less structured Wonder Exercise. This next exercise is less structured and more closely approximates natural intimate conversation. However, its looser structure makes it easier to avoid intimacy if you're too inhibited.

Wonder Intimacy Exercise

This exercise starts like the Q & A exercise with the same guidelines and initial preparation up to the point that you both write for 10 minutes. These are the steps:

1. **List out your "wonders" for 10 minutes.** Start at the top of your paper by writing the words "I wonder…" Then finish the sentence with something you can wonder about in the moment. It doesn't have to be serious. You're free associating, so let the ideas come to you without evaluating them. If you try too hard to deliver a "good" or a "right" wonder, you will lock yourself up with anxiety. Here's an example of what I might start for a list:

- I wonder if there's life on Mars.

- I wonder if I'll still be alive when we get to Mars.

- I wonder if I'll still be able to climb onto my sailboat when I'm 85 years old.

- I wonder if I'll get my book finished anytime soon.

- I wonder if we'll ever sail as far as Jamaica.

- I wonder if my first real girlfriend ever thinks about me.

- I wonder what would have happened if I hadn't run from that other girl at age 16 when she told me she had been raped by her uncle. Would she have been my first true love?

Notice how my associations evolve to more meaningful material. This commonly occurs as partners become less inhibited and gradually turn on their receptive curiosity. The 10-minute preparation is a kind of intimacy foreplay. It helps you to transition your brain to a more receptive state.

2. **Flip a coin to see who shares first.** Remember—no volunteering the other guy.

3. **The first partner shares a wonder and elaborates on it.** The second partner helps by asking expanding questions. No opinions, criticisms or reactions are given. This is a collaborative effort of expanding the details and meaning being shared. I'll give an example of what this might look like after I describe the next step.

4. **The second partner picks a wonder from his or her own list and elaborates on it. You both continue taking alternate turns to share wonders from your lists.**

Here's the example I promised of a shared wonder. It's from the last item on my list: "I wonder what would have happened if I hadn't run from that other girl at age sixteen when she told me she had been raped by her uncle. Would she have been my first true love?"

This is something that I've wondered about from time to time. I harbor a regret from my youth. When I was sixteen, I started dating this girl who was a year younger. She was cute but, above all, very honest and genuine. Her parents were immigrants from some eastern European country. They lived in a little cottage next to a forest. I would ride my bike over to her place to visit. One night I rode over to her place and her parents weren't home. We had a wonderful time making hot chocolate and listening to her record from a new folk singer named Joan Baez. When it came time to leave, she walked with me to my bicycle outside. I went to kiss her goodbye but was shocked by her drastic response. She made a horrible grimace and started flailing her fists on my chest.

"What are you doing?" I asked.

She slumped her head and shoulders with a pained look on her face.

"I'm fighting you off," she replied.

"Why do you have to do that?" I asked. "I was only going to kiss you goodbye!"

**She made a horrible grimace and
started flailing her fists on my chest.**

She got this sorrowful look on her face. "I'm so confused."

She started to cry and told me her story. Her uncle had sexually molested her for several years starting at age 11. She said she was only doing what she thought she should do by defending herself. We talked for awhile about her reaction, but, unfortunately, I wasn't as sympathetic as I now wish I'd been. I thought she should leave such matters in the past and get a better grip on herself! (Not a very auspicious start for a future therapist.)

After a lengthy conversation, we said goodbye again. This time she kissed me long and passionately as if trying to make up for her earlier debacle. Surprised again, I tried to make light of it. "You don't have to make like I'm going to spend the whole night!"

After a few days, I talked with her again about how she was doing. In a subdued voice, she told me she was trying to get used to the idea that she wasn't going to see me again. And the sad thing was, she didn't. I ran from the relationship and what I considered to be all her defectiveness. Besides, I was also insecure about my own sexuality, and this girl obviously wasn't going to help me. This was my level of narcissistic thinking at the time. Decades later, I look back and wish I could take a time capsule back to the moment that this incident occurred. I fantasize holding her that night in a completely non-sexual way, just letting her feel my affection and acceptance despite her obvious injury. It was a lost opportunity for healing and possibly for a wonderful relationship based on beautiful honesty. I wish I could somehow go back and undo the compounded injury I must have caused her by my rejection. But now all I can do is add the experience to my wisdom and avoid hurting others in a similar way.

Pretty intense stuff! I chose this story to illustrate what can be done with the exercise if you're willing to share your own personal meaning. If you're not ready to share at this level, then don't. If I were a more vulnerable person, then I might have chosen a less disclosing item like "I wonder if there's life on Mars?" Intimacy depends on the emotional states of the people sharing as much as what's being shared. If you're fascinated with the personal meaning of what is being shared, then you're probably in the zone.

You're NOT in the intimacy zone when you're analyzing the problems in your relationship. Many men have learned to feel terror in their hearts when they hear the dreaded words, "We need to talk!" These words conjure up the specter of having their social inadequacies verbally dissected. This isn't a way to nurture attachment.

Nostalgic Memory Exercise

This exercise is a bit daring because it opens up a lot of complex emotion. It's not the best exercise if either you or your partner is too reluctant about reinvesting in the relationship. The exercise may bring you too close together. If you both are willing to risk exposure, then you might collaborate as follows:

1. **Talk with your partner and decide how long your "happy honeymoon" period lasted in the beginning of your relationship.** If you say four years and your partner says two years then go with the shorter period of time.

2. **Find a moment in time that you both can remember.** This will probably be a memory that has some emotional significance for both of you. For example: "Remember when we had just moved to Urbana (for graduate school) and classes hadn't started yet. Remember we didn't know anybody, and we were exploring the town for the first time. That Saturday night we decided to ride our new bikes across town to see "M*A*S*H." Remember?"

3. **Both of you discuss the sensory components of the episode.** For example: "I remember us trying to stay out of the traffic on those little bikes, then trying to find a safe place to lock up the bikes so they wouldn't get stolen while we were watching the movie. Do you remember that? We waited in the lobby of the theater for at least a half hour. Remember how they let us in the lobby because it was starting to sprinkle?"

4. **Both of you share whatever you can recall of how you were thinking during the episode.** For example: "I remember thinking how odd it was that we had been seeing the poster ads for M*A*S*H

in the subway in New York for months. Remember that funny poster with the sexy legs on the bottom of the figure and the victory sign with fingers at the top of the figure. Then we were finally seeing the picture out in the cornfields of Illinois. I remember thinking about how strange that was. Subways to cornfields. I recall thinking about how much fun it was going to be to explore more of what the town had to offer. I know I was still worrying about whether the bikes were safe where they were chained in the parking lot."

5. **Both of you share what emotions you were feeling during the episode.** For example: "I remember feeling excited and a bit scared at the same time. Here we were starting our new lives together, really getting away from our families and being on our own. It was a new beginning with a lot of new things to explore in a new town and with new friends to make. We had to really depend on each other more than before. But I remember feeling scared that I didn't know how well I was going to do in graduate school. I kept wondering what our future was going to be like. Excitement and a bit of anxiety. Those feelings were going through me around that time. That and my worry about the bikes in the parking lot."

There are a couple of pointers for doing this exercise. It will work best if you both spend time elaborating each of the steps three through five. There's benefit in the details. You're both stimulating your memory systems. You should realize that you're not just trying to recall. You're actually working against a part of your mind that doesn't want to recall! That's why it's important to magnify seemingly trivial details and spend time on each step. I highly recommend that you both agree when you've exhausted each step before moving on to the next one. The simple way to think about this exercise is: sensory to thought to feeling. That's the order, but don't rush it. Develop each stage fully before going to the next.

The next pointer has to do with emotions that might be released. You need to be prepared for a mixture of ambivalent feelings. Most nostalgia brings about bitter-sweet feelings. If your relationship involved a positive honeymoon period followed by later struggle, then the bitter-sweet feelings may be intense. Don't panic and don't be surprised if tears start to flow. If you can tolerate the intensity, then consider it a good thing. Whoever is tearful is actually beginning to "thaw out." Emotions are starting to come out of dissociation. The brain is reconnecting. It's a step toward risking more trust.

The positive memories are surrounded by a field of subliminal associations. These subliminal associations are about loss and missed opportunities. They may not be explicit but they still activate in the unconscious and give rise to emotion. If you don't know what to say when your partner becomes tearful, consider some form of reassuring touch such as holding hands.

Once you have thoroughly milked one memory for its sensations, thoughts, and feelings, then move on to another that you both can recall.

The Curious Regeneration of Love

This chapter has offered some ideas about how to go beyond the mere expression of love. Most self-help literature about relationships says that communication is the key to growing affection. "Say this. Do that. Give your partner these symbols of your undying devotion." I believe that this emphasis is misplaced because it ignores a partner's experiential core and overemphasizes external behavior.

Some authors say that you should know your partner's closely held sentiments in order to nurture his or her affection. That's certainly desirable, but such a static model is very limited. A more dynamic perspective is that adult nurturing is more about *exploring* and *receiving* a partner's experience than merely having knowledge about it. This is a difficult concept to grasp because it's so intangible. We're usually much more focused on tangible outcomes instead of process. It's also one reason why men and women often get stuck in their communication. A man may want to solve the problem with a concrete solution while the woman wants the experience of being heard. The man is in a telic state and the woman wants them both to share a paratelic state.

Curiosity is an extremely important resource in a relationship. It allows us to momentarily forget about ourselves and to really pay attention to the person in front of us. This receptive attention is the most powerful way that we can reinforce love in a relationship. It allows us to tune into our partner's core and reflect back our nonverbal signals of delight. It's a subtle but powerful process. Couples who do this keep regenerating their love.

This chapter has offered some intimacy exercises to help you kick start your curiosity about your partner. If you find that your curiosity turns on, then it's important to keep scheduling your intimacy meetings. You may eventually find that you can maintain intimate curiosity without the structured exercises. That's great! Just keep doing it. If you find that your curiosity stalls and won't run, you will need to discover what's keeping you stuck. It may well be "The Great No-No" of covert shame and inhibition. In the next chapter, I'll describe how this hidden assassin can gradually kill a relationship.

Chapter Five

Love's Hidden Assassin

Question: What's the best way to kill love?
Answer: You strangle it in the dark where no one's looking.

The reasons why some of us lose love are not obvious. Most of us think of concrete or external causes. Our partner became too preoccupied with his or her job. Our partner became a nag and stopped caring. We grew apart in our interests. Love just up and left for some magical reason. We rarely think of love's destruction as seeded within ourselves. In this chapter we will explore an insidious syndrome that covertly strangles affection.   Strangulation is a harsh, but apt word for what happens when love dies. To segue into this discussion, you're invited to first participate in a little self-evaluation test that I often give couples. For some, the results may be surprising and illuminating.

The "I Want...Will You" Test

This is a self-administered test where you can evaluate the results yourself. It's a self-observational experience where you notice how you feel when expressing certain words together. The test involves the following steps:

1. Familiarize yourself with the following scales. You're going to be rating your feelings about saying some phrases out loud. As you

go through the test, you're going to be figuring out how you <u>feel</u> about the phrases on three scales: Comfortable – Uncomfortable, Negative – Positive, and Unfamiliar – Familiar. You want to come up with a number or score on each of the scales. You can visualize the scales and corresponding scores as follows:

0	1	2	3
Totally Comfortable	Slightly Uncomfortable	Moderately Uncomfortable	Extremely Uncomfortable

-AND-

0	1	2	3
Totally Positive	Slightly Negative	Moderately Negative	Extremely Negative

-AND-

0	1	2	3
Totally Familiar	Slightly Unfamiliar	Moderately Unfamiliar	Extremely Unfamiliar

2. First find a quiet place where you won't be self-conscious about saying something out loud to yourself.

3. Close your eyes and say the following two phrases <u>out loud</u> with at least three seconds separating the two. The phrases are: **"I want"** ....(pause)....**"Will you?"** Just like that. It's important to bring your intonation up at the end of the second phrase because it's both a question and a request. The elevation of intonation at the end of a question is the way that we acknowledge uncertainty. The uncertainty of the request is an important element in this exercise. It's as if you're expressing the core syntax from the two sentences "I want (something)...Will you (give it to me)?" You're leaving out the content and less important parts of the request.

4. Let the sense of silliness pass through you from doing this unusual task. Your first reaction will probably be one of feeling slightly ridiculous. Don't worry. That's a common reaction because you're breaking out of your usual role structure. It may take a minute, but let the silliness do its thing until it processes through and out.

5. Once again repeat the two phrases <u>out loud</u> while still keeping your eyes closed. This time, focus inward to notice your emotional reaction. Pay attention to your body. If your emotional reaction could talk, what would it say? Does the syntax feel comfortable or uncomfortable, positive or negative, familiar or alien? Let yourself go with the <u>feel</u> of the words instead the logic. Once you've noticed your emotional reaction, then ask yourself whether or not this kind of expression would normally show up in your usual syntax. Make sure you come up with a number for each of the three scales we listed in step 1.

6. Don't stop yet. Repeat the previous step another five times, each time allowing yourself to "taste" the lingering connotation of the syntax. Each time you repeat the phrases out loud, notice if it feels comfortable or uncomfortable, positive or negative, familiar or unfamiliar. Work out a final number for each of the three scales listed in step #1.

When finished with the self-test, you should wind up with three final numbers corresponding to the three rating scales. Strive to be completely honest about what you've observed. You may be a little bit challenged to be completely honest with yourself. This little test may take some people where their minds don't want them to go.

Now, go ahead and take the preceding test before you read any more. Reading the next part of the discussion before completing the test will interfere with your observations and invalidate the results.

- Stop here and take the test before reading further. -

Roger was a middle-aged stock broker and one of the earliest clients to take the "I Want...Will You" test. He had come from a dysfunctional family with an uninvolved father and a critical, sarcastic mother. He had suffered a lot of humiliation under their care. He and his wife had initially come to me for marriage counseling. He had been extremely avoidant of any closeness in his marriage. I had both him and his wife do the "I Want - Will You" test, one after the other. While doing the test, his discomfort was made obvious by the grimace on his face. "I have pain right in the middle of my chest! It hurts right here," he said, pointing to his heart region. It was the strongest negative reaction I'd seen up to then. After reviewing social histories and plotting an intervention strategy, I decided to treat Roger separately because of apparent attachment traumas.

Two months after I gave Roger the first test, I decided to try giving him another variation of the same genre. This time, I asked Roger to state the words, "I want fun and pleasure!" With his eyes closed, Roger attempted it for the first time.

"I …I …I want…." His breathing became heavier, his face more strained.

"I want…." His breathing became more rapid and his voice became louder.

 Roger finally pushed himself through the obvious resistance to complete the full statement.

"I want…fun and pleasure!" He finally blurted the last words with bulging eyes and a look of panic on his face. His body started trembling and his right arm cinched up close to his chest in a crooked position. Roger stared down at his arm, now in spasm.

"Look at me! I'm starting to spasm!" he yelled. Roger was experiencing an abreaction, a psychological phenomenon in which a patient emotionally reacts and relives a prior trauma as if it were occurring once again.

Look at me! I'm starting to spasm!

Roger and I had hard therapeutic work ahead of us. From that day forward, we worked in a kind of therapy I call "hedonic disinhibition." The therapy focused on freeing his pleasure circuits from the shame and inhibition his early traumas had generated.

Since I started giving the "I Want…Will You" test, I've observed the reactions of several hundred clients. Roger's reaction was by far the most extreme. About two-thirds of my clients claimed to feel relative comfort during the test. If you felt comfortable during the test, consider yourself to be lucky. You just dodged a big one. Your summed score on the test is a good indicator of how much hedonic inhibition is working against you. You ideally have a summed score of zero and you're totally comfortable and familiar with expressing "I Want…Will you…" Approximately one-third of the people coming to see me have not felt comfortable during the test. Many people reported feeling "uncomfortable" while others reported stronger reactions such as anxiety, nausea, or even chest pains.

Over the years I have also found differences in how people reacted to each phrase in the test. For some, "I want" was what felt uncomfortable because it felt too "pushy" or "selfish." For others, it was the question "will you" that generated the anxiety. The single thing that all these people had in common was that they were all having difficulty maintaining closeness with their partner. What's also interesting is that certain themes of family background were likely to be associated with discomfort on the test. These backgrounds usually involved how parents interacted with the clients when they were small children. The different themes were as follows:

- Neither parent played with the client, didn't ask the client about his or her day, and didn't seek time with the client one-on-one.

- The client was one of six or more siblings where parents struggled to maintain the family.

- The client was given a lot of parent-like responsibilities for younger siblings.

- The client took on the responsibility for protecting one parent against the other. This usually occurred when one parent raged and was verbally abusive against the other. Alcoholism was frequently, but not always, involved.

- The family of origin had a culture of self-sacrifice. Parents can model missionary-like selflessness in a way that's absorbed by their children through a process called introjection.

A frequent commonality through all of the above themes was that the clients usually claimed that they had held back from expressing their wants and desires to both parents. The patterning in their current marriage was less obvious. For some, they were the pushy, dominant partner. Others were avoidant and withdrawn. In fact, the distribution was fairly bimodal. The partners who were comfortable with "I want," but not with "Will you" tended to be dominant in the relationship. They could tell their partners what they wanted just fine. "I want you to do this! I want you to do that!" You get the drift. I refer to these partners as being "dominant intruders." In contrast, the clients who were uncomfortable with both phrases tended to be avoidant. They didn't speak up much and often sought refuge in work, child care, or some other covering responsibility. I refer to these partners as "submissive avoiders." It seems as though emotional deprivation in childhood can be associated with either of these two styles.

One more interesting observation about the "I Want...Will You" test has recently emerged. I've had several couples come back to me and report a common phenomenon. The first time it happened, the conversation went something like this:

One partner reported, "We've been practicing your exercise and we've been doing a lot better."

"Which exercise?" I asked, quite puzzled and suspecting my own fairly incompetent memory. "Did I give you one?"

"You know... the 'I Want...Will You' thing."

I was still puzzled and a bit slow on the uptake. "But that wasn't an exercise and I didn't tell you to do anything with it."

"Well anyway, we've been practicing it when we talk to each other.... and we're getting along a lot better!"

Since that couple's report, I've had several more couples tell me the same thing. So, not to be totally dense, I now relay to new couples what some of the earlier couples have told me. Weaving "I want...will you" into their speech seems to go along with better relations.

So what's going on? What does it all mean? And how do all these observations relate to love being strangled in the dark? One interpretation is that "dominant intruders" and "submissive avoiders" are **both** avoiding the anxiety of closeness and intimacy by adopting different strategies. It may be that they want closeness, but there's something that gets in the way that's subtly frightening. Most of the time, this fear isn't conscious. The mind is so efficient that it automatically routes the person away from risk without the person even knowing it. For the "submissive avoider," it's less frightening to be under-expressive and to hide in responsibilities. For the "dominant intruder," it's less frightening to be commanding and treat the person as an object instead of facing the uncertainty of their having a choice.

For these people, the use of "will you" implies uncertainty and the possibility of disappointment. According to my interpretation, **both** styles involve a subtle unconscious fear. And it's also my premise that this fear can strangle affection from below where most people don't want to look. Of course, we've come full circle back to "The Great No-No" of shame and inhibition. But to see how these dynamics work below the surface, we're going to take an unusual detour in this next part of our discussion.

The Heart is a Rat

In college, Psych 101 was the first course I had to take to be a psychology major. Later, in graduate school, I had to teach the course. I remember one particular experiment that I found fascinating. It was a rat study that demonstrated the dynamics of motivational ambivalence.

You take a rat and tether him to a device that measures how hard he pulls. Then you put him in an alley way that leads straight to a wall that has a light and a small speaker mounted. Below the light and a speaker is a food tray and on the floor is an electrical grid. In the first part of the experiment, you train the rat to associate food with a tone emitted by the speaker. When the tone comes on, a tasty piece of food drops into the tray a second later. Eventually, the rat learns to pull towards the food tray when he hears the tone. How hard he pulls is a good indicator of his motivation to approach at any given distance that he's away from the tray. What's interesting is that his pull isn't constant. He'll usually pull harder as he gets closer to the food. The grams of pulling force can be plotted as a function of distance as shown in this section's first illustration.

The next phase of the experiment involves training the rat to fear the light. With the tone kept off, the light is turned on to signal that a shock is coming through the grid. It doesn't take long before the rat learns to fear the light and runs away when it's turned on. You can plot his avoidance motivation by how hard he pulls to get away when the light turns on. He will pull very hard when close to the light, as shown in the illustration. As he gets further away from the light, his motivation quickly falls off. What's especially important is that the slope of his avoidance motivation is much steeper than his motivation to approach. We'll soon see why this is important.

Now we get mean. We turn on both the light and the tone at the same time. I can imagine some of you thinking "Poor thing!" Many of us can empathize from our life's conflicts and tough choices. But the relevant question is: Where's the rat going to be? The answer to this question is predicted from our previous measurements. The rat will spend most of his time where his motivation to avoid equals his motivation to approach. Where the two gradients cross will be where he spends most of his time. He may not be frozen but may vacillate back and forth around that set point. I can't help but think of many relationships where the couple vacillates back and forth between breaking up and getting back together.

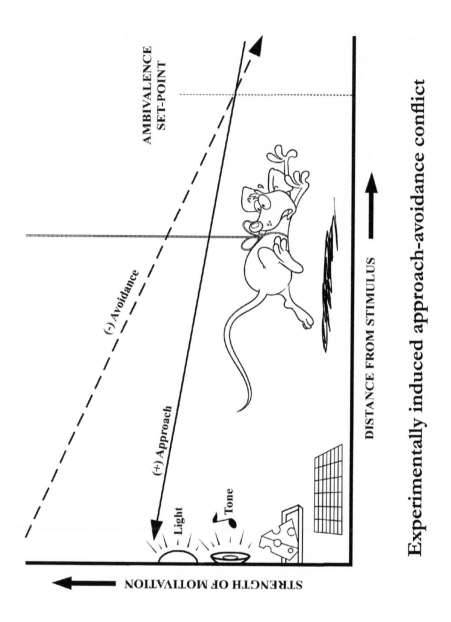

Experimentally induced approach-avoidance conflict

So how's all of this relevant to love? It's relevant when you realize that we humans have similar approach-avoidance conflicts but on a different scale. Instead of physical distance as in the rat experiment, we humans react to psychological proximity. This proximity involves either temporal distance or degree of similarity. If a situation is in some way similar to a previous painful situation, our anxiety can kick up without our knowing why. And here's a really important point. The origin of our emotional reaction doesn't have to be consciously remembered. Ambivalence can be triggered in what is called implicit memory. Think of conscious memory as the tip of an iceberg. In contrast, implicit memory extends far below the surface of consciousness. Some of our most powerful emotions can be triggered by this unconscious memory, just as if we're a dumb rat. And one of these emotions is our fear of shame. It's the anxiety we can feel when we're vulnerable. Our brains fear the shock of shame just like the rat fears the electric shock. For many of us, getting very intimate or exposed is like the red light coming on.

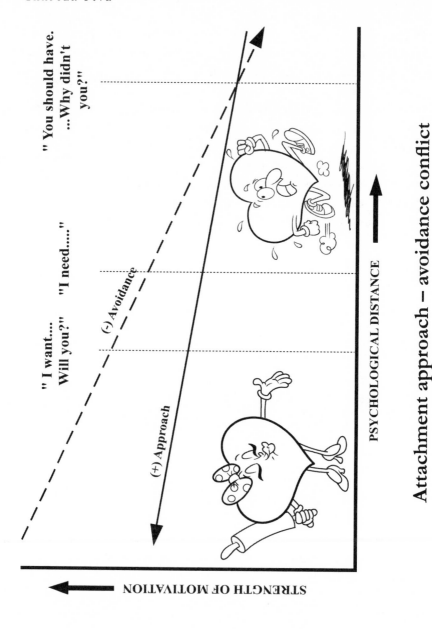

Conscious shame is actually the tip of a large inhibitory system that works mostly in our unconscious. This system operates like a car brake and is triggered by shaming, traumatizing, or repetitively frustrating experiences. These experiences activate circuits in the brain that suppress our usually dominant activation system. The result is an emotional shut-down much like a car coming to a screeching halt. It really hurts! We might sense a curling of our bodies away from their usually straight posture. We may also have a sense of shrinking, vanishing or of wanting to hide. These are all conscious reactions to shame. However, the mind is also capable of anticipating experiences that even MIGHT lead to the painful shutdown. It can block out potentially dangerous associations before they become conscious. This is how words and phrases such as "I want...Will you" can be conditioned to provoke anxiety. The inhibitory system works in the unconscious, generating anxiety to ward us away from situations that can potentially lead us to acute shame.

The following figure is a good way to conceptualize our inhibitory system. Think of it as an iceberg with only the tip showing. What shows above the surface of consciousness is what we experience as shame. It's extremely painful. When inhibited circuits are kept totally inactive, we're relatively comfortable. When something starts to trigger activation of those inhibited circuits, our unconscious begins to fear the possible onset of acute shame. That's when we experience anxiety. When the inhibited circuits activate further and break the surface of consciousness, we painfully experience conscious shame.

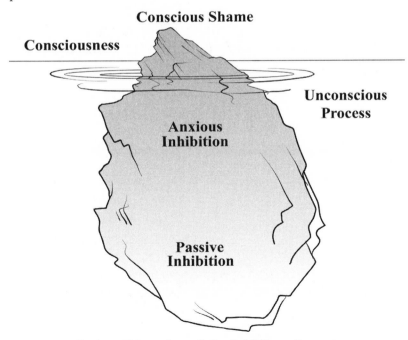

Iceberg Metaphor of the Inhibitory System

Our inhibition in a relationship can come from two sources. First, it can come from early shaming experiences with caregivers. I call this core shame. There's extensive research on how different attachment styles are instilled into children. Some children demonstrate anxious or avoidant attachment styles very early in life. They tend to perpetuate these styles later in adult life, quite consistently with our description of core shame. There's also research demonstrating how marital satisfaction is usually most positive for couples who both have secure attachment styles. This same research also shows how marital dissatisfaction is strongest for partners who both have insecure avoidant styles. With all this available research, it would seem reasonable to base all of our discussions on attachment theory. However, one reason why we're using the concept of core shame instead is that it's more useful for discussing how relationship dynamics can change over time. When a person carries core shame, there's a lot more that can be affected than mere attachment to people. A person with strong core shame might also experience generalized inhibition from attaching to enjoyment, meaning, and possibly even hope. Some of our most important attachments involve more than people.

Core shame turbo-charges the conditioning of relationship shame.

The other reason why we're using the core shame concept is that it's useful for describing how shame and inhibition can evolve during a relationship. Inhibition can accumulate not just from childhood experience, but from adult events that condition shame during the relationship. For want of a better term, I call this "relationship shame." Core shame and relationship shame are not merely additive. Core shame can actually potentiate more rapid conditioning of relationship shame as a person experiences the inevitable friction inherent in an adult relationship. One could say that core shame turbo-charges the conditioning of relationship shame. Here are just a few examples to illustrate how each type of shame can be generated.

Core Shame:

Child: Mommy, will you play with me?
Parental Response: (no response)

Child: Daddy, can we go to the fair?
Parental Response: (grimacing, raised voice, throwing up hands) We've got way too much on our plate right now. Maybe next year.

Child: Can I go play at Jennie's house?
Parental Response: You have to do your share and watch your brother. You can't just always think of yourself.

Child: Mommy, do we have to pay taxes? Jenny says her dad is mad about having to pay taxes.
Parental Response: (Mother doesn't respond but turns and discusses an unrelated topic with the father.)

Child: It's unfair! You let Bobby go ice skating.
Parental Response: (Furious expression on face) One more word out of you and I'll smack your face! I won't tolerate your disrespect!

Child: (Crying in response to some previous harsh words from the parent)
Parental Response: If you don't stop crying, I'll give you something to cry about!

Child: (Playing with toy car in the corner of the room) Brrrrrrrrr!
Parental Response: (Father swears under his breath) Damn kids!

Child: (Crying in response to both parents fighting)
Parental Response: (Parents ignore and keep increasing their volume.)

Relationship Shame:

Partner A: We haven't done anything fun lately. Do you want to go down to the flea market with me tomorrow morning?
Partner B: (eye roll) Don't you see how much pressure I've been under! Somebody's got to earn the money around here.

Partner A: I don't think it's fair to me that you expect us to visit your parents three times in....
Partner B: (interrupting the husband's speech) But it is fair and we've been over it time and time again, etc.

Partner A: Can I tell you how I really feel about this?
Partner B: I already know how you feel! I don't believe you when you say you don't feel what I already know you feel.

Partner A: (Partner A is busy doing something.)
Partner B: I need you to do this. (Implied command to subjugate)

Partner A: I see it differently than you. I don't agree.
Partner B: But that's the right way you should do it. The other way is stupid! (Parent to child communication implying defectiveness for non-compliance)

Partner A: I really regret what I did. I think it was wrong and I'll do it differently next time.
Partner B: Then say you're sorry! You should apologize and make it up to me. (Demand for subjugation instead of accepting that the partner is already taking responsibility)

Partner A: Can we put new carpeting downstairs? We could get the money by holding off on the 401-K.
Partner B: Don't tell me what to do with my paycheck. You don't make the money around here. I do. (Implied inferior status of the homemaker)

Partner A: I don't want to talk about it right now. I'm too upset. I just need to be left alone.
Partner B: (Ignoring the refusal and request for privacy) You're not going to put me off! We're going to talk about it right now!

In the preceding examples of shaming experiences, the dynamics are sometimes subtle. Even so, the painful shock of shame is generated when a need is in the process of being expressed but then gets unexpectedly disrupted. A bit of shame is jabbed into memory like a splinter that the brain unconsciously tries to protect from being irritated. Any behavior that threatens to irritate that splinter becomes like the red light in our rat experiment.

Several days before writing this section, I was sitting with a client in my office. She and her husband had both come from tumultuous family backgrounds. She reported an interesting observation:

"When Rick and I go out for dinner, I notice that we're both really anxious until the food arrives. Then, when the food arrives, we're OK. If we're eating dinner, we relax and then we're OK. It's like it's too intense until the food arrives."

I suggested that perhaps she and her husband were uncomfortable with receiving full attention from each other. Once their food arrived, their eyes were probably focusing more on the food instead of each other. With only partial attention from each other, each could be more comfortable; like the rat that is more comfortable at its distant set-point in the alley-way. They want closeness and attachment with each other. However, their core shame creates too much anxiety when they're close. Their comfort zone is when they're distantly affiliating while they're partially preoccupied with doing something else. Full attention would generate too much anxiety by bringing them too close to the unconscious splinters of their core shame.

This type of dynamic is played out in many relationships. It's subtle enough to even influence the language that people use. When attachment anxiety is low, a person will have little ambivalence about openly communicating their needs. They can use respectful requests like "I want…. Will you?" Other respectful requests include "I want…..What do you want? and "I want…..Do you want that too?" When attachment anxiety is moderate, they'll be more ambivalent about exposure. They may tell their partner that they "need" something but never actually ask for it. Asking would imply uncertainty about getting what they want. It would imply their dependence on their partner's choice. That would evoke too much anxiety. So, the unconscious works out the solution of implying a command: "I need…."

When attachment anxiety is high, the unconscious is likely to work out an even more defended position. Instead of "I want…Will you?" or "I need…" the unconscious solution may be critical: "You should have….Why didn't you?" With this posture, exposure of need can be completely avoided. If one can bully his or her partner into a rigid role of responsibility, then any hint of dependence can be avoided. The second illustration in this section shows how each of these solutions represents a different position in the psychological proximity to attachment.

Where we are with our attachment ambivalence will partially determine how out of balance our relationship will get. It's hard to maintain an integrity-based relationship if we're reacting to our own fear of shame. For example, if we're using the "I need…" or "You should have…Why didn't you?" solutions, we're likely to be injecting little splinters of shame into our partner. There's a risk that he or she will depersonalize and withdraw. If we're so filled with our own core shame that we can't ask for what we want, we may allow our partner to structure the common agenda. If we let this happen, then we'll be the ones who will depersonalize and withdraw. Either way, the crucial balance is lost.

Assassin #1: Hedonic Inhibition

"Hedonic inhibition" is an uncommon expression. It's related to the word "hedonism" which commonly carries a negative connotation. Think of hedonism and you associate gluttony, orgies, sleazy sexual indulgences, etc. But healthy hedonic enjoyment includes feeling wonder, play, joy, and even love. The inability to feel pleasure, referred to as anhedonia, is a primary marker of clinical depression. Having the ability to feel pleasure is an important part of being human and being able to connect with others. However, when a person's inhibitory system forbids certain types of pleasure, hedonic inhibition is taking place. This usually occurs quite unconsciously as with a workaholic who never seems to have free time to share with his family. The person doesn't notice himself or herself being inhibited. It's just that fun or pleasurable activities seem unimportant or even silly.

Hedonic inhibition is a "sleeper" assassin. It usually doesn't show up when a person is in love. This is because inhibitions are suppressed by disinhibiting neurohormones in the brain when a person falls in love. Nature has its way of making sure that we get together and make our contributions to the gene pool. However, the disinhibiting neurohormones typically decline after the in-love stage has completed its run. If partners are living together, tripping over each other and bumping up against each other when making their daily decisions, then the in-love stage will usually last at most two to three years. After that, the bruising effects of life together can trigger old shame and/or build up new inhibition. It's the challenge of sentimental loving for partners to either prevent or reverse this trend.

In the previous section, we discussed how core shame results from emotional bruising during childhood and relationship shame is generated later in the person's adult relationships. Both of these classes of shame are derived from relationships, but at different times in a person's life. It's useful to distinguish core shame from relationship shame because the effects of core shame are so profound. As implied by the term "core," core shame becomes embedded deep in the core of a person's psyche. It's extremely difficult to overcome. If a person has a lot of core shame, relationship shame will develop more quickly and result in stronger inhibition. The reason is that every time the person experiences disapproval from the partner then the core shame from childhood also resonates in the person's unconscious and adds more pain. This reactivation of old shame makes any disapproval from one's partner much more toxic. If a person has very little core shame then disapproval may seem like only a mild 12-volt shock. If a person carries a lot of core shame then it may feel more like 220-volt main current. We all vary in our vulnerability to disapproval and criticism, but people with a lot of core shame have it the worst.

Samantha and Nate wanted counseling to revive Samantha's dormant interest in sex. Both had been very sexual during the early years of their relationship. However, the last two years had seen a gradual decline in sexual relations as Samantha had became more and more disinterested. Nate was a successful executive coach whose presentation was both assertive and dominant. Despite his assertiveness, he listened carefully and showed real concern for Samantha's feelings. He genuinely wanted her emotional involvement and not just sexual gratification with her body. Samantha was quite affable with a definite feminine softness to her demeanor. She seemed to complement Nate's character by having no hard assertive edges of her own.

As sessions progressed, several important facts emerged. First, Samantha disclosed how she would frequently dissociate to the corner of the room while having sex. She would often imagine seeing herself having sex instead of allowing herself to directly experience the sensations. Second, she revealed how she had been sexually molested by her father during early childhood. She was working on that early traumatic memory with another therapist in private sessions. Third, she complained that Nate treated her as if she were the less important partner. When I asked Samantha for some examples of this latter kind of disrespect, she could only reference somewhat ambiguous examples of Nate behaving insensitively. In other words, there was no overt domination or abuse.

As a matter of course, I usually ask couples about how they derive plans for having fun and recreation. Here, Samantha provided an important clue. She reported that she usually let Nate schedule their common agenda because it wasn't easy for her to know what she wants. I found this very significant. It was as if one side of her mind complained that she was a footnote in Nate's world, while the other side of her mind wanted Nate to organize all of her enjoyment. It seemed that the two parts of her mind couldn't make the connection. By now, I strongly suspected severe hedonic inhibition so I decided to assign her an exploratory exercise. She enthusiastically agreed to meditate several times each day, each time fantasizing about what might be some fun activities she could conceivably explore. She didn't have to actually explore anything. All she had to do was fantasize possibilities. She agreed to write down her most attractive fantasized possibilities. I wanted to reduce her performance anxiety by lowering her expectations. Therefore, I gave her some simple examples of what I might fantasize as fun if I were to perform the exercise.

Samantha telephoned me halfway through the week. She wanted help. She wondered that perhaps she wasn't doing the exercise correctly because she couldn't come up with anything. Each time she meditated to fantasize, no ideas would come. I told her to stop the assignment until we could revise it at our next session. When we next met, I recommended that she change the exercise to include a priming technique. I told her to start each meditative session by first revisiting five of her most "fun" past experiences. I figured that this might encourage her to more freely fantasize. Unfortunately, it didn't work. Samantha returned the following week with no reported ideas. It was by now apparent that Samantha's ability to express her needs was caught in the grip of a very powerful inhibition. She would require a lot of integrative therapy to recover from the core shame of her early sexual trauma. She would also need additional work to become comfortable with the pursuit of healthy pleasure.

While Samantha's case was extreme, it illustrates how generalized hedonic inhibition can become. It isn't just about sex. Samantha's inability to fantasize pleasure meant that she couldn't negotiate any agenda for enjoyment as an equal. She couldn't fantasize about pleasure so, of course, she couldn't propose her own ideas for fun. Samantha was projecting blame onto Nate for her own incapacity. She didn't see that she had already lost so much of her separate self that she naturally didn't want to sexually merge and lose more separateness. And that's how it works. Hedonic inhibition robs people of their sense of identity. If you don't express what you want and defend your separateness, you will lose attraction for your partner.

The inherent bruising that takes place when partners live together will naturally promote hedonic inhibition as a companion to relationship shame. However, when core shame exists before the relationship, the compounding of shame and inhibition can be much more severe. Even so, the deterioration of a relationship isn't inevitable. There are ways that a person can service their autonomy and roll back hedonic inhibition. We'll be discussing these strategies later in much detail. For now, it's important to realize that hedonic inhibition is like a slowly accumulating odorless and colorless gas. It's not obvious, but it's highly lethal. I'm reminded of a popular parable. If we put a frog in a pot of hot water, he'll immediately jump out. If we put a frog in a pot of cold water and raise the temperature one degree every minute, he'll stay there until he boils. If you unknowingly habituate to your accumulating inhibition, your relationship will eventually become parboiled. You can do this just by making sure you always play it safe. Never ask for anything that's fun. Never do anything that's unnecessary. Never disagree with your partner. Never express anger. Never do anything of which your partner might disapprove. Always make other people's needs more important than your own. Play it safe. That's what hedonic inhibition is all about. If we don't expose what we really want by asking or hoping for it, then we won't get as badly smacked by shame when we're met with disapproval or disappointment. Of course we'll also lose the sense of our separate identity, and we'll lose attraction for our partner in the process.

A Self-Exam for Hedonic Inhibition

By now you're aware of how subtle hedonic inhibition can be. Our minds are fully capable of dissociating shame and resulting inhibition from our awareness. Any self-exam must take this subtlety into account. We must detect it by its footprint and its shadow, not by our conscious recognition. First, ask yourself how you did on the "I Want – Will You" test. Did the "I want" part feel too selfish or pushy? Did the uncertainty implied with "Will you" stir up any discomfort? Do you avoid these words? Your answers to these questions start off the first part of this self-exam. Additional items will help you to locate some tell-tale signs that hedonic inhibition may already be at work.

Answer True or False to each of the following. It's best if you give your initial quick response. You might want to ask your partner to also take this exam so that you can discuss your results.

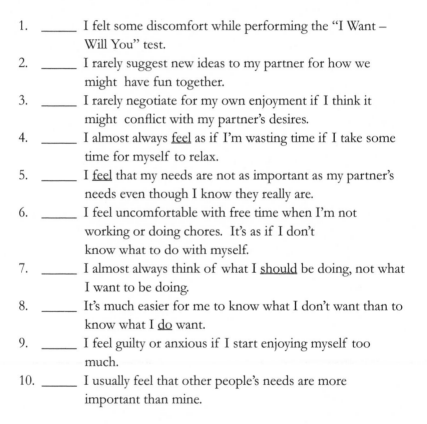

1. _____ I felt some discomfort while performing the "I Want – Will You" test.
2. _____ I rarely suggest new ideas to my partner for how we might have fun together.
3. _____ I rarely negotiate for my own enjoyment if I think it might conflict with my partner's desires.
4. _____ I almost always <u>feel</u> as if I'm wasting time if I take some time for myself to relax.
5. _____ I <u>feel</u> that my needs are not as important as my partner's needs even though I know they really are.
6. _____ I feel uncomfortable with free time when I'm not working or doing chores. It's as if I don't know what to do with myself.
7. _____ I almost always think of what I <u>should</u> be doing, not what I want to be doing.
8. _____ It's much easier for me to know what I don't want than to know what I <u>do</u> want.
9. _____ I feel guilty or anxious if I start enjoying myself too much.
10. _____ I usually feel that other people's needs are more important than mine.

If you answered true to any of the above items, you would do well to contemplate why. If you answered "True" to several items, then your hedonic inhibition is probably fairly strong. Now we'll go to the other end of the scale. The following questions will help you determine how free you are from hedonic inhibition. Again, answer True or False.

1. _____ I felt totally comfortable with the "I Want – Will You" test.
2. _____ I'm proud that I have a sensual and fun-loving side to my personality.
3. _____ I'm almost always looking forward to some fun and enjoyment that I've helped plan.
4. _____ I'll usually negotiate for my fare share in the relationship.
5. _____ I love to relax and have a good time without having to attend to responsibilities.
6. _____ I feel comfortable when someone gives me a present.
7. _____ I enjoy sex for the fun of it. I even look forward to it.
8. _____ I enjoy exploring new places and activities, even if just by myself.
9. _____ I'm comfortable asking my partner to share intimate time with me.
10. _____ I enjoy talking about what I want and what I love.

By now you should have some idea of how much you may be limited by hedonic inhibition. In later chapters we'll be discussing what you can do to free yourself if you think it's a significant problem in your relationship.

Chapter Six

The Other Usual Suspects

There are other dynamics that can kill love besides hedonic inhibition. In our discussion, we're going to diverge from the usual "one size fits all" approach adopted by most relationship self-help authors. Human beings are complex. Human relationships are even more so. Many systems are hierarchical, interactive or both. It's not realistic to say just follow these ten steps and your relationship will be repaired. It's more realistic to understand what type of problem you have so you can more specifically target your intervention strategy. Understanding these additional assassins of love can help you do this.

Assassin #2: Attachment Neglect

Attachment neglect can kill love primarily because of ignorance. Many couples are not initially hampered by core shame or attachment ambivalence. However, they may still kill their relationship because they just don't know any better. This is a subtle dynamic because the damage is done not by something that happens, but by something that doesn't happen. An appropriate metaphor is that a person can be hurt by injury but can be hurt just as badly by starvation. Many relationships just starve to death because the partners don't know that their relationship needs to be fed.

In chapter four, we discussed how nurturing of attachment needs to occur primarily when partners are both in a free paratelic state. Many relationships deteriorate when children arrive on the scene and partners relate to each other only as co-parents. If partners share all their experiences as a family, then they set themselves up to lose passion. If they're smart enough to balance out their roles (sometimes co-parent, sometimes business partner, sometimes playmate) then they're set up to maintain love. I've seen many couples rekindle affection by simply restructuring their schedules to share regular private time with one another.

When relationships begin to suffer attachment neglect, relationship shame is usually accumulating as well. Most people don't want to admit to themselves that they're as emotionally dependent as they really are. It may not occur to them to tell their partner that they're beginning to hurt from loneliness and a yearning for more connection. That's why the accumulating relationship shame may stay unconscious. When a person no longer sees affirming signs that their core self is important to their partner, their shame of feeling unloved will build. This unconscious shame will usually begin to exhibit itself in the form of angry, critical behavior. It's as if the unconscious mind says, "If I'm not important enough to be loved then at least I'll prove I'm important enough to demand respect!" Consequently, partners may find that they're fighting about issues such as who put the salt shaker back in the **WRONG** spot?!!

There's a good metaphor for the fighting that often accompanies attachment neglect. When relationship shame builds up due to attachment neglect, it's as if humidity builds to one hundred percent in a room. With the humidity at saturation point, all it takes is a few cosmic particles to ionize the air to bring about a lot of condensation. In the same way, a charged atmosphere between partners will lead them to find some small provocation for a fight. Their minds will look for an excuse to act out their defenses to unconscious shame. Their angry defensive energy will condense into a fight.

The end result of attachment neglect is usually an escalation of defensive criticality. The bruising fights beget more shame, more inhibition of emotional attachment, and more escalation of defensiveness. Marriage counselors who naively focus on the couple's fights are hopelessly doomed. The source of the strangulation is far below consciousness in each partner's unstated fear. And the fear is that maybe, just maybe, they really might not be that important or loveable after all.

One hopeful point should be mentioned about attachment neglect. It's quite reversible if neither party is strongly inhibited by core shame. If the partners are merely ignorant, then they can be taught about what's really going on. They can learn to be more honest with themselves, learn to courageously express their needs instead of resorting to defensive criticisms, and learn to routinely structure attachment experiences with each other. Many couples experience rapid improvement in their relationships as a result of these interventions. However, improvement becomes more difficult if either partner is hobbled by core shame as described with our next assassin.

Assassin #3: Conflict Avoidance

Get ready for some serious initial confusion about this one. We're going to discuss why avoiding conflicts will actually kill a relationship. Sounds paradoxical, doesn't it? But like many paradoxes inherent in human nature, it makes sense when viewed from a broader perspective.

First, let's be clear that we're not talking about screaming, cursing, hitting, raging kinds of conflicts. We're instead talking about integrated, tactful, respectful, **productive** conflicts. We usually don't think of conflict as being productive because many of us are so poor at it. But when we're good at conflict, our relationships are more vital and passionate. This is because well-executed conflict serves four important functions:

1. **It rebalances boundaries.** When you confront intrusive behavior, it prevents your partner from establishing patterns of behavior that will degrade and shame you in the future. Healthy confrontation is sometimes necessary to prevent your partner from adopting a parent-like role over you.

2. **It reinforces your sense of having a separate self.** The act of expressing disagreement and facing disapproval can actually strengthen your autonomy on a neurological level. Some ways are more effective than others, and we'll be discussing them in the later chapter about autonomy.

3. **It prevents the accumulation of relationship shame.** When you confront intrusive or domineering behavior, you largely prevent the injection of shame into your system. When you shrink back from confronting such behavior, you allow the conditioning of what's known as "learned helplessness." Learned helplessness is the viscerally rooted perception that you're totally powerless in

115

your situation. Think of it as a close cousin to hedonic inhibition. Learned helplessness is about safety and control, while hedonic inhibition is about enjoyment and pleasure. Relationship shame is also avoided when you openly conflict and negotiate for what you want. This prevents the accumulation of hedonic inhibition that we've already discussed.

4. **It allows you to risk getting closer.** Think of it this way. Would you feel as scared walking down a dark alley if you knew you were packing a .45 in your back pocket? OK, perhaps that's not such a great metaphor for the peace loving, but you get the idea. When you're packing well-honed conflict skills, you can afford to get close. You intuitively feel more secure. This idea flies somewhat in the face of the common belief that the purpose of intimacy is to get vulnerable. That's a myth. It just so happens that when we're intimate we're usually <u>more</u> vulnerable than at other times. In his superb book *Passionate Marriage*, David Schnarch makes the point that it's not virtuous to be vulnerable. People who are too vulnerable can't get close at all. They can't risk closeness because they don't have the protective autonomy skills needed when conflict and disapproval arise. I would add to David Schnarch's premise that the real virtue is to reduce our vulnerability in a way that allows us to risk exposure and love more deeply. In this way, well-honed conflict skills can allow us to get closer. And we won't have these skills if we don't use them sometimes. It's like the adage "Use it or lose it!" If we don't use our conflict skills, we'll probably lose our emotional intimacy as well.

> **Vulnerability isn't a positive trait. The real virtue is to reduce our vulnerability in a way that allows us to risk exposure and love more deeply.**

I find that conflict avoiders usually fall into two categories. First there's the "consistent conflict avoider" and then there's the "episodic rager." Both can be considered conflict phobic, but they handle it in different ways. The partner who totally avoids conflict is more likely to come from a family where conflict was taboo. There was no yelling, screaming, or fighting. However, there wasn't any real exposure of negative emotions during conflict either. Everyone was "nice." The total avoider usually grew up in a family that taught them absolutely no conflict skills. Their family probably modeled suppression of conflict instead. For this reason, the consistent conflict avoider is just that, one who rarely expresses anger or risks a confrontation.

The episodic rager shows a different pattern. Their MO is to hold back, hold back, hold back, hold back, hold back, hold back, **BLOW!!!** Like the consistent conflict avoider, the episodic rager also tries to avoid conflict or feeling anger. But they'll blow up after the accumulated shame of their perceived victimization reaches a critical pressure. Then it can be a small trigger that suddenly releases a huge explosion of stored up resentment. It can be merely a small trigger that suddenly releases a huge avalanche of stored up resentment. This pattern is the result of poorly integrated anger combined with core shame. Many of these people have experienced painful humiliation during childhood at the hands of a tyrant parent. Their core shame has been driven deep by these early traumas. But there's another factor that's just as pernicious. Their tyrant parent has actually taught them a perverted mental model for how to be powerful. This isn't to say that this is actually how they want to be. Quite the contrary. The episodic rager is trying NOT to be angry like his tyrannical parent. That's why he keeps holding back and avoiding conflict. However, when the sense of humiliating victimization builds to the breaking point, the closest template for expressing anger is close at hand. It's the model that was introjected years before. He acts like the tyrant parent he so very much doesn't want to be like. Afterwards, he'll usually feel a lot of shame for his rageful outburst. This generates even more resolve to never get angry or engage in conflict. Of course this becomes a recursive self-perpetuating cycle, the problem tightening on itself like a knot.

Both patterns of conflict avoidance, the consistent avoider and the episodic rager, can kill a relationship. The consistent avoider will lose his or her autonomy, stop taking risks, and fall prey to hedonic inhibition. The episodic rager will, of course, seriously bruise his or her partner while an atmosphere of fear settles around the relationship. For both patterns, the answer isn't for them to keep avoiding conflict. The solution is for them to learn how to use anger and other emotional resources so that they can skillfully engage in productive conflict.

Assassin #4: Enmeshment

To illustrate an important principle in this next killer of relationships, I'd like to recount an experience I had with one of my clients. She was an extremely attractive young lady, a successful dentist with her own practice. She was dissatisfied with her marriage and had unsuccessfully tried to get her husband to come for marriage counseling. I vividly remember the moment in our conversation when I felt the pull to become an enmeshed care-taking therapist.

"You look a bit distracted. What are you thinking?" I asked.

"I'm not really thinking about much. I'm just tired. I didn't sleep well."

"How come? Any idea what's going on?"

In a remarkably matter-of-fact tone she answered, "Well, Jim woke me up at 2:00AM last night and wanted sex."

"And what happened then?"

"Well, I tried to tell him I was too tired, but he said that I'm his wife and that's something I'm supposed to do." She shrugged her shoulders. "I'm his wife so I did what he wanted."

Her manner was so resigned and there was no protest, no complaint. It was her resignation that was most significant. I remember vividly my own reaction. My blood started to boil. I wanted to yell in outrage. I wanted to infuse her with my anger so that she would go back and blast him! And then I started thinking about how I was feeling. We therapists are supposed to do that sort of thing. And then I started getting curious. What would have happened if this lady had given the same resigned presentation in a therapy group? I knew the answer. Everyone would have reacted similarly to how I felt. Most people would have been halfway out of their chairs in rage. I could picture it clearly. Then I decided to play with the fantasy. Suppose she had told her little story to a group with a different emotional presentation. Suppose she had said the following in an outraged tone of voice:

"Do you know what happened to me last night? You won't believe it! Jim woke me up at 2:00AM last night and insisted that I have sex with him. What gall! He even said that it's my duty as his wife! That son of a bitch! How can I have a relationship with him when he's such a pig-headed, fucking, chauvinistic bastard!'"

I knew the likely consequences of that fantasy. The group would take her side, but their demeanor would be different. They would be understanding, compassionate, approving of her outrage, but they probably wouldn't be halfway out of their seats with outrage. They wouldn't be trying to supply the missing piece!

So here's the principle. We all unconsciously feel a pull to supply missing resources to a person with whom we're identifying. We naturally want to complete the picture. If I were a more naïve therapist, I would have become her paternalistic protector. I would have given her detailed instructions on how to assertively handle every outrage her husband was levying on her. Instead, I recognized the trap and referred her to a therapy group to help her build stronger emotional resources and bolster her autonomy. Seven months later we had a follow-up session. She had separated from her husband and was proceeding with divorce. It was remarkable how her demeanor had changed. She now had an air of determination instead of resignation. Healthy anger was visible. As an epilogue to this story, I should mention that the ex-husband came to see me several months later, a full-blown, five-star narcissistic personality disorder. He was able to acknowledge the nature of his disorder but continued therapy for only three sessions. Life on the beach was much more attractive and he moved out of town. Such clients rarely persevere in therapy. Much too boring.

I use this story, not because this couple illustrates enmeshment but because my own reaction illustrates the power of the dynamic. I could feel such a strong pull. It was so tempting to become her champion. We're all similarly pulled to complete the missing parts in others. But there's a reciprocal side to this dynamic as well. We can also be pulled to merge with others who supply our missing pieces. If we're under-assertive, then we might be pulled toward someone who supplies our anger. If we're irresponsible, then we might be pulled toward someone who's super responsible. If we're disorganized, we might be pulled to someone who's super-organized. But the downside is that those initially attractive traits may eventually wind up driving us nuts! Where an assertive person may initially be attractive for their "strength," they may eventually be resented for being "pushy" or "abusive."

Where someone seems attractive for their happy-go-lucky freedom, they may eventually be resented for their juvenile lack of discipline. Such is the nature of what's called projective identification. The missing piece that attracts you to the other person may later be resented as a royal pain in the butt!

Many relationship authors have written extensively about projective identification. Some claim that it's the major dynamic causing the most marital dissatisfaction. I disagree with this perspective. While projective identification deserves a place in our discussion of relationship killers, it is one dynamic among many. There are many ways for a relationship to go out of balance. Even the various relationship killers discussed in this chapter are a mere subset among many.

Caretaking is one type of enmeshment that is especially frequent. It occurs when there's an overdeveloped sense of responsibility to protect and care for one's partner. This may sound quite innocent, perhaps even virtuous. Except that several things gradually occur when this dynamic is perpetuated over the years. First, there's a tendency for partners to become polarized. As the helper nurtures and protects, the less-mobilized partner often becomes less and less responsible. The helper grows more parent-like while their partner acts more and more like a child. It's an imbalance that tends to grow more and more extreme. What eventually occurs is a loss of respect and along with it, the loss of sexual attraction. That's because sexual attraction thrives on respect and autonomy. Enmeshment kills it. Most of us can't fathom having sexual attraction toward a child or a parent. When a partner begins to resemble one of these, sex dies or gets thrown out of the relationship. As a result, affairs are very common.

Enmeshment can squash intimacy in surprising ways. The following situation involved a man who felt obliged to surrender his privacy for the sake of his marriage. Andrew was clearly the avoider, while Samantha was the pursuer. Samantha frequently complained to Andrew that he didn't spend enough time with her, didn't want to have sex with her, and especially didn't reveal enough about how he felt. She gave Andrew long lectures about his emotional shortcomings because allegedly he didn't share enough about how he felt. If she ever deduced that Andrew was hiding some thought or feeling, she pried and cracked him open like a clam! Andrew partly bought into this mandate to disclose everything because the alternative would have led to conflict. He couldn't face that conflict.

Andrew rarely felt sexually interested anymore. The boundary loss had been too great. One exception involved a humorous yet somewhat sad incident that Andrew described to me the day after it occurred. While asleep he had dreamed a very steamy scenario involving his best friend's wife as well as his friend. In the dream, all three had engaged in some very interesting and unusual sexual activity. These kinds of images were not in Andrew's usual repertoire of thoughts. When he got up the following morning, he felt a bit guilty about the dream, but still found himself quite aroused. The arousal lasted quite a while and his thoughts turned to Samantha who was still asleep. It was a lazy weekend morning and she was going to sleep late. Fully clothed, Andrew lay down and curled up next to Samantha on the bed. Samantha apparently woke up and noticed that it was unusual that Andrew was curling next to her in his clothes. She asked him what he was doing. Andrew got flustered and inarticulate. And here's the important point. **HE COULDN'T TELL HER THAT HE WANTED HER!** They eventually got out of bed and started their day.

The following day, Andrew and I dissected the missed opportunity. It wasn't hard. If he had made an obvious sexual invitation, Samantha might have wanted to hear about what led up to his sudden surge of interest. That would have meant she might have caught scent of his dream. Once that occurred, she would have pried him open by stoking his guilt about withholding thoughts and feelings. He wouldn't have been able to maintain his privacy. Once the dream was out, there would be hell to pay. He figured it was best to lay low and not be forward. This incident illustrates an important principle. Enmeshment can increase your guilt and vulnerability to the point that intimacy can't be risked. It does so by leaving you wide open to guilt.

> ## Enmeshment can increase your vulnerability to the point that intimacy can't be risked.

Guilt is the strongest glue of enmeshment. Even when a client has a history of complaining bitterly about a partner, it has frequently amazed me to see the outpouring of guilt and sadness when they finally "let go" of the covert feelings of responsibility they've been carrying. The day before I wrote this section, I was doing some trance work with a lady who had been working on anger management. We were using a memory of when she had erupted in rage at her sister while they were in a restaurant. Her sister had supposedly displayed some disrespectful behavior and I was having the patient relive that moment. With the client in trance, I was guiding her through the experience of letting go of anger and defocusing off of her sister's feelings. I guided her instead to reattach to her own higher consciousness. Suddenly, I could see the flushed face, the trembling lower lip and the tearing around the bottoms of her eyelids. She blurted out, "It doesn't feel right. I feel selfish!" I replied back, "Good! Now we know we're exactly on the right track!" This illustrates an important principle to keep in mind. When people grow to the point that they let go of an enmeshing focus on their partner, they often feel guilty and disloyal. The price of leaving enmeshment is often a period of guilt and grief. These feelings need to be tolerated for awhile until the person can more fully consolidate their autonomous sense of self.

> **The price of leaving enmeshment is often a period of guilt and grief.**

Assassin #5: Low Level of Consciousness

Level of consciousness is the degree to which a person has morally and emotionally matured their sense of self. It's essentially how much a person has developed a framework of meaning so that they feel connected and a part of the greater world beyond their mere self. It also involves loving principles and ethics as a part of that world. Level of consciousness is a current area of personality research although the therapeutic community makes little reference to it. That's most unfortunate because it's a useful concept that can explain many problems in marital relations. For example, how stable can a marriage be if a partner tells lies of convenience? If they lack a mature frame of meaning where truth is prioritized over comfort, how can that person's relationship develop a foundation of safety? It will be hopeless. Low level of consciousness allows a person to grab all that they can without empathy for their partner. It also prevents the principles of equity and responsibility from giving the relationship a safe environment.

Neuroscientists have developed specific tools to measure and track level of consciousness. One interesting fact is that a person's level of consciousness can change over time in a quantum-like manner. During times of calm security, a person may operate at a relatively high level of consciousness. When threatened or shamed, a person may regress to a relatively low level. This is what happens to many people who regret their frequent outbursts of temper. There's also a general tendency for people to grow their level of consciousness over their lifetime. This is why we may consider older people wiser or more mature. Even though we have changes in our level of consciousness, we each have our own average level. Albert Schweitzer and Mahatma Gandhi would be considered to have high levels of consciousness. St. Augustine has been rated to have had an exceptionally high level of consciousness. Pure psychopaths or malevolent narcissists such as Hitler or Stalin have very low levels of consciousness.

My opinion is that level of consciousness is one of the most underappreciated factors affecting a marriage. Some authors approach this concept by talking about the "level of individuation" in each partner. However, level of consciousness is a much richer concept because it accounts for emotional growth far beyond getting rid of pathology. Couples with very high levels of consciousness are usually going to fare very well in their relationship. Those with very low consciousness will be turbulent because their emotional insecurities produce hostile defenses.

Measuring level of consciousness requires a precise scientific methodology that far exceeds the capability of this text. However, it might be interesting for you to get a general feel for very low and relatively high levels of consciousness. The following two-part quiz may help you to re-examine some of your world views. This first section asks about relationship beliefs that indicate a relatively high level of consciousness. Answer *true* or *false*. It's best if you give your initial quick response.

1. _____ I never lie to my partner because my integrity and my relationship are more important than keeping the peace.

2. _____ I would rather lose a quarrel than violate a principle of fairness to get my way.

3. _____ I feel good when I tell someone they were right and I was wrong.

4. _____ I feel good when I compensate someone for damages I caused them by mistake.

5. _____ I believe that admitting the truth about my shortcomings is more important than winning an argument.

6. _____ I feel it's my responsibility to be respectful and constructive even when I'm criticized.

7. _____ I'll allow my partner to hurt if it's necessary to prevent behavior that's destructive to the relationship.

8. _____ I refuse to believe that I'm more worthy or deserving than others.

9. _____ I refuse to believe that I'm less worthy or deserving than others.

10. _____ I frequently surprise my partner with creative ideas for us to have fun.

11. _____ If my partner doesn't feel comfortable sharing a private feeling or thought, I want my partner to keep it private until he or she is ready to share.

This second section asks about relationship beliefs that indicate a relatively low level of consciousness. Of course the paradox here is that if your consciousness level were low, you probably wouldn't be reading this book. You also wouldn't be honest with yourself on this self exam.

1. _____ When someone else hurts me, I'll usually try to get even.

2. _____ I sometimes lie in order to avoid being interrogated.

3. _____ I often sacrifice my own rights to avoid my partner's disappointment.

4. _____ What my partner doesn't know won't hurt him/her.

5. _____ If I'm not getting attention from my partner, then I'll secretly get it elsewhere.

6. _____ I'll defend my pride at almost any cost.

7. _____ If my partner treats me disrespectfully, then I'm justified in dishing it right back.

8. _____ I basically feel that I'm more special and more deserving than others.

9. _____ My partner should follow my lead because I know the right way to run a household.

10. _____ Whoever earns more money in the relationship should have more say over how it's spent.

11. _____ I should be able to veto any of my partner's friendships that might be a bad influence.

It's interesting to look at yourself from these different perspectives. It's also very tempting to take your partner's inventory. No doubt there's some bias. You may wonder how your partner would rate you versus how you rated yourself. We all have blind spots.

If you're wondering how to raise your level of consciousness, realize there's no quick fix. It's a phenomenon that involves gradual maturation. People who have an attention deficit disorder or who reduce their frontal lobe metabolism with drug abuse will probably slow down their maturation process. Drug abuse may even reverse it. Conversely, we know that certain kinds of social environments can accelerate the process. Intimate radical honesty communities can *catalyze* more rapid emotional growth in its members. Self-help groups such as Alcoholics Anonymous use intense socialization of "spiritual" principles to perform this function. Certain types of group therapy can do the same. There's a neurological reason why this kind of social catalysis can occur, but it would be too technical and boring to discuss here. Just be aware that the relations you keep with others have a profound effect on your developing level of consciousness. If you hang out with low functioning sociopaths, you will probably remain concrete and immature. If you keep company with friends who are boldly honest and enlightened, then you will likely mature at a far more accelerated rate.

Assassin #6: Addictions & Compulsions

To depict the nature of addictions and compulsions in the context of relationships, a good metaphor is that of a monkey wrench thrown into a delicate apparatus. Broken pieces dislodge and break other pieces. Gears grind each other to shreds. There's compounding collateral damage in a chain reaction. Everything turns to chaos. Implied in this metaphor is that it doesn't make sense to analyze every thing that goes wrong. Just expect it to turn into an interactive mess. Because of this impossible complexity, I refuse to analyze a couple's dynamics when an addiction is involved. I'd just show how incompetent I am for the job. The appropriate sequence of intervention is to deal with the addiction first and the relationship much later.

There's another reason why the monkey wrench metaphor is appropriate. When a partner has an addiction or a compulsion, it fragments their personality into separate pieces like a fractured apparatus. This occurs due to neurological events. Both addictions and compulsions involve powerful reactions in the limbic reward centers of the brain. In the case of compulsions such as gambling or sexual addiction, a specific behavior triggers the release of opiate-like endorphins. The emotional payoff of these endorphins is so powerful that it outweighs the influences of logic or conscience from the upper cortex. The lower brain wins out and takes the most direct route to complete its emotional mandate: get those endorphins released! In the case of a drug or alcohol addiction, the drug either locks directly into the neuronal receptor sites or the drug stimulates release of the endorphins much like a behavioral compulsion. Either way, the lower brain takes control. In order to accomplish its *coup* over the upper cortex, the addicted part of the mind must turn off the dissonant circuits of logic and conscience. It accomplishes this by dissociating awareness of any consideration that might bar access to the drug or compulsive behavior. This dissociation is the central feature of an addiction or a compulsion. It's precisely as if the person forms a mini multiple personality disorder that breaks away from the main host.

For many people looking from the outside, an addicted person looks weak or stupid. Most of us don't empathize with dissociation. If you'd like to get a better feel for it, try imagining this scenario. Imagine that you're on some reality TV show where you're offered ten million dollars if you will hold your breath until you pass out. You know that your autonomic nervous system will kick in after you're unconscious and you will be OK. However, you will find that you won't be able to do it. About two minutes into the challenge you will experience an "attitude adjustment." Your limbic system will be monitoring your blood oxygen levels. When those get too low, it'll decide it's taking over. Your limbic system won't consider the ten million dollars; it will enact a temporary compulsion to get more air and it will overpower your upper cortex. What you will have experienced in two minutes is what someone experiences with an addiction or compulsion. It just occurs on a different time scale.

The time scale for developing an addiction or compulsion is slow and gradual. The first casualty is usually the person's primary relationship. It's not their job. Jobs are easier to maintain because they involve more concrete skills. An intimate relationship requires emotional balance which the addictive dissociation ruins. The drug or compulsive behavior becomes like a secret lover behind the scenes. Healthy love and attraction dry up. Curiosity and pursuit of mind grind to a halt. It's as if the addicted person's ability to love is being devoured by a black hole in the psyche. What makes this process so insidious is that the addicted person is usually unaware of what's happening. Many couples arriving for marriage counseling are in denial that an addiction is taking them down. They may think the addictive behavior is one problem among many, but not the main problem. About ninety-five percent of the people I see with an early-stage addiction or compulsion are unaware of its hold. Denial is the norm.

While dissociation is the process that fragments an addict's personality, shame is the process that fragments their relationship. Addictions and compulsions are both shame generators. It's unconsciously shameful to be so dependent on a drug or compulsive behavior. It's typical for the afflicted partner to project their shame onto their spouse to get some immediate, temporary relief. Blaming, criticism, and emotional withdrawal are the result. Then the other partner's shame from feeling unloved, unimportant, and failing in the relationship gets projected back onto the addicted partner. It's common to feel one's self turning into a bitter, critical person. The shame ricochets back and forth between the two partners, shredding each partner's self-esteem. No one wins.

In the case of drug and alcohol addiction, there's another factor that compounds the destruction. The toxic effects of addiction will often degrade the metabolic functioning of the afflicted partner's brain. This can start occurring from as few as four to five drinks per evening or even three to four joints of marijuana per week. It occurs from various dosage levels for other drugs. With long-term drug use, brain tissue becomes less functional as can be seen on SPECT scans of brain metabolism. I encourage you to go to your favorite internet search engine and type in "SPECT brain images" so you can see some eye-opening images. Some web sites will display images corresponding to brain metabolism affected by drug and alcohol use. I think you will be surprised at how profoundly the brain is affected. It's also useful to know that the metabolic suppression may require up to a year of abstinence to fully recover.

The toxic reduction of brain metabolism is important because you need your brain for balanced emotional functioning. In the SPECT scans shown on the internet, you can view how the prefrontal areas of the brain are disrupted by marijuana and alcohol. These areas are particularly important in regulating emotional behavior. For someone who has anger management issues, taking these prefrontal areas off-line is like rubbing grease on your car's disc brakes. It's a disaster! Drug and alcohol addiction put to sleep the very parts of the brain that you need to manage shame and other difficult emotions. While the addiction is cranking out shame in the addict's brain, their upper cortex is being pushed off-line so as to be even less able to manage the shame. The process consequently progresses and accelerates.

Addiction's toxic effect on the brain has another notable effect. When the brain's cortex loses metabolism, it has less ability to reach higher levels of consciousness. In our discussion of Assassin # 5, we reviewed how lower levels of consciousness will destabilize a relationship by ruining the foundations of safety and responsibility. As a partner's addiction progresses, it's common for lies and betrayals to increase in frequency.

To consider whether or not an addiction or compulsion is affecting your relationship, ask yourself if the partner in question (it could be you) has failed to learn and correct any negative consequences from his or her behavior. Afflicted partners can show early dissociation in this manner. They'll look somewhat dumb because they don't seem able to self-correct. Despite a previous DWI and an embarrassing incident of drunkenness at the company party, they proceeded to have another drunken incident with the in-laws. Failure to self-correct and inconsistency with keeping limits are strong indicators of a problem.

If you're suspicious of an addiction or a compulsion but there are no obvious negative consequences, there's one more thing you might try. You might talk with your partner about your suspicions and contract for a six-month period of abstinence to see what happens. In the pharmaceutical business, this would be called a time series experiment. You get a baseline measure of the symptom before you do an intervention or begin treatment. Then you introduce a change and see what happens to the symptom shortly afterward. In the case of trying abstinence, you would evaluate what happens for the six months after stopping the drug or behavior. Does your relationship dramatically improve? Does the fighting stop after a month or two? Perhaps you might find that either you or your partner breaks the agreement. If the result of your little experiment is suddenly deceit and inconsistent behavior, then you know you're seeing the effects of a dissociative process. You've made progress by detecting and defining the major problem.

If you know that there's an addictive or compulsive problem in the relationship, don't try to fix it without help. This is a problem that requires help from outside the family. A mental health professional is a good bet, especially if physiological withdrawal symptoms are a possibility. Twelve-step programs are most highly recommended. If you're not the addicted partner, consider that you're still afflicted by shame. Attending a twelve-step program such as Al-Anon, Nar-Anon, or S-Anon is the best way to get your own shame levels down so that you don't keep distracting your partner from focusing on his own inconsistencies.

Assassin #7: Physical Abuse

This killer of relationships destroys the most basic foundation of safety that a relationship requires. If you are suffering physical abuse, then marriage counseling won't fix it. Your partner will need professional help. If you're the one committing the abuse, don't think that your "willpower" will be enough if it hasn't worked up to this point. Physical abuse doesn't come from a communication problem, and it isn't caused by a partner who nags too much. It develops because the offending partner lacks sufficient integrity to be adequately stable. Let's dispense with the myth that all problems are fifty-fifty in a relationship. Whatever problematic traits the abused partner may have, the abusive partner still has nonviolent alternatives. It's their problem that they can't choose them.

Let's define what physical abuse means. It's not limited to hitting, slapping, choking or pulling hair. It actually means any physical force being applied in an unwelcome manner to a partner. It includes blocking a partner's movement, holding onto a partner, pushing, sexual groping, destruction of personal property, or threatening physical harm such as holding a fist as if about to hit. I prefer to include one more debatable item, the denial of retreat to privacy. If a partner is overwhelmed and wants to seek a private place to calm down, I consider it very abusive if the partner won't allow it. In fact, it's quite dangerous to deny privacy. Many violent incidents occur when one partner tries to retreat from a conflict but is followed and literally cornered in a back room. Many animals can be dangerous when cornered. I don't recommend that a person stay in a relationship if the partner can't be persuaded that each person has the fundamental right to privacy.

Physical abuse can be derived from somewhat different origins for different people. That is to say that their integrity may be fractured due to different reasons. Here are the three most common patterns I've seen:

1. **Malevolent Narcissism.** This involves perpetrators whose level of consciousness is so low that they feel entitled to execute physical abuse. Their view of the world is egocentric. They are enraged that their partner isn't obeying and submitting to their will. There's no real empathy and no guilt. Their level of consciousness has not yet embraced the concept of respect for individual differences.

2. **Dissociated Physical Abuse.** This is much more frequent than pure malevolent narcissism. These abusers feel guilty about their abusive behavior, but they can't stop it when they're enraged. That's the dissociative aspect of it. They don't want to be abusive, but they become like a different person when upset. They have a dissociated self part and the experience of anger isn't integrated with the rest of their personality. Many of these people have been abused themselves in childhood. When they feel threatened in marital arguments during adulthood, they start to feel the old humiliation from their unconscious childhood memories. To ward off these horrific feelings, the easiest escape is to grab and use what they've been taught about how to be powerful and important. Unfortunately, that happens to be the mental images from their abusive parent. So perpetrators beget perpetrators and the cycle continues until someone decides to get help.

3. **Drug-Related Physical Abuse.** This situation can occur alone or it can be combined with dissociated physical abuse. There are many relationships in which physical abuse occurs only when the perpetrators are drunk or drugged. The person's intoxication impairs their frontal lobe functioning and reduces their level of consciousness. Adult judgment goes out the window and emotional impulse rules. A great many of these people can avoid violence if they sustain sobriety and let their brains heal.

A word should be said about the abused partner in a physically abusive relationship. The trauma of chronic abuse can seriously distort someone's judgment over time. After years of abuse, the accumulated trauma and shame will frequently train a person that he or she doesn't deserve any better than the abuse. This shame can even lead to the misattribution that she's brought the abuse upon herself. The abused person will usually need a massive psychological support system before she's ready to risk taking unilateral action. A naïve approach is to prematurely tell an abused person to immediately get out of the relationship. A wiser approach is to first dig her out of isolation and get her surrounded with an advocacy support network. That way there's less chance that her ambivalent feelings will sabotage an intervention when she tries to make her move. This might include seeking a treatment intervention from the legal system or possibly separating for a divorce.

Assassin #8:   Affairs

Many toxic dynamics in a relationship can't be neatly packaged as being fundamentally separate and independent. The previously discussed "assassins" are more fundamental than others. The sad fact is that the fundamental assassins can combine and produce new dynamics that further damage the system. This is especially true of affairs. Affairs need to be viewed as a derivative of other factors in the person and the relationship. Ultimately, it's the responsibility of the person having the affair because it represents his/her failure to manage the factors that eventually take them down. Many people view affairs as a simple phenomenon of falling in love with someone else. It's not that simple.

It's very natural for two attractive people of the opposite sex to develop sexual attraction for each other if they're in a conducive situation. If two co-workers are about the same age, are physically attractive, work together daily and share their personal thoughts and feelings as "friends," it's natural for sexual attraction to start developing. If one person is needy for emotional attachment, then it doesn't take much to heat things up. A little bit of human warmth can stimulate more powerful feelings that can build with ever-increasing momentum. In the case of our dangerously close co-workers, one person's developing passion can spark the other into an extremely powerful reciprocal reaction known as counter transference. It's natural to feel a strong pull to succumb to an affair. In fact, counter-transference is one of the biggest threats to therapists losing their licenses. Patients who "fall in love" with their therapist can exert a psychological pull that's occasionally strong enough to pull an ill-prepared therapist into an affair. Counter-transference occurs, even if you're a well-trained therapist. These are feelings, not behavior. How one manages those feelings is the crucial factor.

Think of affairs as the result of a battle between two forces. Instead of the usual good versus evil dichotomy, think upper brain versus lower brain. Impulsive gratification is driven by endorphin-releasing reward systems located in what's known as the limbic system deep in the brain's center. Mature judgment and ethical responsibility are heavily mediated by upper areas of the brain, especially the prefrontal cortex behind the forehead. It's the job of the upper brain to modify or overrule the lower brain's primitive emotional impulses for immediate gratification. The upper brain ideally modifies these emotional drives so that happiness can be maximized over time. When the upper brain rules, you protect your marriage and your family.

You don't fracture your integrity and your capacity for close intimacy for a few hours of sensual gratification. Some neuroscientists call this "temporal integration." When an affair occurs, it represents a failure of the upper brain to mediate emotionally-driven impulses from the lower brain. It's a failure of higher consciousness, as well as a fracture in the integrity foundation of a relationship.

The following illustration shows factors that can determine the outcome of the upper and lower brain's struggle about possibly having an affair. Each affair that occurs will usually have its own constellation where the combined facilitative factors have overwhelmed the preventive ones.

FACILITATIVE FACTORS   **PREVENTIVE FACTORS**

Factors that influence the probability of having an affair

Let's briefly describe each of these factors.

High level of consciousness. This is the degree to which people have matured their view of the world and their place in it. It's not just a conscious belief system involving high morals. There are many hypocritical people who espouse high morals but who privately betray them. A high level of consciousness involves a viscerally felt relationship with higher principles of meaning such as responsibility, truth, creativity, and contribution. Level of consciousness is an area of current neuro-scientific research and can be reliably measured.

Disclosing involvement in an intimate community. Involvement in a radically honest community can strengthen one's level of consciousness against emotional impulse. This is one of the reasons for such twelve-step groups such as Alcoholics Anonymous, Gambler's Anonymous, Overeaters Anonymous, and many others. However, these are not the only intimate and radically honest groups. Some Bible study groups that involve self-disclosure can also strengthen higher consciousness. The early Christian movement's emphasis on small-group open confession probably had a profound effect on the rapid spread of Christianity. Wherever it can be found, radical honesty in an intimate group can neurologically catalyze the growth of higher levels of consciousness. People who are emotionally involved and self-disclosing in an intimate community will usually behave more consistently with their most deeply-held values. Their involvement bolsters the strength of their upper brain to down-regulate their more primitive emotional impulses.

Low level of consciousness. A low level of consciousness involves little consideration for values beyond narcissistic gratification or self-preservation. There's not much awareness of a broader context beyond one's immediate physical situation. There's little relationship with higher principles of meaning or with the greater world beyond one's self. Low level of consciousness is more likely found in someone who's been under-socialized or who's been raised by parents and influenced by peers who also have low levels of consciousness. Drug addiction and social isolation will usually lower one's level of consciousness. With regard to affairs, having a low level of consciousness is like having wimpy compact car brakes on a two-ton truck.

Strong counter-transference or projective identification. Projective identification involves someone trying to satisfy a disowned need by vicariously experiencing it in someone else. For example, a woman who's too afraid to exercise her own power may be attracted to a man who acts very assertive and self-assured. An inhibited girl may be attracted to a "bad boy" with a leather jacket and motorcycle. An emotionally-inhibited, cerebral man may be attracted to the flamboyant and hysterical lady in red. Each of these examples involves attraction to someone who is unconsciously perceived as potentially supplying the missing piece. It heats up sexual attraction to a phenomenal degree. Counter-transference is the tendency to reciprocate emotional attraction. If a co-worker develops a crush on you, it's natural for you to feel a powerful attraction back. Like invisible magnetism, both counter-transference and projective identification can combine to create the unconscious emotional pull on two people towards an affair.

Hedonic inhibition producing depersonalization. This refers to a person who is unconsciously inhibited from expressing and negotiating what she wants for pleasurable satisfaction. This state can gradually leave a person with the depersonalized sense that "she doesn't know who she is anymore." Such a person will typically start to feel "trapped" in her relationship. It's dry tinder for sparking an affair.

Conflict phobia and avoidant defenses. When a person lacks autonomy skills and is too vulnerable to her partner's disapproval, she usually won't risk open disagreement. Instead, she'll use avoidant defenses such as compliance, distancing, nondisclosure, and lying. The problem is that this defensive behavior generates cumulative shame. Fear comes to dominate attachment, and sexual attraction gets eclipsed. The person will emotionally leave the relationship. Again, dry tinder is waiting for a spark.

Attachment Neglect. This refers to the loss of affection when two people don't feed their relationship bonding experiences. If both people merely work together and co-exist, one or both will usually start to feel unimportant to the other. Where there's no nurturing behavior or mental connection, the natural friction of living together will start to accumulate relationship shame. The unmet need for an emotional connection will begin to hurt.

There are different configurations of facilitative factors that can lead to an affair. However, some are more common than others. It may be surprising to hear that attachment neglect isn't the most powerful determinant of affairs. While my observation is admittedly based on a biased sample from couples in a private psychological practice, it's probably true of the general population as well. The most frequent correlate with affairs is that someone is experiencing autonomy failure. They're starting to feel trapped and depersonalized. It seems that affairs are more often caused by the loss of one's sense of self than by a lack of closeness. I see this in two most common configurations.

Affairs are more often caused by the loss of one's sense of self than by a lack of closeness.

Low consciousness with hedonic inhibition. These people are starting to depersonalize in their marital role because they're living all the time in a responsible telic state. They no longer feel alive within their marriage. Life and joy exist elsewhere. It's as if guilt and shame have slowly calcified them into a dreary responsibility state. They haven't exercised and maintained the other joy-seeking side of their personality. Without higher consciousness to act as their braking system, they'll skid into an affair when an opportunity presents itself.

Low consciousness with avoidant defenses. These people feel trapped and dominated because they're underpowered in their defenses. They live with a constant background of hidden fear. The opportunity for an affair supplies them with a way to feel passion again, but without the fear.

There are other less common configurations such as the partner who has a very low level of consciousness and engages in sexual trysts. No real attachment is involved and an affair doesn't take place within an emotional relationship. This is the case with sexual addiction where the motive is basically physical gratification. Another configuration is of a partner with low consciousness who is in a relationship suffering attachment neglect. The pain of feeling unloved may be acted out with someone who offers the missing attention and affection. However, this type of affair is less frequent than those involving partners who have lost their sense of self.

In all of the configurations we've discussed, low level of consciousness is a central factor. One might reasonably ask if any affairs occur for partners who have a high level of consciousness. The answer is "yes," but they occur less frequently and look different. The following case illustrates.

Gerald first saw me alone and had a remarkable story to tell. His wife, Angela, had asked him to seek counseling because he had been carrying on an affair for over a year with her best friend, a nearby neighbor. At first I was shocked, but the story made sense as it gradually unfolded. Angela's friend had lost her husband to a sudden heart attack, leaving her to raise their four-year-old son alone. For the following three years, Gerald had helped the friend by being like a loving uncle to her son. Angela had even encouraged him to take on a somewhat parental role with the boy. It should be mentioned that Angela's friend didn't have a steady romantic attachment during this time period so many of her emotional needs went unmet. The cozy arrangement with Gerald somewhat mimicked a spousal role and so naturally stoked affection between the two. The friend had a rocky history with drugs and delinquent behavior and was not endowed with much integrity. She finally completed the seduction one day by coming out of the shower dressed only in her bath towel. After this incident and a few more sexual encounters, Gerald struggled to pull away. The friend reacted by making threats that she would expose the affair to Gerald's wife if Gerald cut off relations. He felt caught in a trap.

What's most significant about Gerald's story was how he handled the final disclosure. He felt tortured that he had lost the honest relationship he had previously enjoyed with Angela. Instead of waiting to be found out, he voluntarily told her one evening while they were lying together in bed. He wanted to get back to being the person he used to be. Of course Angela was devastated. There were many tears and recriminations, but Angela decided she would stay in the marriage if Gerald agreed to go to counseling. He agreed and started seeing me shortly after.

When I heard Gerald's full account of the affair, it struck me how he had struggled to get his integrity back. He was not merely concerned about avoiding disapproval. If that were the case, he wouldn't have disclosed the affair to Angela. When he expressed how he was afraid that he might have a severe pathological defect, we examined how he had historically functioned and the circumstances of his recent affair. Instead of immediately concluding he had a severe pathology, we were able to methodically rule that out. Instead, it became apparent that he had naively put himself in a dangerous situation, had been caught in the grip of a powerful counter-transference, and didn't have quite the level of consciousness to avoid being sucked down by the powerful feelings. I later saw Gerald and Angela in some joint sessions when we reviewed all the dynamics of the crisis. To Angela's credit, she could see Gerald's integrity at work when he told her of the affair. She was able to mitigate her shame and trauma with what I taught her about how such a risky situation had quite naturally created the powerful emotions. It took only two months of counseling until Angela and Gerald were both cheerfully re-engaged and sharing affection.

Gerald's case illustrates what can happen when a person with a relatively high level of consciousness descends into an affair. They usually struggle to get back to their integrity. The observing partner is often able to notice this struggle, and the recovery time is shorter than with partners of lower consciousness. It's the more deliberate and psychopathic betrayal that mortally wounds a relationship.

The Affair as a Contaminant

Everyone knows how the betrayal of an affair can generate shame and distrust in a relationship. However, most people are unaware of how profoundly an affair will contaminate the judgment of the person having the affair. Many people in an affair will get caught in the trap of having their attachment split between their marital partner and their secret lover. They try to be logical by comparing attributes of each in order to determine which way they'll go. Unfortunately, this is usually futile. The emotional rip tides are much too strong for such a pretense of objectivity. The following case illustrates the power of these emotional currents.

Suzette was angry! Ralph's affair had been irrefutably uncovered in the records of cell phone calls and e-mails. He had been seeing the other lady for over a year before Suzette caught on. They had two small children and Suzette didn't want to give up before trying counseling to salvage the relationship. They arrived at my office in rough shape.

First, I negotiated with Ralph to agree to a firewall around the relationship to restore some safety for Suzette. He agreed to send the third party a farewell letter and to allow Suzette full access to his e-mails and other communications with anyone of the opposite sex. We next worked on several imbalances in the relationship that included a poverty of attachment behavior, as well as Ralph using avoidant defenses. As we worked, Ralph and Suzette's affection began to return. It even reached the point where both were freely expressing in-love feelings for each other. This positive status continued until I began to taper down the frequency of their appointments. Rather suddenly, they both came in after having had a week of terrible fights. He declared he was fed up with living with such a wretched woman and stormed out of the session. He never came back. Weeks later the truth came out. Ralph had covertly renewed his connection with the third party behind the scenes. The week he started the terrible fights with Suzette, he had already been back in the other relationship. It was remarkable to see the dramatic difference his renewal of the affair had made in his feelings toward Suzette. His growing affection for Suzette shifted very negatively once he had restarted the affair. His different perceptions of Suzette were like night and day, depending upon whether he was in or out of the affair.

Suzette and Ralph were one of many couples who have displayed the same type of pattern. A partner's covert resumption of an affair has usually coincided with a dramatic downturn in the marriage. The partner having the affair usually has a sharp perceptual shift to seeing the other partner more negatively. The logical conclusion is that affairs do not leave a person very objective about evaluating choices. One's evaluation process is hopelessly contaminated because conscious perceptions are distorted by the unconscious dynamics.

After the Affair

Whole books have been written on this subject but we're just going to outline some basic principles.

1) Immediate trust is an inappropriate goal after an affair.

If you're the betrayed partner, why do you have any obligation to pretend you feel trust? Because it's the charitable thing to do? Forgive and forget? You have more important things that need attention, like truth and your responsibility to protect yourself. One truth is that adult trust isn't naïve. It recognizes limitations and gradations. You may trust that your partner won't stab you in the middle of the night. However, you may not even trust yourself with walking through a bakery if you're on a diet. Trust is about expectations of safety. If you've been betrayed, there's a reason why it happened. That reason has probably not gone away just because your partner feels remorse. It makes sense that you keep your distrust until you understand the cause for the affair and see its full remediation.

If you've perpetrated an affair, then you have a lot of personal work to do. The affair signals that you had a major integrity breakdown. Whatever stressed you about your relationship pales in significance next to your failure to work through the relationship. If there was a lack of connection, then it was your job to confront your partner about the need for more shared intimacy. If you partner failed your wake-up call, then it was your responsibility to confront her about the need for professional help. If her pride prevented her from accepting professional help, then it was your responsibility to show her the brink of eventual legal action. If you were so conflict phobic that you had to lie and use an affair to get your oxygen back, then you failed to get the professional help you needed. The bottom line is that you have personal work ahead to become strong enough to take the heat.

2) Affirming distrust is paradoxically a smart strategy for rebuilding trust after an affair.

If someone were to tug on your outstretched hand, think about what your natural reaction would be. You would naturally pull back and resist. Tugging on distrust is like this. If you've had an affair, then your smartest strategy involves three steps:

- Admit to yourself that the affair was your failure. Blaming the relationship is an inadequate analysis. You fractured your own integrity. You don't like being a liar and a cheat. That's not the kind of person you've always wanted to be. When you are clear that you were responsible, <u>then</u> talk to your spouse about her distrust.

- Develop a plan to get professional help. Time passage is an inadequate plan. Your integrity failure probably involves one or more of the emotional dynamics previously discussed. Low level of consciousness along with conflict phobia and/or hedonic inhibition requires that you put yourself in a therapeutic or catalytic environment to grow stronger.

- Give your spouse permission to distrust you. If you don't do this, your spouse will recognize how you're dodging the core truth of what's happened. She'll intuitively see that you're more focused on placating and manipulating her feelings than on assuming your responsibility to fix your incapacity. When you affirm your partner's distrust after the affair, you're actually reassuring her! It's as if your behavior is saying: "I know I messed up and I know it indicates a danger that I have to get on top of. I don't fully understand it, but I'm working on it." On a deeper level, affirming your partner's distrust helps you to feel permission to stop struggling with her mind. The resulting disenmeshment reduces your shame. It's a subtle benefit, but very powerful.

The time scale for healing after an affair will usually range from years to never. Some authors say that the relationship usually doesn't recover to the pre-affair level of trust. I find exceptions to that rule. When people do courageous work to radically change their relationships with themselves, their relationships can become stronger and closer than ever before. While only the minority of couples show this kind of courage, it is possible.

Time passage isn't the most important factor in rebuilding trust. Two factors are more important. First, it's important that the offended partner observe a profound shift in his or her partner's mind. We're not referring to mere regret. There needs to be an observable shift in the perpetrator's value system. Level of consciousness needs to increase to the point that the offended partner can see his or her spouse struggling to be a better person *for him or her self.* Intimate conversation is helpful to allow the offended partner this internal view. However, it's not enough. It's more important that the offended partner sees his or her spouse's new integrity tested across challenging situations. When this happens and the partner who had the affair has to voluntarily pay an emotional price to regain his or her integrity, then trust begins to rebuild. Telling the truth when it hurts can go a long way. A willingness to face disapproval for the sake of one's integrity may stir up initial resentments. However, it leads to long-term respect and the rebuilding of the relationship's foundation.

Chapter Seven

Freeing Your Hedonic Self

In Chapter 2, we discussed how a vital relationship is based on each partner's integrity. A fundamental part of this integrity is that each partner feels his or her own autonomy. You need to feel a sense of having your own separate self. If you want to accomplish this for yourself, it's not enough to merely oppose your partner. Saying "no" isn't the best way to strengthen your autonomy. If you don't have a good sense of your self in the first place, being oppositional won't help you. Knowing and expressing what you value are the best ways to generate a sense of self. That's the simple and profound truth. But how you strengthen your valuing process is far from simple.

> **Knowing and expressing what you want and love is the best way to generate a strong sense of self**

In order to value something, you have to activate a reflex system that some neuroscientists call your "approach system." I call it the hedonic system because it's associated with pleasure and positive feelings. Most people associate a very negative connotation to the word "hedonism." This is because the word is most commonly associated with gluttony, debauchery and other low consciousness indulgences. However, at higher levels of consciousness, hedonic experience brings true happiness. It includes the ability to enjoy intimate love, the ability to enjoy wonder and learning, and the ability to enjoy aesthetics and beauty. Hedonic enjoyment is necessary to appreciate what is most meaningful in life.

On a neurological level, the hedonic system involves the firing of specific dopamine circuits in the brain whenever you're in pursuit of what you want. If these circuits are free to fire often, it's my premise that you will build a strong sense of self. The problem is that when you're in a relationship, there are other inhibitory serotonin based circuits that can shut down your hedonic system. Inside your brain you also carry a mirror neuron system that makes a model of your partner's mind. Neuroscientists now consider this mirror neuron system to be central to the experience of empathy. It helps you to feel loved. The model of your partner's mind in your mirror neuron system generates the positive sense of being valued by another. But what happens if your model of your partner's mind generates disapproval or contempt? The result is that your inhibitory system shuts down your hedonic system and shame takes hold. And when you anticipate every little thing that might result in your partner's disapproval, you can chronically shut down your hedonic system without realizing it. It can become a habitual part of your marital role. When this happens, you lose your sense of self and you're on your way to "not knowing who you are anymore." I call this relationship depersonalization. You lose your sense of being your own person.

> **To strengthen your sense of self, you need to prevent the shut-down of your hedonic system. You need to exercise it instead.**

To strengthen your sense of self, you need to prevent the shut-down of your hedonic system. You need to exercise it instead. This involves learning several skills. First you need to know how to partially deactivate the model of your partner's mind in your mirror neurons so your hedonic system can operate freely with less interference. You also need to know how to explore potential desires and then decide what you want. Finally, you need to express your desires and protect yourself from any negative reactions from others. Openly expressing your desires is critical to maintaining your sense of self. You won't feel strong if you always hide. You won't feel autonomous.

In subsequent chapters we'll discuss how to strengthen and defend your hedonic system against shame-imbuing shut-downs. In the current chapter, we're going to focus on how you can locate and free up your core hedonic self. It may already be buried under a ton of inhibition. A good way to see if this has happened is to try some hedonic brainstorming. I'm going to ask for you to do something so that you can get the maximum benefit from this book. Please resist the temptation to skip over this next simple exercise that I'm going to ask you to perform. If you read ahead, it might ruin you chances for some beneficial self-discovery. The exercise is this:

For the next 3 minutes think about what new experiences you would like to try that might be fun. See how many ideas you can collect.

That's it! Sounds simple doesn't it? Maybe so but it's also profound. Humor me and do the exercise. We'll discuss your results in a bit. Are you ready? Go ahead and give it a try.

- Stop here and perform the exercise before reading further. -

OK. How did it go? Did you come up with five ideas? Ten? Twenty? Did you get any? For too many people the answer will be close to zero. That's why the current chapter is necessary. If you came up with at least six or seven ideas, then your hedonic system is probably free of strong inhibition. That's great news! You won't have to read the rest of this chapter because it's a procedural outline for an exercise you won't need. If your hedonic system is this free, please skip forward to Chapter 8. But if you struggled to get even a few ideas about what might be fun, then you badly need to learn the exercise in the current chapter. I would recommend that you practice it during a daily meditation period for many months and perhaps even longer. It will help you where you most need to grow.

Steps to Freedom

The following steps describe a way to strengthen your autonomous self in a relationship. Many people intuitively perform these steps without much conscious deliberation. You may not be as lucky, especially if you carry hedonic inhibition from a frustrating childhood. You may need to arduously train before you can perform these steps competently. It's much like learning a dance. First you focus on getting each step right. Then you practice, practice, and practice some more. It's only after a lot of practice that the overall process becomes intuitive, fluid and natural.

Here are the steps all together so you can see the whole process at once. Then we'll discuss each step separately.

1. Be aware when you're depending on some one else's mind instead of your own.
2. Imagine distancing or separating the other person away from you.
3. Begin to fantasize about what <u>might</u> be enjoyable.
4. "Taste" the emotional experience of the fantasized activity.
5. Make a decision about whether you would want the experience if it were really possible.
6. Decide whether or not to disclose your desire to your partner.

Now we'll discuss each step separately. When we're through, we'll package the process into an exercise you can practice.

Step 1 - Be aware of when you're depending on some one else's mind instead of your own.

This initial step involves becoming more aware of what you're thinking and feeling. It's the experience of observing yourself. Neuroscientists call it "metacognition," and it involves activating certain regions of the brain that allow flexible and creative thinking. If you don't take this step, then you will just go on with your usual automatic way of thinking and feeling. Metacognition allows you to make a conscious choice instead of merely repeating a habit. In order to start this process, you need to decide that you're going to self-reflect <u>right now.</u> Once you've decided to observe yourself in the moment, then you can become curious about what may be your source of motivation.

A good way to strengthen metacognition is to ask yourself questions. Verbalizing questions about yourself can heighten your curiosity so that you can become even more mindful and self-observant. My suggestion is for you to ask yourself the following two questions:

1. **If my feelings could talk right now, what would they say?**
2. **Whose mind has my attention right now?**

These two questions can lead you into a profound self-awareness. I would suggest you become proficient at asking them regularly. The first question kicks you out of automatic mode and starts up your metacognition. You start to observe your own thinking. You can usually put your feelings into words that make sense but also give your clues about whether you're thinking autonomously. The second question about whose mind has your attention may lead you to observe one of several possibilities. One possibility is that you're focused on your own concerns and not focused on anyone else's mind. That's fine. You're still in the driver's seat. Another possibility is that you're momentarily focused on your partner's or parent's mind and thinking about what they want and how you can help them. That's fine too as long as you eventually get back to your own mind and concerns. You will then need to weigh out any conflicts between what your partner wants and what you want. A third possibility is that you're not thinking of your partner's mind but rather the mind of some abstract judge. It may also be as if you're being evaluated by that judge, a common phenomenon that may or may not be problematic, depending on how severely you're judged and how easily you can leave this mindset to have some healthy fun. The "abstract judge" is usually the collective imprint from minds of parents and intimate friends.

A fourth possibility is that you're focused on your partner's mind with a desire to please him. You may be thinking about how happy he'll be when you do something for him. This kind of thinking can bring you great pleasure when you vicariously identify with your partner's happiness. There's no problem as long as you can and do easily switch back to directly serving your own desires. However, you will be in trouble if you can only obsessively think about your partner's welfare and you exclude your own. This type of enmeshing self-sacrifice will eventually lead you to feel like you're just a footnote in your partner's life. Let's flag this as a problem if it sounds familiar.

Using your partner's mind to give you "should's" like a parent

A fifth possibility is that you're using your partner's mind to give you "should's" like a parent. If you let this automatically happen without any cognitive self-awareness, then you're on your way to losing your autonomous self.

If you notice that you're reacting to an internal model of your partner's desires or "should's" in an automatic way, that's where you have an opportunity to strengthen your autonomy. However, the objective isn't to necessarily oppose your partner. The objective is rather to have a conscious choice that includes your own desires in the process. In order to have this kind of choice, you need to first reconnect to your core self. The sequencing is critically important. Some readers may have the misconception that I'm advocating narcissistic selfishness. Not at all! I'm advocating for you to have a heterocentric choice in which love for your self and love for your partner are jointly considered. The enemy isn't your partner. The enemy is automatic defensive thinking that excludes your own needs and slowly strangles your self.

Step 2 - Imagine distancing or separating your partner away from you.

It's at this step that many people hang up. You may feel guilty or disloyal when you imagine separation from your partner. However, we're not talking divorce or permanent separation. You're only going to get some privacy (and safety) from your model of their mind so that you can focus on your own. There will be plenty of time to reconnect in the future.

Imagine separating your partner from you.

If you feel a guilt reaction at this stage, then recognize it for what it is. It's your enmeshment talking. It's whispering in your ear: "You shouldn't be so selfish as to have your own wants and needs." I have seen clients who couldn't bring up an imaginary intervening wall higher than their waist.

Step 3 - Fantasize about what <u>might</u> be fun or enjoyable.

This is the brainstorming stage. It requires that your mind is free enough from anxiety so that your unconscious can communicate to your consciousness. Weak associations in your unconscious are put together in novel combinations and then raised up to consciousness. Unfortunately, this delicate process can be easily disrupted by anxious inhibition or guilt-generating "should's." That's why imagining separation from your partner's mind is a useful preliminary step. Enmeshment can suppress creativity but dis-enmeshment can free it up.

Fantasize about what might be enjoyable.

At this brainstorming stage, it's important to withhold any evaluations about practicality. Evaluation needs to come at a later stage. You need to give yourself permission to entertain "silly" ideas as being perfectly OK. Fear of being "silly" is actually your inhibitory system squashing your creativity. It's ideal if many of your wants and desires seem "silly" to others but fine to yourself.

Step 4 - "Taste" the emotional experience of the fantasized activity.

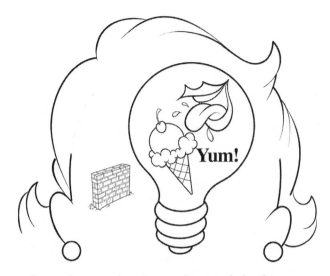

Savor the emotional experience of the fantasy.

In your fantasy, notice how the activity feels. Does it seem pleasurable? Is it interesting? Is it boring? Notice the feelings. This is important information. It's useful data that can help you make future decisions. "Tasting" the emotional experience is just a metaphor for how you can notice the quality of pleasure you get from it. Most people can do this rather easily. However, it's a mistake to think that everyone can. Some people carry so much unconscious inhibition of enjoyment that they can't detect pleasure. **Step 5 - Make a decision about whether you would want the experience if it were really possible.**

Notice that we're still dealing with a hypothetical situation and not reality. "If it were really possible" still involves a hypothetical ideal world fantasy. This is where your hedonic self thrives. At this stage you may decide that you want something even though practical concerns later dissuade you from seeking it. The important thing is that you're allowed to form a relationship bond with what you want. It's less important that you actually get it. If you can let yourself know what you want, then your hedonic core self is free! You will know who you are and you won't depersonalize.

Make the decision to want it.

Step 6 - Decide whether or not to disclose your desire to your partner.

You have a right to privacy. If you feel too vulnerable or unsafe to disclose what you want, at least you've communicated with yourself. If you decide to tell your partner about your desires, then you need to decide on how to do it. You basically have two options. The first option is to share them as mere fantasies. This could be an intimate sharing much like we discussed in Chapter 4. The second option is to negotiate with your partner to try to satisfy one of your desires. Of course negotiation would be risking conflict so you might not want to practice this option right out of the gate. If you do, you need to accept and to prepare for the possibility of conflict and disapproval.

Taking the risk to negotiate

The Hedonic Strengthening Exercise
Part 1: Connecting to Your Self

The following exercise is designed to help you free yourself from hedonic inhibition if it has built up within your marital role. It's not a one-time miracle cure but is a useful tool if you practice it diligently. Consider it like a physical exercise. One work out won't bring observable results. It takes many repetitions to build up strength. Be aware that you're also working against the opposing force of your unconscious inhibition. In fact, there's a real limitation to this level of intervention. If you had severe attachment traumas in your early childhood relationship with your parents, then it's possible that the following exercise won't work. Therapy would be the logical alternative. However, if your hedonic inhibition has been built up only by

151

recent relationship shame, then it won't be buried so deep. You can probably make some headway.

The exercise is presented in two phases. The first phase involves your mentally separating from your partner and others so that you can more easily connect to your core hedonic self. The second phase involves sharing with your partner what you've discovered. It involves your mentally coming back into the relationship. Taken together, these two phases comprise the more complete picture of healthy balance in a relationship. The mental switching back and forth between autonomy and attachment is a necessary skill for maintaining a robust relationship.

Here are all the steps of the first phase of the exercise so that you can see the whole process. Then we'll discuss each step in more detail. You may want to copy this list of steps so you can lay them on your lap to use as a guide when you're first trying the exercise.

1. **Find a comfortable position and close your eyes. Take a deep breath. Relax and clear your mind for a minute.**
2. **Find the other mind(s) in your mind that are generating any "should's."**
3. **Visualize a very strong and thick wall in front of you so that other minds are not in view.**
4. **Find 5 joyful memories not involving achievement and pride. One memory for each of the senses: sight, hearing, taste, smell, and touch. Spend at least a minute in each one.**
5. **Draw the memories close together.**
6. **Meld the memories until you can visualize them as a bright orb of light.**
7. **Let the joyful light float "forward" into the future of infinite possibilities.**
8. **Wait patiently to see what possible fun experiences begin to resonate to the light and begin to rise up to join it.**
9. **When a fun fantasy floats up, let it become clear to you what's happening.**
10. **"Taste" the experience. Notice how it feels. Is it all sweet and joyful? Does it have some sour negatives to it?**
11. **Allow the fantasy to position itself close to the joyful light.**
12. **Repeat steps 8 through 11 until you have a decent collection of fantasies (ideally 5 or 6).**
13. **Consider the taste of your fantasies and choose only the**

sweetest tasting ones.

14. **Ask yourself if you're willing to commit to form a relationship with the fantasy that we can refer to as "wanting." This doesn't require any external behavior. It does require that you're willing to love the fantasy a little bit in your mind.**

OK. Now we'll go into each step and detail it out.

Step 1 - Find a comfortable position and close your eyes. Take a deep breath. Relax and clear your mind for a minute. It's best if you do this exercise in private and not at work. You may need even a few minutes of letting go of the day's concerns before you're ready to focus.

Step 2 - Find the other mind(s) in your mind that are generating any "should's." This is the point where it's useful to ask yourself "If my feelings could talk right now, what would they say?" Notice if you're feeling a mandate from any one else's preferences or opinion. Then sharpen your imagery so that you can clearly visualize and "hear" the other person telling you their mandate. It may be your partner or it could be a parent. Whoever. If there's no one else giving you any "should's" then you can skip step 3 and go right to step 4.

Step 3 - Visualize a very strong and thick wall in front of you so that other minds are blocked. Here is where you do a very important shift in your thinking. You're going to use a visual image to help you momentarily free yourself from the other person's mind. Visualize a very strong and thick wall sliding between you and the other person. This is a powerful metaphor for your own personal boundary. It can come up from the ground or come down from the sky or ceiling. It could even slide across the scene from the side or perhaps come together in the center like two sliding doors slamming shut. You choose. But however it comes, let yourself hear the sound and feel the vibration from the heavy weight of the wall sliding into place. Details are important here because they help you to web the imagery down into your unconscious memory. I recommend that when you first practice this wall for the first half dozen times, spend some time interacting with it on a sensory level. Get up close to it and look at its texture. Notice any colors and irregularities. Then place your mental hand up flat on its surface. Notice its temperature. Take your fingertips and brush lightly across the wall's surface. What do you feel in its texture? Next, rap you knuckles against the wall and notice what you hear. Then ball your hand into a fist and use the edge of your fist to bang against the wall. What do you get? Notice all the details. You're imbedding a powerful tool into your memory banks.

After you practice your wall the first time, you can start adding one more important element. Feel yourself shouting out a loud emphatic "**NO** !" with your mental voice at the same time that you erect the wall. This is all done with imagery, not in the physical world. Let yourself hear the "No !" in your own voice as you feel yourself sub-vocalizing it. When you have all the imagery together, your loud internal "No!" will coincide with your strong boundary wall rumbling into place, complete with vibrations felt through your feet. All of these sensory details will speak to your unconscious that you're safe to be your own person.

Step 4 - Find 5 joyful memories not involving achievement and pride. One memory for each of the senses: sight, hearing, taste, smell, and touch. Spend at least a minute in each one. This step may require a lot of work the first time. You need to find enjoyment and fun in your past. Sift through all these memories until you find one good memory for each sense. It's a good memory if it brings back the sense of pleasure you once had. It might have been the smell of lavender on a spring day, the sensation of a full body massage, the sound of some great music, etc. Some people can't find a memory for each sense. That's OK. If you can just find two or three, you can still proceed with the exercise. Once you have your final set of memories, you don't need to reinvent them each time you do the exercise. You can use them again and again. The technical word is "priming." You're going to use these memories to help prime associations to possible future enjoyment.

Step 5 - Draw the memories close together. This is just a matter of holding them in your mind at the same time and willing them to be associated together. You may first visit each memory one after the other in rapid succession and then imagine several picture screens coming close together.

Step 6 - Meld the memories until you can visualize them as a bright orb of light. Let yourself see the screens start merging into one screen and the image become brighter and brighter. Let the screen coalesce into an orb of very bright light. You're creating a visual metaphor with the joyful memories in close association, even though you don't see them distinctly any more. If they don't all merge into an orb, that's still OK. Just let them come very close together

Step 7 - Let the joyful light float "forward" into the future of infinite possibilities. We're floating forward in time to imagined future possibilities. The joyful light is a metaphor that stimulates positive associations. These associations prime the brain to come up with similar positive ideas. They help free you up from inhibition.

Step 8 - Wait patiently to see what possible fun experiences begin to resonate to the light and begin to rise up to join it. As you float your joyful light into the future, you need to give the process time to work. Be patient and allow yourself to get curious. Curiosity helps open your mind so that your unconscious can begin to speak to your conscious mind.

Step 9 - When a fun fantasy floats up, let it become clear to you what's happening. Spend some time to allow the visual and sensory images to become vivid and clear.

Step 10 - "Taste" the experience. Notice how it feels. Is it all sweet and joyful? Does it have some sour negatives to it? Here is where you tune into your feelings. Does the imagined experience bring you pleasure or discomfort? My reference to "taste" is a metaphor for your noticing your pleasure when you imagine the experience.

Step 11 - Allow the fantasy to position itself close to the joyful light. You may want to reduce the fantasy scene to a small thumbnail image and finally into a small light that hovers right next to your main flowing orb.

Step 12 - Repeat steps 8 through 11 until you have a decent collection of fantasies (ideally 5 or 6).

Step 13 - Consider the taste of your fantasies and choose only the sweetest tasting ones. Go back over your collected fantasies and decide which ones gave you the most obvious pleasure. Consider these to be like collected gems.

Step 14 - Ask yourself if you're willing to commit to form a relationship with the fantasy that we can refer to as "wanting." This doesn't require any external behavior. It does require that you're willing to love the fantasy a little bit in your mind. This is a really important step. It may seem strange to talk about forming a relationship within your own mind. However, this is exactly what needs to happen. You need to decide to "own" the relationship between yourself and what you can want. You're overcoming a little bit of dissociation in your mind. It doesn't mean that you have to actually get what you want. Rather, it means that you're willing to tolerate the mild frustration of not getting immediate gratification. When you're really good at this process, most of your wants are going to go unfulfilled. Even so, you're going to be getting more enjoyment than you would otherwise. You will also have a greater sense of who you are.

Part 2: Communicating With Your Partner

When you've effectively separated your own desires from your partner's mind, then you're ready to go beyond thinking only about yourself. You will be ready to consider your partner's needs along with your own. This way you can have balance. If you let your partner's mind inhibit your own needs then you're in trouble. On the other extreme, considering only your self interests will similarly spin your relationship into the abyss. You have to get both your partner's needs and your own out on the table if you want to have a balanced relationship.

You might be asking "Why share my desires at all?" The answer would be the same reason that you add weights to barbells when you work out at the gym. You need to push against the resistance in order to strengthen yourself. Another relevant metaphor was expressed by one of my male clients who regularly came to heroically detoxify his terrible childhood abuse traumas. He had a military background and phenomenal self-discipline. When I asked him how he was able to face his humiliating memories, I'll never forget his answer: "If you want a diamond, you need heat and pressure. Otherwise you just get a lump of coal." Although he didn't understand all of the relevant neuroscience, he intuitively understood that some struggle is necessary for developing emotional strength. Since our conversation, I've started using the term "catalysis" to refer to the method of stimulating emotional growth. Emotional growth is similar to physical growth in that some catalysis is necessary if you want to grow stronger. If you lie in bed for months after an operation and you get no exercise, your body will degenerate and atrophy. You need to moderately stress muscle tissue in order to switch on the genetic machinery for new tissue growth. Similarly, you need to moderately stress neuronal reflexes in the brain to stimulate the growth of neural pathways.

> **If you want a diamond, you need heat and pressure. Otherwise you just get a lump of coal.**

Expressing your hedonic desires will be necessary if you want to prevent yourself from calcifying into a subjugated marital role like an unused arthritic joint. I recommend that you start regularly sharing your hedonic fantasies before you begin negotiating to implement them. In order to practice sharing your fantasies, follow these basic steps.

1. Make sure both you and your partner are each in a paratelic state. You both need to be curious and relatively free of worry. Don't start sharing fantasies if your partner is in work mode. You can use the suggestions made in Chapter 4 for how to plan for intimate exercises.

2. Tell your partner that you'd like to share some fantasies you've been having. Make sure that your partner understands that you're not trying to negotiate any solid plans.

3. When you start to share a specific fantasy, start each fantasy with a disclaimer that again reassures your partner that there's no expectation to actually implement the idea. This strategy helps reduce your partner's anxiety so that he or she can be more receptive. The following are some examples.

    Someday, if we ever had enough money, I'd love to........

    If a miracle occurred and circumstances would allow, I'd love to......

    If it were ever possible without disrupting our other plans, I'd love to......

    It would be great if someday we could.......

If I could have anything I wanted, one of the things I would want would be.......

4. If your partner asks for more information about your fantasy, that's great! Go with it and share more. If your partner don't ask, then you can ask her if she has some fantasies she might like to share with you. Either way, your main mission has been accomplished for the day. You've catalyzed some strength into your hedonic self by practicing its expression.

If you want to start negotiating for what you want, then you're moving into the realm of possible conflict. Your partner may feel threatened because your idea may conflict with some that he or she may want. Your partner may like saving money or time for something else. That's not to say you're doing anything wrong by negotiating. It's just that you need to accept that there is often some friction involved. You have to be ready for possible disapproval. This comes with the territory and it's hard for many people. We'll be discussing different strategies for conflict management later in this book.

If you want to negotiate, it's best to come out and be very open about your agenda. One of the best ways is to approach your partner with an "I want...will you..." approach. For example: "I want to negotiate an agreement with you about something. Will you listen to my request?" In this example, you're negotiating for your partner's attention. Assuming you get it, you can then elaborate more specifically what you want and ask for his or her help to get it: "I really want (XXXX). Will you agree that we can do this?" or perhaps "I want (XXXX). Would you do (YYYY) so I could have it?" This part of our discussion may seem unnecessarily simple to many readers. However, it may be surprising for you to know how many people can't face the anxiety of negotiating directly. For example, I frequently see one partner throw a statement of desire at the other partner while avoiding an actual request for agreement. They merely assume they have an agreement when the partner doesn't object. "We should do (XXXXX)" or "Let's do (XXXXX)" are often unconscious strategies for avoiding the risk of open negotiation. It's as if the mind resorts to guerilla tactics in lieu of open exposure. You need to express yourself more directly if you want to grow stronger.

There's a final point I should make about negotiation. Once you clearly have your hedonic interests in mind, you need to additionally consider your partner's interests. In the preceding exercise, we've emphasized the importance of first getting in touch with your hedonic core. That's because all too many of us never get around to considering our own desires once we've focused on our partner. If you want to grow a really vital relationship, you can't just separately consider either your partner or yourself. You need to be able to first connect with your core, but you need to subsequently consider your partner's desires along with your own. When you can hold both sets of desires in your mind along with the future welfare of the relationship, then you're well into the higher consciousness of heterocentric thinking. This kind of thinking helps to keep the relationship in balance. Remember. It's not always just about you.

Catalyzing Strength

The exercise in this chapter is designed to help you get started. It would be dishonest for me to give you the impression that all will be well if you just practice this exercises a few times. That would be like saying you merely need to go the gym a couple of times and then you're set for life. In truth, you need to get yourself to the point that you're expressing your hedonic desires on a daily basis. To do so requires that the process is intuitive. You don't want to perpetually stay at the level of methodically executing each of the fourteen steps of this chapter's exercise. You want to develop your autonomy to the point that you can intuitively free yourself from your partner's mind, distill your desires into consciousness, and then give them some expression out in the open. You also want to get to the point that you can toughen your hedonic core by regularly expressing it when expression is totally unnecessary. That's the best way. For example, I still make a regular habit of pushing myself to ask for hugs and say "I love you" when there's no situational provocation for it. Don't wait for a Hallmark sanctioned Valentine's Day to legitimize your expression of affection. If you want to catalyze some real emotional growth, try this idea. Make a commitment to yourself to always purchase blank greeting cards. Practice expressing your sentiment openly and honestly.

> **We must learn to tolerate uncertainty if we want to toughen our hedonic core.**

One principle is especially important if you want to toughen your hedonic core. You must learn to tolerate uncertainty. Uncertainty is what partners avoid when they throw expectations at each other instead of asking for a choice. That's why the "will you...?" part of the "I want...will you" exercise is so important. We need to suffer the anxiety that our partner may refuse us if we're going to practice real autonomy. "Will you do this for me?" "Would you be willing to share this with me?" "Can we have an agreement about this?" These requests are all like weights on a barbell that we're using to exercise our emotional fitness. Waiting for our partner's answer and tolerating the anxiety is like doing an exercise with good form so we can get maximum benefit. And when we're inevitably refused for some of our requests, we need to catch ourselves before we freefall into shame. We have another opportunity for growth even when we experience rejection of our requests. We can actually strengthen our autonomy by validating our own desires in the face of disappointment. So here's a novel idea. Instead of minimizing disappointments, you can express and emphasize them. "I would have really enjoyed that!" "I'm really disappointed!" "I'm still going to hope for that sometime in the future." These are all examples of growth-inducing expression. Practice loving what you've lost. Even in disappointment, you can strengthen your autonomy and your hedonic self if you refuse to hide from the truth in your core.

Chapter Eight

Defending Autonomy

See if the following description applies to you. You hate to fight and so you do your best to keep the peace. However, your spouse seems to always be on your back by telling you to "do this" or "do that," and then criticizing you if you didn't do it quite the way she wanted. You put up with this, trying to do your best and trying to keep the peace. Your spouse eventually becomes even more critical about something that you think is unjustified. You finally go "over the top" and let out all the fury that you've been storing up while letting yourself feel victimized. Your rage only creates a mess that takes a very long time to clean up. If this describes your situation, then you're probably well on your way to losing your autonomy and your attraction for your spouse. You won't have any passion left when you feel that you've finally been backed into a corner.

In order to understand the danger of this kind of situation, it's best to first understand some things about personal boundaries. Boundaries are a hot topic in self-help literature and pop psychology. You will hear frequent references to "setting boundaries." I'm going to discourage you from using that phrase as it is commonly used. Not because boundaries are a bad concept, but because I think there's a real drawback to thinking that boundaries are something that you consciously set. That way of thinking is misleading on two fronts. First, it misleads you to think that your boundaries are always conscious. The second misdirection is to define boundaries as necessarily occurring in external behavior. These two errors suggest that we must have boundaries by acting like a reactive adolescent who has something to prove. Let me suggest an alternative.

I encourage you to think of a boundary as an involuntary visceral feeling. It's the <u>felt sense</u> that you own or deserve something. It's an implicit assumption about what belongs to you. It's not an explicit act. You can have a strong boundary by merely feeling your deservingness. For example, if you strongly feel that you deserve privacy, then your boundary is strong in that area. Let me also suggest that you use the word "limit" to refer to the assertive act of refusing unreasonable requests or unacceptable behavior. If you refuse to disclose something that you want to keep private, then you're setting a limit. Setting a limit is your external behavior, while feeling your entitlement to privacy is your boundary. Limits are external while boundaries are internal. Using these two terms will help you to think more clearly about the subject. For example, you can aspire to strengthen your boundaries to the point that you have a good *internal* defense system. If you can get to that point, you won't always have to react with external limit-setting.

Limits are external while boundaries are internal.

I'm also going to encourage you to make use of the term "boundary intrusion." A boundary intrusion occurs when your partner, without asking, intrudes on your boundary in an unwelcome way. It's as if a neighbor walks through your front door and into your living room without first ringing the door bell. Sometimes it's obvious; at other times it's subtle. Here are some very common boundary intrusions that most of us commit from time to time:

- We speak before our partner has finished talking. We interrupt his or her sentences.

- We give a command instead of making a request. "Hand me a towel," instead of, "Would you please hand me a towel?"

- We give a "should" statement that prescribes a standard on our partner. "You should do it this way" or "You should do that."

- We tell our partner why we think he or she did something, but we don't ask for our partner's assessment of his or her own motivation.

- We pressure our partner to do something immediately instead of asking our partner if he or she would prefer a more convenient time.

- We use sarcasm, a loud voice, or a glowering facial expression to momentarily make our partner feel ashamed that he or she is defying our will.

- We use shaming words such as "silly," "stupid," and "ridiculous" to intimidate our partner when his or her perspective conflicts with ours.

No one is a saint. From time to time, we all intrude on our partner's boundaries and he or she will do the same to us. Intimate relationships are a messy business. We're not going to adopt the position that boundary intrusions are so outrageous that they should never occur. It's true that we need to reduce their frequency, but we also need to know how to defuse them. Even the best relationships are going to occasionally trade boundary intrusions.

There's a problem with how many people try to deal with boundary intrusions. I call it the "Perry Mason Strategy" after the 1950s TV character Perry Mason who never seemed to lose a case in court. He would always come up with an elegant case presentation for the jury at the conclusion of each show. People who use the Perry Mason Strategy will view boundary intrusions as an outrage that must be completely wiped out of the relationship. They also tend to be people who are very uneasy with conflict. Because they're so conflict phobic, they don't confront boundary intrusions when they occur. They want the solution to be relatively conflict free so they gradually accumulate resentment until they're finally triggered to make their case presentation. Then they deluge their partner with all the accumulated evidence of how they're always so inconsiderate. The complaining partners believe that the overwhelming evidence will somehow humiliate their partners so much that they'll be forced to change their behavior across the board. Then they won't ever have to deal with any more intrusions. It's a naïve strategy.

People don't usually change habitual behavior because of a humiliating scolding. The Perry Mason strategy of confronting a partner usually dumps shaming information into his or her semantic memory. That's a different memory system than the performance memory system where habitual behavior is governed. This is one reason why the Perry Mason approach won't work. Another reason is that people don't usually grow in the direction of shame and humiliation. People grow toward positive emotion. Humiliating your partner with a memory dump will only motivate him or here to dissociate the whole unpleasant mess from awareness. Your partner won't work with the information. People are more prone to change behavior when they're offered positive feelings about themselves for doing so. Moving toward self-actualization is a much more effective change strategy than escaping humiliation.

There are a few things I need to get off my mind.

This is probably the best place in our discussion to introduce a crucial change in perspective for most readers. Let me preface what I'm going to say by telling you how couples often present themselves in therapy. One partner is usually more dominant and also somewhat more intrusive than the other. The more submissive partner usually complains about being bossed around and often admits that he's given up trying to be heard. At some point, out comes the Perry Mason approach whereby the submissive partner presents all the accumulated evidence. They expect me to be the judge and change their partner with magical psychological tools they assume I have. However, I have to inform him that trying to "dumb down" a dominant partner rarely works although the partner can be taught to have more tact. If the dominant partner is violent or threatening, then he or she will need psychotherapy. But most dominant partners don't fit into this category. Submissive partners are very surprised when I tell them that they're going to have to do most of the work instead of the other way around. This seems paradoxical. If the dominant partner has a problem with being intrusive, the submissive partner wonders, "Why should *I* have to do more of the work if I'm not the one with the problem? It doesn't make sense!" But I have to say, "Yes it does!.... just not the way you expect." It makes sense because the more submissive partner has his or her own problem, which is fairly serious in its own right. From a systems perspective, solving the submissive partner's problem first makes a whole lot of sense for solving the overall problem. I'll explain.

We've already discussed how we can strengthen our core selves by expressing hedonic desire. That's the most important tool to use. Even so, it won't be adequate if we don't have assertive defenses to prevent relationship shame. A person will still become mired in shame if he only uses avoidant defenses. I almost never see a person who runs away from conflict but also feels very attracted to the partner. The two don't go together. In fact, total conflict avoidance often leads to the loss of passion in a relationship. My interpretation is that conflict avoidance results in the gradual accumulation of relationship shame. When a person ignores or minimizes subtle disrespect shown by the partner, a covert reflex system begins to inhibit self-esteem. It's as if little doses of poison accumulate in the person's system. If this keeps happening, the accumulating inhibition will eventually snuff out a person's attraction to the partner. He/she may even start to depersonalize and turn numb as their core self goes comatose.

> **Total conflict avoidance often leads to the loss of passion in a relationship.**

In order to prevent the accumulation of relationship shame, we need to use active defenses. If we do so, we can prevent the injection of shame that

165

would otherwise occur. An active defense speaks to our unconscious and affirms the importance of our boundaries. It's as if an antidote is added into our system to neutralize poisonous shame before it accumulates. If we're exceptionally advanced in our maturity, our active defense can be totally internalized. However, most of us are not that evolved and we need to transact some external behavior in order to effectively defend our boundaries.

The most effective way to defend boundaries isn't with the Perry Mason strategy. Instead of hoarding up resentment for a big historical barrage, we can more effectively defend boundaries by dealing with each intrusion the moment it occurs. We can use the term "micro-corrections" to refer to this more consistent approach.

The Power of Micro-corrections

Micro-corrections have four important properties:

1. **The correction occurs in "real time."** The offended partner doesn't wait until later for a confrontation. He or she deals with the boundary intrusion when it's happening.

2. **The offended partner always starts the micro-correction with a question about his or her partner's intentions and behavior.** It prompts the intruding partner to reflect on his or her behavior instead of reacting defensively. This initial question is critically important because micro-corrections will rarely work without it.

3. **The emotional expression has very low intensity.** The offended partner is respectful in how to confront. There's no rage or indignation. The tone is matter-of-fact.

4. **The offended partner finishes by asking the intruding partner to redo the transaction a better way without the boundary intrusion.**

Here are some examples so you can get the feel for how it works.

Intruding Partner: "Take out the trash. It's almost on the floor."

Offended Partner: "Uhh….Are you asking me to do something? Because I didn't hear a request. I heard a command. Would you please redo that as a genuine request so that I won't take offense?"

Intruding Partner: "You should do (XXXX)."

Offended Partner: "Excuse me. Did we ever negotiate an agreement about that? I don't recall our negotiating any agreement. Would you negotiate with me now instead of giving me a parent-to-child 'should' statement?"

Intruding Partner: "You did that because you're feeling (XXXXX). I know that's what's going on."

Offended Partner: "Are you meaning to tell me what I'm feeling without checking it out with me? Do you really think you have more authority over knowing what's going on in my gut than I do? If you want to interpret my feelings, I think you'd better check it out with me, whether you're right or wrong. Otherwise, it's very demeaning to me. Would you be willing to redo your interpretation so you can check out how I really feel?"

Intruding Partner: "We have to talk about this NOW!"

Offended Partner: "Excuse me. Do I get a choice about whether I'm ready for this right now? I'm hearing a command instead of an invitation. Would you please rephrase that as an invitation, so I won't have to reject it as a command?"

Most partners won't respond well to being micro-corrected unless a couple has made adequate preparations. In order for micro-corrections to work, both partners need to understand what's really going on. They both need to understand how uncorrected boundary intrusions can slowly strangle a relationship with accumulated shame. This enlightened understanding can help the couple view any micro-corrections as attempts to protect the relationship. They're not viewed as actions by one individual trying to dominate the other.

The other way to prepare for micro-corrections is to practice them before you get hit with challenging emotions. This is like practicing dance steps from book illustrations before you get up on the dance floor and tango to the music. Without this kind of practice, you are not likely to implement micro-corrections with any success. The reason is that you need skills embedded in your performance memory and not just in your semantic memory. These are two different memory systems. As you read this book, information goes into your semantic memory, but it isn't integrated into a performance skill. It's like the difference between reading about piano performance and your "feeling the notes at your fingertips" following years of practice.

Practicing Micro-corrections

A great way to develop micro-correction skills is to practice them proactively. This means that you don't have to wait around until you notice that your partner has done something to offend you. Both of you can agree to practice micro-corrections more frequently by going at it more deliberately. Here are the steps:

1. Both partners decide who uses avoidant defenses more often. Who is more reluctant to protest being given a command instead of a request? We'll designate that person the responder and the other partner the intruder. However, let's recognize that we're all occasional intruders in our intimate relationships.

2. The designated responder makes two lists. The first list is a list of ten frequent intrusions from the intruding partner that are "pet peeves." These are usually commands or "should" statements that the avoider frequently gets from the intruder. They need to be simple (e.g. "Get me that" or "That's a ridiculous idea. You should do it this way instead.")

3. The responder then makes up a second list of five micro-correction responses that he/she wants to practice in response to the ten intrusions on the first list.

4. The responder gives the designated intruder a copy of the list with the ten frequent intrusions. That's the practice playbook. The intruder is also shown a copy of the micro-corrections list. The intruder can request changes to any micro-correction that appears disrespectful. Otherwise, the responder's preferred micro-correction is given priority.

5. The intruder uses the list of ten intrusions to episodically pitch out intrusions to the responder. The responder then responds with one of their micro-corrections. The intruder finishes the sequence by responding to the micro-correction by correcting their intrusion. This is like batting practice in baseball. The intruder pitches out the intrusion and the responder tries to hit it square with a micro-correction. It's important that the intrusion should be pitched out of context. In other words, the intruder doesn't wait around for a real conflict situation to occur. Both parties may be driving in a car and the intruder may start with "Go take out the garbage." This helps alert the responder that the intrusion is really a practice opportunity. The frequency of practice needs to be at least three times per day over an extended period of time. The training is gradual.

The longer a couple trains with micro-corrections, the more benefit they'll get. It's ideal for the couple to switch roles after several weeks so that both get the experience of being in the intruder and responder roles. What happens with practice is very interesting. The benefit isn't just on the responder side. The more dominant intruders will often report more awareness of boundaries as a result of the exercise. They'll often become more tactful when communicating with their partner. On the other side, the more avoidant partners come out of hiding. They may even experience a re-emergence of attraction and affection for their partner as their emotional inhibition declines. It's as if their oxygen supply comes back. The micro-correction strategy is especially effective at turning around some relationships when the partners also negotiate their hedonic interests as described in the previous chapter.

Pacing and Privacy

One of the previous examples of boundary intrusion involved a partner who demanded to talk immediately about an issue. That example illustrates a particular type of boundary issue that I refer to as "pacing." One type of boundary intrusion occurs when one partner refuses to honor his or her partner's right to determine when they're ready to communicate. Like sex, constructive conflict needs to be mutually consensual. If one partner forces it on the other against his or her will, then the other partner will be damaged by shame and resentment. Each partner has a right to decide when he or she feels ready for an activity. Each also has the right to postpone communication unless already committed to a firm schedule.

> # Like sex, constructive conflict needs to be mutually consensual.

Shame is generated when one partner unilaterally disrupts the other's immediate agenda. Because men tend to be more concretely action oriented than women, they're likely to bond with anticipated activities in their immediate future. A last-minute disruption in their agenda is a bit like *coitus interruptus*. Women often don't understand why their male partner erupts when he is asked to have a talk "right NOW!" For the male partner, the disruption is threatening and painful. The more tactful approach is to respect each other's right to pace readiness (e.g. "When would be a good time to talk to you about something?") This respectful approach allows the other partner to avoid a painful upheaval in their immediate agenda. It also allows them to emotionally prepare for a serious talk.

High Noon at 128 Black Rock Circle

The right to choose privacy is another important boundary. It's similar to pacing in that one partner can choose whether she's ready to be in the other partner's presence. This is an important safety issue because one partner may be too emotionally upset to feel safe around the other. If we examine the foundation of our integrity-based relationship model, it requires that we have two people with stable integrity. If one person's integrity is shaky, then he or she is likely to act out defensively with disrespect. On a neurological level, too much emotional pain can reduce a partner's level of consciousness to that of a child. Insisting that an unstable partner stay in your presence is comparable to giving a child matches. The results are likely to be damaging.

Requests for privacy are often combined with the pacing of conflict. Getting a disagreement quickly resolved is ideal when it's possible. However, when a partner is too upset to continue a conflict, she may choose to postpone it while she seeks privacy to calm down. However, it's the responsibility of the upset partner to seek her own privacy. I sometimes hear of one partner telling the other that he's not "allowed" in his own bed or bedroom. Instead of seeking privacy, this could be categorized as retribution or punishment. If we seek privacy for ourselves, then it's our responsibility to remove ourselves from our partner's presence. We don't order our partner around and disrupt his or her usual activity. A good way to negotiate privacy is to ask your partner which room(s) he or she is not likely to use. (e.g. "Where are you NOT going to be so I can have some privacy for the next few hours?")

Some couples have a serious problem because one partner doesn't believe in the other's right to privacy. This enmeshing perspective is consistent with a love-based relationship model. "If I'm upset, then my partner SHOULD stay so we can work it out immediately. We SHOULD always feel close." There's usually no recognition that their partner may need privacy to self-stabilize. I don't recommend that couples ignore this issue. If one partner doesn't recognize the other's right to privacy, it's a fundamental fracture in the health of the relationship. It's similar to the right to choose when to be touched or to choose when one is ready for sex. Denial of privacy can be very dangerous. Many violent episodes start when one person attempts to retreat and the other follows from room to room like a heat-seeking missile. Finally, the person seeking privacy may be cornered in the back bedroom in the house. This is the kind of situation where violence often occurs. I've heard many stories of desperate violence at the site of final entrapment. Even cornered animals can be dangerous.

If you're involved with someone who refuses to allow you privacy, I strongly recommend that you seek counseling with your partner in order to get the issue resolved. It's going to be very hard to have a quality relationship while there's any ongoing violation of your right to privacy. I don't recommend that you appease your partner by forgoing this right. If your privacy is violated and you can't get away, then I recommend that you even consider taking a hotel room (without children) until you feel more stable. If you decide to do this, you can unilaterally enforce your right to privacy. Some issues are important enough that you're better off allowing the crisis to build in order to ensure that it will be resolved one way or the other. I suggest that you consider your right to privacy to be a deal breaker, just like your right to not be physically abused.

The When and Where Rule

The When and Where Rule is an excellent rule for pacing conflict when both partners don't feel ready to start the discussion or aren't emotionally equipped to continue it. The rule has two parts that go together. It's like epoxy glue. There's a part A and a part B. The two parts are necessary for the rule to work over time.

Part A: Each partner has an absolute right to withdraw from a conflict at any time, no matter what. This part of the rule has top priority.

Part B: The withdrawing partner has an obligation to offer a negotiated rescheduling of the discussion. Before withdrawing, this partner must offer to negotiate a specific time and place for resuming the conflicted discussion.

This rule recognizes the absolute right of both partners to pace themselves for conflict so that it can be more productive. However, the rule also recognizes that each person has a responsibility to the relationship to address an issue if it's disturbing their partner. Stonewalling on an issue isn't good for a relationship. Couples usually can't get this rule to work unless they're very deliberate. The devil's in the details. Most couples make the mistake of being too vague about resuming the conflict. For example, most conflict-avoidant partners will offer to talk about the issue "later" or "tomorrow." Their partner understandably distrusts such a dodge because it has zero probability of being carried out. The more dominant partner assumes he or she will have to grab the avoidant partner when possible. The dominant partner won't be tricked (again) by vague promises. Instead of a vague deferral, extreme specificity is the key ingredient in the When and Where Rule. As its name implies, both time and place are negotiated. Here's an example of how such a negotiation might be offered:

> "I'm too angry to continue this conversation right now. I want to negotiate a 'When and Where' on this. How about we talk about it tonight after supper…Say 8:00? I'm going to suggest we meet in the den. We can sit at the table and work it out then.….Or is there another time and place better for you?"

Notice that a specific time and place is being offered in the previous example. The specificity offers a believable picture to which a partner's mind can bond. Without such a specific image, the other partner will feel abandonment. Also notice that the process of scheduling is shared. The negotiation won't work if one partner dictates to the other. "I'll see your ass tonight in the den at 8:00. Be there!" But people do this. Even control over the conversation can become a weapon in the dominance wars. For the When and Where Rule to work, one partner must truly negotiate and allow the other to have some say in the rescheduled time and location. For this reason, it's useful to have couples practice the question "Or is there another time and place better for you?"

There's another useful tool for stopping a conflict when it's going over the top. Imagine your partner is engaged in a tirade that's going on and on. Instead of elevating your voice to compete in volume, you may want to use a nonverbal tool. There's an instinctive need to see another person's eyes during a conversation. It's called attunement. Even infants attempt attunement long before they learn verbal language. If you can't be heard while your partner rages at you, you might try the "T" signal for "time out." The following illustrates how you block eye contact with your hand. The disrupted eye contact stops attunement and usually has the effect of momentarily inhibiting conversation. Then you can get your when and where proposal out in the open.

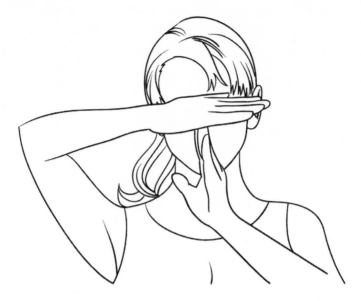

The "Time Out" signal for breaking attunement

Practicing the When and Where Rule

This is an appropriate place to inform you that even though you've read about the When and Where Rule, you will still have close to zero probability of actually implementing it without practice. That's because there's a difference between semantic learning versus performance learning. When the music starts and you're feeling overwhelmed by emotion, the dance steps outlined in this chapter will be far from your mind. Unless you do some preliminary practice, you will just fall back into old automatic behavior. Our minds are like that. Too much emotional disturbance will turn off a part of the brain called the upper anterior cingulate. When this part of the brain is turned off by negative emotion, we have a hard time using metacognition to override old habits. Negative emotion makes your thinking rigid. Of course that's probably not really news to you. So unless you practice the When and Where Rule, you will use your old defenses instead.

Practicing the When and Where Rule is like practicing dance steps without the music. Both you and your partner need to agree that you will be practicing in order to improve your relationship. You want to remove any sense of silliness so you agree that you can practice the rule without the negative emotion. The way to do this is to wait until you and your partner are having a pleasant conversation without any hint of conflict. Then, right in the middle of the conversation, use your time out signal and negotiate a when and where deferral. You and your partner may be talking about the Redskins game or perhaps an interesting piece of gossip you heard from a friend. The topic really doesn't matter as long as the conversation is relaxed and peaceful. Go ahead and negotiate a when and where rescheduling of the conversation as if you're dealing with a terrible conflict. After that, make sure that you and your partner show up at that time and place to finish the conversation. It may seem silly when you get together the following day to finish talking about the Redskins. But you will have accomplished something very important. You will have imprinted an important piece of trust in both of your brains. If both you and your partner each practice at least two when and where deferrals this way, then you will have at least quadrupled the chances that you both can use the tool when you're in emotional distress.

The benefits of implementing the When and Where Rule are enormous. When couples learn to defer tough conflicts until both are ready, the heat of conflict can be greatly reduced. It's as if the brain has a chance to prepare itself to be more methodical and mature. As a general rule, a frightened brain is more likely to overreact and go "over the top." When a person feels more reassured after some thought, they're less likely to lose it. For this reason, the When and Where Rule is probably the single most important tool to learn for managing conflict.

Refusing Enmeshment

Sometimes a conflict between partners involves no substantial issue other than disapproval. For example, imagine a couple getting ready for a Sunday barbecue with friends. The wife turns to her husband and exclaims, "Why do you have to wear that same old ugly outfit? Don't you have any imagination? Try wearing something different for a change." Although the wife is genuinely expressing her feelings, she's also intruding a bit into her husband's boundaries by using syntax and vocabulary that invoke shame. This would be an ideal occasion to put a micro-correction to good use. However, let's suppose the wife persists with her complaint because she feels strong disgust about her husband's mindlessness regarding his appearance. The issue may be much deeper that it appears. She may interpret his mindlessness about his appearance to be a part of a greater mindlessness about the relationship itself. (e.g. If she were more important to him, he might care more about how he appears in her presence.) Of course the wife probably wouldn't want to admit to herself that she's as vulnerable and emotionally dependent as she really is. That would bring her too close to "The Great No-No." Her unconscious avoidance of her own shame is what throws her out of balance. Consequently, she chooses the less vulnerable approach of expressing disapproval. This is how a lot of fights start in a relationship. Very often, the couple can't even remember how the fight started. It takes on a life of its own. In our previous example, the husband might respond with some form of counter-attack to reassure himself that he's not a total wimp. Back and forth it will go, each person trying to avoid the shame of victimization by mounting a more aggressive attack on the other. This is one form of enmeshment. Even though they're opposing each other, neither party can pull away from focusing on each other's reactions. It's like a self-tightening knot.

Disenmeshment (refusing enmeshment) is an important skill to have in a relationship. This skill allows you to side-step unnecessary conflicts that would otherwise only cause damage. However, it's not an easy skill to learn because it requires that you employ metacognition to observe your own thinking and feeling. You need to first consciously realize that you're feeling threatened or ashamed by your partner's disapproval. This initial step of self-honesty is probably the hardest part. You have to wrestle with "The Great No-No." After this initial realization, you have several more steps in order to disenmesh. The whole sequence can be outlined as follows:

1. Consciously focus on your own emotional state. Notice how you're starting to feel ashamed and diminished. Are you stable enough to continue the conflict?

2. Consider whether the conflict has any valid issue. Does it really need to be resolved? If so, continue with the negotiations or perhaps a micro-correction.

3. If the conflict has no valid issue, then choose a new focus to replace your previous focus on your partner's mind.

4. Amplify the new focus of your attention with overt behavior or internal affirmations.

The key process in disenmeshment is the shifting of attention in your brain.

The key process in disenmeshment is the shifting of attention in your brain. When you form a focus of attention, specific areas of your brain become activated. When your attention shifts, so do the areas of activation. Neuroscientists have extensively studied the complex systems for letting go of attention, shifting attention, and fixating attention. The relevance here is that, in order to disenmesh from a disapproving partner, you're going to have to shift attention away from your mirror neuron system. That's the system that replicates a model of your partner's mind. In other words, you have to get your attention away from how your partner's mind is viewing you as such a schmuck! Some people can't do this. They're like a deer stuck in headlights that can only look at the oncoming car! They can only fixate on what their partner is thinking and how to change it. They remain in a low consciousness state and strike back.

A typical enmeshed partner

When you disenmesh, shame can be avoided if your new focus of attention sufficiently inspires you. This usually means that you need to feel good about a new purpose to guide your behavior. I refer to this shifting of attention as an "autonomy shift." You shift from attachment to autonomy within your own mind. Here are some examples of some disenmeshing responses to our hypothetical picnic attire conflict. Let's assume the conflict has already escalated into a full-fledged shame fight.

Internal Response: Why is she taking such a guarded position? Maybe she's not feeling very important in the relationship. After all, I haven't spent much time with her lately. I probably need to nurture the relationship a bit more than I have.
External Response: Hey, I'll make a deal with you. I'll let you choose my outfit if you will wear that sexy halter top that's such a turn on.

Internal Response: We're only causing damage in this argument. There's no real issue that we have to resolve. The important thing is to settle it down so we don't ruin the afternoon.
External Response: This argument is really unnecessary. I don't want for us to ruin the afternoon. Why don't you and I just get ready separately and maybe we'll be calm enough when it's time to leave.

Internal Response: We're both locked in a shame fight. She doesn't see it, but I do. Even though she's indulging herself, I have a responsibility to do what I know is best for the relationship. That's the kind of person I want to be. I know there's nothing I can say that won't provoke her right now so I'll just go into the other room.
External Response: (leaves)

Internal Response: We're in an enmeshed fight right now. She disapproves, but it's important that we don't keep fighting about that. I need to let go of this struggle. I can do that by using permission.
External Response: It's OK that you don't like what I wear. Go ahead and disapprove. We're different people with different tastes. You wear what you like and I'll wear what I like.

The previous examples illustrate how there's no one "right" focus for your attention when you disenmesh. The important thing is that you feel that your new focus brings you closer to your own integrity. The positive feelings that result from this shift can then successfully compete against your previous sense of shame. When this happens, you don't have to go "over the top" to avoid humiliation.

> **Sometimes we need to say out loud what our unconscious needs to hear.**

A very useful principle is illustrated in the last example from our list of picnic fight responses. The principle is that sometimes we need to say out loud what our unconscious needs to hear. Permission giving is a powerful device for helping us to disenmesh. "It's OK that you don't like what I wear. Go ahead and disapprove." This kind of permissive statement really speaks to your own mind more than to your partner. It helps you let go of your partner's mind without the usual sense of shame that comes from running away. It reframes your disengagement as something powerful and dynamic. Your unconscious will hear the message and even though your partner won't appreciate their lack of influence on your emotions, your autonomy will be better protected.

Responsible Capitulation

The concept of talking to your own unconscious has more than one application. In the previous discussion, we illustrated how you can tell your partner what you need to hear yourself. This can help you to reframe the interaction so that you avoid shame. The same strategy can be used when you sometimes need to capitulate in a conflict. Does that sound like anathema? Am I really advocating that you learn to capitulate? You betcha! There's a good reason to do just that. Even the best armies don't always attack. They need to maneuver and know how to retreat. Relationships involve a lot of compromises. Many victories can be pyrrhic if you insist on winning a conflict that's not critically important. The juice may not be worth the squeeze.

Imagine that you're in Venice, Italy on your 25th wedding anniversary. You've just started a two- week tour through Italy and Greece when your wife changes her mind about the agenda of your last day. You had previously agreed that you would take the gondola ride that last afternoon, but she just heard about the glass blowing on the Isle of Murano and she wants to completely change the agenda and go there. If you're the wife, you can reverse the story. Your husband wants to junk your shopping visit to Murano because he just got a hot urge to tour the canals in a gondola. In either story, imagine that you had negotiated the original plans far in advance and that you really don't like your spouse's proposal. You're tempted to complain that they don't have a right to press you so hard to give up a mutual agenda at the last minute. You think they're being a bit selfish. What are you going to do?

What's more important to you? Do you want to "stand up for yourself" or do you want to capitulate in order to help ensure harmony during a once in a lifetime shared experience? This is an extreme example that's loaded in an obvious direction. However, you need to be ready to capitulate and compromise in many lesser dilemmas. The challenge is how to do so without wounding yourself with shame and resentment. We're going to discuss how to do this.

Let's first discuss how to **NOT** capitulate. Here are some expressions that are especially destructive:

"Whatever! I don't care." (may be accompanied with either a shrug or an eye roll)

"Fine! We'll do it your way, as usual." (sarcastic tone)

"You're always right. It doesn't matter what I think."

"What I want isn't important. We'll do what you want."

In all these examples, the most destructive element is the minimizing of your hedonic desire. If you discount your real feelings, you're unconscious is listening and takes it in as shame. You're accumulating the unconscious inhibition that can snuff out your affection or later explode as dissociated rage. The problem is that most people don't know that there are more than two ways of responding. Most people think that you either have to fight or that you need to hide your selfishness. They don't know that there's a smarter way.

The third option is something I call responsible capitulation. That may sound like an oxymoron. How can it be responsible to capitulate? I have two answers for this. The first is that it's responsible to surrender when it serves a constructive higher purpose. Preserving tranquility for a once in a lifetime anniversary trip might be such a purpose. My other answer is that it's responsible to capitulate when we assume responsibility for making the choice. If we don't assume responsibility, then we won't surrender responsibly. We'll hurt ourselves by accumulating shame. If we surrender while connecting to our sense of responsibility and higher purpose, then it won't be damaging. It will stimulate us to grow stronger.

Let's first codify some guidelines for how to surrender constructively.

Guidelines for Responsible Capitulation

1. **Express the importance of what you're giving up when you choose to capitulate.**

2. **Openly articulate the meaningful considerations that led you to give up what you want. Use syntax that joins what you're giving up and the more important concern that you're prioritizing.**

That's it! The guidelines are simple but profound. They can make a phenomenal difference in how we feel and behave long after we capitulate. They can also help us to be more flexible negotiators when we're confident that we don't have to eat a lot of shame each time we give in. Let's take the example of the imaginary conflict in Venice. After your spouse insists on changing the agenda at the last minute, you decide that a fight about what you consider to be her selfishness isn't worth the risks to your very special trip. Imagine telling your spouse something like this:

"Since you're really passionate about going to Murano, I'll agree to do that... **AND**... I'm going to really miss that gondola ride with you. I had imagined it as a really special romantic memory. I had even imagined how we'd be able to look back in our old age at some really romantic pictures of us in the gondola. That was important to me **AND** what's MORE important is that we enjoy the two weeks with each other and not upset the whole applecart. I want for us to get along and get close during this once in a lifetime experience, even if we have to miss out on the gondola thing."

Imagine what it would be like to say that. Notice that you fully articulated the importance of what you're giving up. That's the first guideline. Expressing the importance of your frustrated desire helps to prevent dissociation. It ensures that your mind doesn't lie by saying that what you wanted was unimportant. That kind of lie would inject shame and inhibition into your system. In this imaginary discussion you also expressed a higher order desire as the reason for your sacrifice. That's the second guideline. You valued the overall harmony of the trip more than winning on a particular issue. You expressed your sense of responsibility for protecting an important symbol of relationship.

> ## Expressing the importance of your frustrated desire helps to prevent dissociation.

There's another important aspect of this imaginary discussion in Venice. Notice that you used the word "AND" to join your two considerations together. You didn't use the word "BUT" to contrast them which would have been more natural speech. There's a reason for this strange syntax. First let me ask you a question. Which would you prefer: to speak proper English or to become more astute? Sometimes the English language imposes restrictions on how we think. Dissociation occurs between two ideas when we separate them with the word "BUT." When we use the word "AND" the mind is encouraged to join ideas together. It stimulates your mind to grow more sophisticated when you simultaneously hold together two conflicting desires. The tolerance for ambivalence is one of the best indicators that a person enjoys higher consciousness. I'm not advocating that you change your syntax in everyday speech. I'm only suggesting that you use this strange syntax whenever you make responsible capitulations. You will protect yourself from shame while stimulating your own emotional growth.

Responsible capitulation depends on your personal frame of meaning.

Unconscious shame is averted when you perceive that your sacrifice serves a greater good. That's the essence of responsible capitulation. It means that you've embraced responsibility for a greater meaning than your original desire. And what can that meaning be? For many readers, that's a scary topic. Many people are afraid to talk about their own meaning. It's as if they're afraid of being ridiculed for being silly. After all, isn't meaning just an abstraction? Nope. It's a powerful neurological event.

When we embrace meaning in our lives, we activate associations in the prefrontal cortices of our brains. Monoaminergic dopamine circuits fire up, and opiates are released in the deep brain reward centers. This is the power of positive psychology which can affect our lives in profound ways. In his book *Man's Search for Meaning*, Victor Frankel writes about how he observed meaning to be a powerful determinant of who survived the horrors in a concentration camp. Attachment to meaning is also closely associated with longevity. Our immune systems can be turned off by high levels of cortisol that accompany stress. When we feel attached to positive meaning, our stress is reduced. What's especially relevant about meaning is that it can also block shame. When we embrace a positive meaning for why we capitulate, we're neurologically protected. We can prevent our autonomy from becoming mired by the accumulation of unconscious inhibition. That's the purpose for the second guideline for responsible capitulation. By articulating our meaning out loud, we amplify it in our brains. Our unconscious is listening to what we say and do.

> **By articulating our meaning out loud, we amplify it in our brains.**

Some readers may wonder what types of meaning can block shame. What meaning can be that powerful? Let's imagine a fantasy. As much as we want to live forever, we're all going to die. Imagine that you can travel forward in time and see your own tombstone. At the top of that tombstone is inscribed your name and then the following words: "He lived true to his core values." If you're a woman, it would of course read:, "She lived true to her core values." Down below that statement are listed five words. What would yours be? Think about it. This little exercise has a way of clearing out the opinions of others so that you take more responsibility for your own ideas. What words would you choose?

I've found that certain core values are more popular than others. Here are some of the more frequent ones.

Truth	Service
Responsibility	Creation
Faith	Honor
Spirituality	Duty
Integrity	Beauty
Contribution	Loyalty
Generosity	Fairness

There are many others. Core values vary from person to person. The important thing is that you use them to guide your behavior, especially in conflict. If you capitulate merely because you fear disapproval, then your capitulation will be irresponsible. It will allow shame and resentment to accumulate and hurt your relationship in subtle ways. It's like pouring acid on the beams of your house. It's more responsible to do the tough work in the moment and keep your beams uncompromised. If you don't think you're serving one of your core values when you capitulate, then you have no business capitulating. In Chapter 3, we discussed how our relationships require that we alternate between states of autonomy and connection. This autonomy switching is a tough thing to do. It's the Olympic challenge inherent in all intimate relations. When should we give in and when should we hang tough? My recommendation is that you let your core values guide you.

> **Capitulating because you fear disapproval is like pouring acid on the beams of your house.**

It requires a certain kind of skill to think of core values during a conflict. There's a neurological reason for this challenge. Negative emotion causes reciprocal suppression of activity in a part of the brain called the upper anterior cingulate. When this area is suppressed and inactive, you lose cognitive flexibility as well as the ability to override old defensive habits. It becomes harder to activate the prefrontal areas in your brain that mediate your core values. Negative emotion reduces cognitive flexibility. That's a known psychophysiological fact. However, the situation isn't hopeless. For a number of years, I've trained people to access their core values when they feel shameful disapproval. I've named it "conflict inoculation training" and it involves purposefully putting clients in a shame state so that they can practice. The procedure is much too complicated to be presented here, but it illustrates the fact that people can change. They can develop greater skill at accessing their core values during conflict. After conflict inoculation training, clients often stop freezing and can start negotiating. Other people stop raging. In one case, a woman was able to stop spitting on her husband. That's the result when positive psychology is put to work in a practical way.

For your own situation, I suggest that you try implementing the guidelines for responsible capitulation. They'll challenge you to be honest with yourself. If you can give in to your partner while articulating your higher responsibility for doing so, then you will be on firm ground. If you can't articulate a higher purpose and you find that you're only afraid of disapproval, then you will need to hang tough. Your other alternative is to use a when and where deferral so that you have time to regain your flexible thinking. Either way, you will be protecting your autonomy to the benefit of your relationship.

Chapter Nine

Managing Conflict

When we talk about managing conflict, we don't mean eliminating it. We don't even necessarily mean reducing it. In fact, sometimes it's better to increase it. It all depends on which type of conflict is involved. We're going to discuss different types of conflict in this chapter. To start out, let's define two major categories: destructive versus constructive conflict. "Constructive conflict." Doesn't that sound like an oxymoron? How can conflict be constructive? Doesn't conflict wreck relationships? Most of us are so conditioned by painful experience that we overlook the potential utility of conflict. Anger tends to get the same treatment. How can anger be a good thing? The answer is: when it protects and helps the species to survive. Conflict can similarly protect and help our relationship to survive. We just need to know how to do it skillfully. The difference between constructive conflict and destructive conflict is like the difference between electricity and an atomic bomb.

We have to initiate conflict in certain situations if we want a vital relationship. If we settle for an emotionally distant relationship with our partner, then we can afford to be perpetually nice. Conflict and anger won't be necessary. Totally avoiding conflict will get us a peaceful and vapid relationship. If we want emotional closeness instead, then we'll have to pay for it with occasional discomfort. We'll have to use our anger in a disciplined way while we risk our partner's disapproval and correct the situation so that it doesn't perpetuate. This is the heavy lifting aspect of a vital relationship. It's tough work, but it keeps a relationship more balanced. Robust relationships aren't for wimps!

> ## We have to initiate conflict in certain situations if we want a vital relationship.

There are three types of situations for which conflict can be beneficial. They are:

1. **Conflict of Interest** – This occurs when one partner wants it one way and the other partner wants something different. For example, you want to go out for dinner and eat Chinese while your partner wants Italian. The choices may be mutually exclusive.

2. **Broken Agreement** – This occurs when one partner breaks a negotiated agreement with the other. For example, your partner agreed to pick up milk on the way home but forgot.

3. **Boundary Intrusion** – This occurs when one partner intrudes on some form of privacy, ownership, or personal prerogative of the other. For example, one partner gives a command to their partner instead of a respectful request.

Initiating conflict in these situations can help prevent a relationship from going downhill. If we don't negotiate conflicting interests, then we build up resentment and hedonic inhibition that can strangle our affection. If we don't confront broken agreements or boundary intrusions, then we accumulate relationship shame from our sense of subjugation. When we do risk conflict in these situations, we certainly need to use skill and tact in order to get positive benefits. Otherwise, we just get the all too familiar mess. The following discussion outlines some useful strategies that can help.

Negotiating Conflict of Interest

We need to exercise the hedonic part of our personality if we want to keep it alive in a relationship. When we have a partner doing the same thing, we're going to naturally bump up against them. There's a natural friction when two partners are robustly living together. If we do have the courage to openly express what we really want, then the conflict can go in one of two directions. We've already mapped one direction when we previously discussed the concept of responsible capitulation. Sometimes it's important to yield to our partner when we're aware of a higher purpose. At other times, we need to hang tough and firmly negotiate. When we follow the second route, there are four principles to keep in mind. These principles are explained in a classic book on negotiation by Fisher and Ury titled *Getting to Yes*. I've modified them so that they can be applied to intimate relationships.

Principles for Tactful Negotiation

1. **Focus on interests instead of positions.** The initial focus of negotiation should be about what each partner wants and not about each partner's rigid idea for a solution. By initially focusing on needs instead of solutions, there's more flexibility to create solutions that meet the needs of both partners.

2. **Separate your partner from the problem.** There are subtle ways to protect each partner's ego from shame during negotiations. When "the problem" is defined as not being the fault of either partner, then both partners can be less defensive and more creative.

3. **Negotiate objective standards of fairness.** Objective criteria in the real world can be used to define what's fair or equitable. One simple example would be: who was the last person to choose the restaurant for dining out? Objective criteria can protect both partners from fearing that they'll be victimized. Without objective criteria, the threat of shame is greater. One partner could perceive that the other partner is bullying him or her into submission and victimization.

4. **Create alternatives for mutual benefit.** Sometimes both partners can get their needs met if they think creatively. They can reconfigure the conflict in such a way that both get something in the end. Alternatively, one partner might "trade" a favor in a completely

different area so that the final solution doesn't completely leave the other partner deprived. Shame of feeling victimized would again be averted.

Focus on Interests Instead of Positions

The use of tact during negotiation can remove the specter of a possible humiliating defeat. When we don't have to fear shame, we can negotiate more flexibly and creatively. The principle about dealing with interests requires that we control our focus of negotiation. If we focus on our positions during a conflict, then we'll advocate our one proposed solution against our partner's solution. The problem is that our egos are attached to our proposals. With egos involved, we'll be afraid that our proposal will be found inferior. We're afraid of symbolic inferiority rendering us inflexible. If we deal with both partners' interests without bonding to one proposed solution, then we don't have to prove that we're smarter or more capable than our partner. We can think more creatively.

> **When we don't have to fear shame, we can negotiate more flexibly and creatively.**

Here's an example of a conflict that I once had with my wife Helen. It illustrates the difference between positions and interests. We had our sailboat in a boat slip located at the mouth of a scenic harbor. The view was absolutely majestic. However, we could see the sailboat was less protected if a large storm ever blew down the river from the southwest. We figured that our thick dock lines could handle the large swells if that happened. One year, a tropical storm nearly wrecked the boat and proved us wrong. Two huge dock lines had broken and the remaining ones were nearly chafed through by the time the storm subsided. Helen and I started to negotiate about what to do.

When we first started negotiating a solution, Helen and I were negligent about using principles of tact. We both quickly staked out positions.

She thought we should sell our original boat slip and relocate to a "hurricane hole." I felt agony about her position. I had envisioned myself in my later years, writing books in the pilot house of our boat, looking out over the river and the waves crashing over the rock jetty. A hurricane proof boat slip would wreck my dream. My position was that we should keep our boat slip and watch for storms. I figured we could have the boat hauled out of the water if one approached. Helen argued that we couldn't always tell if a tropical storm might quickly generate off the coast. Back and forth we went. Tempers flared. These are good examples of battling positions. Each of us had our own idea for a solution. Each became like a sword with which we parried.

In this case, both of our interests were valid. Why have a boat if it doesn't give you a spiritual benefit. My interest was that I wanted to maximize my aesthetic enjoyment during my senior years. My wife also had a valid interest. What good is a boat if it's sunk? Helen was more interested in safety and protection. I was more interested in the aesthetics. Our interests were weighted in different directions. We eventually got around to addressing both of our concerns with two boat slips. We had another spare investment boat slip which we would sell and use the proceeds to purchase a safe slip in the hurricane hole. During tropical storm season (summer and fall) we would keep our boat in this safe slip where we would also have access to a pool. During the winter and spring months when tropical storms don't occur, we would keep the boat in our exposed scenic slip. The latter would be close to town and give us access to more friends during winter. We would rent out each unused slip during the months when we were in the alternate location. The final solution addressed both of our interests and we were satisfied. However, we would have resolved things more easily if we hadn't locked into opposing positions at the very beginning.

Separate Your Partner from the Problem

This principle of tact is once again about protecting each partner against potential shame. If we let our partner know that we see "the problem" as being outside of them, then they won't be as afraid that they'll be attacked for being the obstacle. Which of these scenarios do you think would make your partner more defensive? In the first scenario you sit facing each other. You each present your respective ideas. In the second scenario, you sit side by side. You both face some visual aid such as a blackboard or piece of paper.

You avoid using words such as "your" and "my" when referring to different perspectives. Instead, you refer to "the" different interests that you're trying to resolve. You both look at those interests drawn out on a blackboard or the piece of paper in front of you. It's a no-brainer as to which scenario would evoke greater defensiveness.

I remember a conversation I had with a man who drove a horse-drawn carriage. He said that if you ever want to know what a horse is thinking about, look in front of him. Most people don't know that emotions can operate on the same level as a dumb horse. Body language is extremely effective at evoking different emotions. For example, I have learned to stoop or kneel down to reduce my stature when talking with an angry paranoid client. This submissive posture doesn't aggravate the paranoid's already overblown fear. If you and your partner are in a conflict with scowls on your faces, you don't want to stand and face each other. The horse brain part of your partner's mind will tell them that you're the problem. The situation gets worse if either of you label the other's ideas as being "dumb" or "stupid." It's much better to sit parallel and face an outline of the problem on a sheet of paper.

A great way to separate your partner from the problem is to validate his or her interests at the start.

A great way to separate your partner from the problem is to validate his or her interests at the start. It's not enough to understand the partner's interests. You need to communicate to them that you think their interests are important. A great way to do this is to elaborate their concerns <u>with feeling</u>. When you do this, it's a bit like acting. You passionately advocate their interests as if they're your own. For example, let's use the previously discussed boat-slip conflict that I had with my wife. Suppose I had said the following:

"Dear, we have to get this boat totally safe. She's a once in a lifetime investment and we'll never be able to replace her if she gets wrecked. The insurance would never pay what she's really worth. And these tropical storms are so unpredictable. They can blow up off the coast in almost no time. Remember Hurricane Charlie? That blew up in 24 hours. Whatever we come up with as a system to protect her, it has to be reliable and most important it has to be <u>FAST</u>!"

In this hypothetical conversation, my wife probably would have assumed that I didn't view her as the problem. I would have articulated the problem in a way that would have kept it separate from her. My passionate emphasis would have been disarming. She wouldn't have needed to express as much of her emotion since I had already emphasized the importance of her concerns.

Negotiate Objective Standards of Fairness

You can think of this principle as being a close cousin of separating the person from the problem. It's another way of protecting egos by making conflicts less personal. If we don't use objective standards for determining fairness or truth, then we'll be afraid of being subjugated to our partner's will. That's the great fear: that our partner's desires will be treated as being more important than our own. If our partner's force of will were to prevail over ours, then we'd feel shame. Our subjugation would tell our unconscious that we're less important. What a shameful position! Our mind rebels at this specter and we become more defensive.

> The great fear is that our partner's desires will be treated as being more important than our own.

Objective criteria involve real world data that are independent of anyone's will. For example, imagine two partners who are arguing about whether they have the money to buy a larger house. They might use bank records from the previous six months to calculate realistic figures for a budget. They might also agree to use a friend who is a realtor and who might give them objective advice about the parameters of any prospective purchase.

Objective criteria might be as simple as remembering which partner

193

had the last choice. If you remind your partner that he or she was the last one to choose a restaurant, then you're using an objective criterion. Turn taking is a factual standard that doesn't rely on force of will. More complex decisions might involve getting a neutral expert involved. My wife and I had to use one to resolve a particularly tough dispute. She operated a speech pathology clinic next door to my psychological practice. I had designed the financial and billing program for both corporations. My wife had a favorite employee who had worked for her a long time and she wanted to give her a raise. I was appalled when I saw what she started paying the employee. I didn't see how she could afford it. I wouldn't ordinarily protest what my wife does in her own business. It's her business, not mine. However, if she was mistakenly setting up a welfare system that would result in a perpetual loss, then I felt I had to demand more accountability. I showed her calculations from her database that indicated her employee was being paid more money per collected dollar than she was. It was no use. My wife said that I was biased and could make MY financial programs say anything I wanted. I refused to drop it.

I asked my wife to choose any financial expert she could trust to act as a mediator. She chose our own CPA who has a lot of corporate experience. I sent my calculations to him and we scheduled a meeting for all three of us. When we finally met, I asked him if my costing model was appropriate. He replied that if there was a better model, he didn't know what it would be. After a few minutes of looking over the calculations, he looked up at Helen and exclaimed: "They're eating off of your plate!" He then described how it was unfair that the risk-taking proprietor (my wife) was being paid less per dollar collected than her employees. Afterwards, when we were walking out the front door, Helen turned and said: "I could hear it from him. I couldn't hear it from you." Even in a good relationship, objective criteria can sometimes be trusted more than a possibly biased partner.

Create Alternatives for Mutual Benefit

When resolving conflict, it's often possible to find a solution that gives something good to both partners. Suppose Sue wants Ed to come with her to her family's reunion in Minnesota. Ed happens to hate these types of affairs. He doesn't like her family, and he doesn't like large parties or groups. Her family had recently visited them and stayed for several days. He figures he's reached his yearly quota and the end of his tolerance. Sue is in agony at Ed's resistance because this is a once in a lifetime occasion arranged around her parents' 50th anniversary. What to do? One solution is to sweeten the deal for Ed by reconfiguring the trip. Sue knows that Ed's passion is fishing. She proposes that they lengthen their trip another three days so that after the anniversary, Ed can drive to nearby Lake Oshkobee to fish its waters that are thick with big muskellunge. He can take a room in the nearby town and fish, while Sue spends an extra day with her parents. Then Sue can drive up on the last day to join Ed before returning home.

The preceding example shows how a "win-win" can sometimes be arranged from a conflict of interest. However, it would be inaccurate to claim that this is always the case. Sometimes, circumstances won't allow it. Imagine that Beth is in genetic research and Mike is in business. Beth has just won acceptance to do ground-breaking research on the genetic engineering of corn. The problem is that the job is in Kansas and they live in Boston. Mike, who loves the night life around Boston, is not enthused about "spending their next four years in the middle of corn fields." This kind of dilemma is actually fairly common with the increasing mobility of the work force and double-income families. One partner may get an occupational breakthrough in a new city that holds little occupational promise for his or her partner. What to do?

In Beth and Mike's case, they decide to do a horse-trade. Mike doesn't make the common mistake of assuming that Beth will restore equity in the future through self-sacrifice. He's smart enough to know that the deal needs to be struck **now**. He's also smart enough to know that he needs to help Beth make her breakthrough. He's willing to take the big hit now of living where he loathes, but he wants to make a trade. He'll get a part-time job in Kansas to help support the family, but he wants to use the rest of his time to get an MBA. He wants Beth to agree that after the grant is finished, **he'll** pick the next place to live. It will be somewhere that can advance his business background…perhaps New York. She might have to teach for four years while he beefs up his business resume.

Most people don't think creatively enough to do trades. Instead, they think only within the confines of the particular situation. It's uncommon to think about doing transactions in two dimensions at once. However, it's extremely beneficial to prevent one partner from feeling the victim while the other partner gets a favorable outcome. Here are some examples of creative horse-trading between partners.

Partner A: Wants to buy a car that she likes. She will be the main driver. Her partner hates the car.

Partner B: Will agree to let his partner get the car if she will go camping with him for their vacation instead of going to the beach like they usually do.

Partner A: Wants his partner to start participating in a structured smoking cessation program. Wants her to stay in a treatment group for a year to ensure her abstinence.

Partner B: Will agree to go to treatment and the group if her partner agrees to take salsa dancing lessons with her and join a dance group.

Partner A: Wants to get a poodle.

Partner B: Will agree to allow the poodle if he never has to walk it and if she will agree to help support his training for a pilot's license.

Partner A: Wants to buy a motorcycle from joint funds.

Partner B: Will agree to the motorcycle if her partner first builds her the screened-in porch that she's always wanted.

Partner A: Wants to get a horse.

Partner B: Will agree to the horse if his partner will agree to the country club golf membership he's been wanting.

Partner A: This one's for you. Think of something you want that requires your partner's cooperation but that they've been opposing.

Partner B: Now think of some things that your partner badly wants. Is there any trade that you would be willing to offer?

You may notice that sex doesn't show up anywhere among the preceding examples. That's because trading sex is a bad idea unless you want to be a secret prostitute. Many people are. We'll be discussing this sad phenomenon in another chapter. For now, let's just say that it's injurious to make sex a commodity. If you do, you generate shame within yourself. You don't want to trade sex any more than you'd commit to telling your spouse you love him or her every time your spouse empties the trash. You'd be training your emotional expression to become a means to an end as well as a lie. Don't do it.

It's injurious to trade with sex.

Negotiating Different Kinds of Wants

Earlier in our discussion, the point was made that there's a difference between wanting lusty sex versus wanting to get off a hot stove that's burning your butt. We use the word "want" in both instances as if the motivation were the same. It's not. Avoidance and escape aren't the same as seeking enjoyment, yet we use the word "want" for each. The English language has some serious deficiencies.

If we want to service our autonomy by negotiating with our partner, then it's important to know that hedonic interests are more important to negotiate than dislikes. There are many people who think they have no problem expressing what they want to their partner. If you ask them for examples, they may say something like, "I tell him all the time that I want him to stop coming home late." Or perhaps, "I want her to not interrupt me when she can see I'm working on the computer." These are examples of non-hedonic desires that relate more to removing something that's distasteful. Unfortunately, there are many people who stay primarily on the negative side of the street. Their unconscious won't let them cross over to even thinking about enjoyable goals. If all they do is negotiate for removal of things that they dislike, then their core self won't be strengthened. They'll be on their way to eventually numbing out.

Negotiating conflict of interest works best when we negotiate for our positive desires. If you're in a committed relationship, then it would be a good idea to ask yourself the following questions: "Do I actively negotiate with my partner when we're determining our agenda for pursuing enjoyment? Does our common agenda for enjoyment include many of my ideas? Does half of it come from me?" These questions can help you determine whether hedonic inhibition or fear of conflict has a strangle hold on your oxygen supply.

Confronting Broken Agreements

None of us have a perfect memory. We all sometimes break agreements because we forget to follow through or may even have forgotten the original deal. We forget to stop by the store to pick up the milk that we agreed to get on our way home. We forget that we agreed to keep our voice low when we're in a heated conflict. We may also appear to break an agreement because the deal wasn't clearly communicated in the first place. Many people will throw a proposal at their partner and then erroneously assume that their partner's acquiescence means that they've made a commitment. It's rare that a partner knowingly breaks an agreement merely because of a sociopathic personality.

Broken agreements need to be confronted for several reasons. One reason is that you don't want to accumulate shame and resentment by perceiving yourself to be the victim. You can reduce this kind of shame when you confront. However, there's a more important reason to confront broken agreements. If left unrepaired, they'll fracture the basic safety of your relationship. Everything will go downhill. You need to confront broken agreements so that a) you can clarify if there was an original miscommunication, b) your partner can come up with a plan for improving compliance in the future, or c) you can find out if you're truly in bed with a sociopath. Most of the time, you will be working with your partner toward improved compliance.

Most people don't know how to confront broken agreements effectively. The classic mistake made by most people is to accuse their partner in a way designed to provoke humiliation and shame: "You forgot the milk, didn't you? Can't you remember anything or do you only think about yourself all the time?" This kind of shaming accusation is usually met with stiff resistance or avoidant withdrawal. Rarely does it accomplish anything positive.

The best strategy for confronting a broken agreement is to get the other person to do the work. Instead of outright accusation it's better to induce the partner to sweat his own inconsistency. If you lay out the whole case of how he messed up, then he can't "own" any part of the process. There's nothing left to feel good about. If you're smart and use some tact, you can get him to declare his inconsistency before you do. That way, your partner will be much more motivated to make plans to keep the agreement in the future.

There are four steps to effectively confront broken agreements:

1) **Ask your partner what he remembers about the original agreement.** This can be as simple as "Do you remember us discussing the car registration? What did you agree to do?" Sometimes it's necessary to provide details to help your partner jog their memory. "Remember? We were standing in the kitchen and I said this and then you said that and then I made such and such a point, etc." If you can't get him to remember any agreement, then you're dead in the water. You won't be able to do any constructive confrontation and you might as well drop the matter. If you get many irretrievable agreements, then you will need to start recording agreements between the two of you. Either that or ask your spouse to get a neuropsychological exam.

2) **Ask your partner about what he actually did.** "Did you do it in time to avoid the late fee like we discussed?"

3) **Ask your partner to reconcile #1 and #2.** "What gives? How come you agreed to do it but it's not done?" Your goal here is to get your partner to sweat the inconsistency. You want him to explain what happened. This is where he can start taking responsibility for the mistake. Most people will do this if you haven't hurled an angry accusation. Unfortunately, some people are so shame-bound that they can't admit mistakes. If your partner is a total narcissist then he might not admit his mistake, no matter how good your tact is.

4) **Ask your partner when he will give you a correction plan.** This is a step that's frequently bungled. When the mistake is a one-of-a-kind occurrence, then it's probably OK to let the matter go after your partner admits regret. However, if the same agreements are repeatedly broken over time, a more deliberate confrontation is in order. Imagine the following situation involving a husband who forgot to take out the recycling bin before its scheduled pick-up time. He has already apologized to his wife. She replies:

> "John, I'm not interested in an apology. That's not going to work because it obviously hasn't worked all the times before when you've forgotten. This must be the

fifth time you've forgotten. Each time you apologize. I don't want any more apologies. They don't work. I want to know what you're going to do differently so that you don't have to rely so much on your terrible memory. I want you to think up a better plan and tell it to me tonight or tomorrow at dinner. Better yet, why don't you tell me when you think you can give me your plan?"

This is an effective confrontation because it's practical. The wife is demanding that her husband take responsibility for solving the long-term problem. She's not settling for an apology without a plan. She's not being manipulated with the usual "I'm sorry" ritual.

The Problem with "I'm Sorry"

Saying "I'm sorry" is a perfunctory social ritual that's good for soothing the feelings of an injured partner. It's based on the premise that the apologizing partner is really expressing regret and empathy. These emotions help the injured partner to feel less hurt and realize that her feelings and needs do matter. This is useful when there's a one time transgression like stepping on your partner's toe or making a simple mistake. A one time occurrence doesn't need further correction. In this case, a simple "I'm sorry" will do.

The problem with "I'm sorry" is that it's a distraction when it's often used in the context of repetitive or systematic transgressions. For example, your partner comes home an hour late for dinner for the fourth time in a month. Another example is that you've just caught your partner lying again about something he said he would do, but didn't. In these situations, many people will profusely apologize with "I'm sorry." They'll also say it will never happen again and will beg for forgiveness. But what's really going on? Where's their attention focused? It doesn't take much thought to realize that the focus is on manipulating their partner's emotions by ego posturing. It's as if they're saying, "I'm self-flagellating and abasing myself so low that you should show mercy and forgive me." The focus really isn't on fixing future problems. It's on placating their partner so that they can escape disapproval. They're not taking responsibility because they're distracted by their effort to manipulate. What's the alternative? Imagine that the late arriving husband says something like the following:

> "Dear, I know I really messed up. I owe you more than a simple apology because it's happening too often. I mean it's what?…the fourth time this month? It's getting ridiculous! I've been thinking that I have to come up with some sort of system to help my leaky brain so that this doesn't happen again. I really don't like doing this to you. It's just that I get so caught up with the stress and crises at work that I forget about everything else. Then, when I realize that I'm already late, I'm too afraid to call because I'm already feeling guilty and I know that you're going to be furious with me. But I've got to come up with a better way of dealing with it. I'm going to ask that you let me take a few hours to think about what I can do differently. I'll come up with some plan to help me wake up at work and call you when I'm obviously going to be late. I can't prevent having to come home late sometimes, but at least I should be able to call you ahead of time when that happens. Can we talk about it at bedtime tonight?"

Later that night, the husband tells the wife that he'll set his watch to sound an alarm at 4:30pm every day. That will be his signal to remind him to call his wife if he sees that he's managing some crisis that won't let him get home on time. It may or may not work but it's a reasonable plan to try.

This example illustrates two important differences from the "I'm sorry" ritual. First, there's no covert seeking of forgiveness! There's an expression of regret, but that regret is expressed as a statement without the ego posturing manipulation for forgiveness. The husband is saying "I really don't like what I'm doing to you." He's also saying that he owes his wife some sort of reasonable plan for correction. These statements express regret but the main focus is not on manipulating the wife's disapproval. The focus is on his responsibility to fix the overall problem. That's the second major difference from the "I'm sorry" ritual. The transgressor takes the responsibility to forgive himself. Then he's in an adult state of mind with more autonomy.

For repetitively broken agreements, there's a more useful ritual that can be summarized: **Share your regrets and a plan.** What's implied with this is that if you're the one making amends, then you take the responsibility to forgive yourself. You don't extend that authority to your partner. He or she may choose to do it but you're not in a child-like dependent state. You're taking the responsibility for being an adult. This is why sharing your regrets and a plan is often more valuable than saying you're sorry.

> **Sharing your regrets and a plan is often more valuable than saying you're sorry.**

There's another aspect pertaining to the partner who's on the receiving end of a repetitively broken agreement. I often train couples to demand more accountability from their partner than the usual "I'm sorry" apology. Why settle on such a cheap response? It's a responsibility dodge! What's much better is to refuse the apology and demand more. Imagine a wife confronting her husband in the following way after he's finished his "I'm sorry" routine.

> "John, I really don't want your apology. Your feelings of guilt aren't what I'm after. It's obvious that having you feel sorry and guilty hasn't fixed the problem up to now. I don't expect that it will change your behavior in the future either. I want you to take more responsibility than that to fix the problem. You can forgive yourself but give me a better plan than your supposed guilt. When can I have a plan about what you're going to do differently so I don't have to keep hearing your apologies through the rest of our marriage?"

The guideline I'm suggesting here is to hold out for your spouse's plan of correction if the same agreement has been repetitively broken. Don't be satisfied with "I'm sorry."

"Setting the Bone"

There's a common bias in the counseling community that intense crises should always be averted through collaboration and calm negotiation. The operative word here is "always." People are shocked when I tell them that I once counseled someone on how to kill another person. The idea is so alien that it seems that it has to be invalid. But at the time that this book is being written we have over 100,000 citizens overseas who have to be prepared to do just that. Then comes the moment of realization: Oh! Yes, of course. The military! But that doesn't really apply over here. Or does it? Then I tell the person who is listening a few more of the details. The person I counseled was a contracted younger therapist in my practice who was being stalked. The police had already issued her a bulletproof vest and had told her that they couldn't adequately protect her. The stalker was a former prison inmate who had a severe pathological transference to the therapist. Word was coming back from the criminal community about details of what was happening in the therapist's house. The therapist was being watched inside her own house! One evening, the former inmate even tried to run her off the road after the therapist had left the office. Vaguely worded threats were being relayed through intermediaries. I think you would agree that this was a dire situation. The final solution came when the therapist finally left the state.

What's the point of the story? The point is that collaboration and calm negotiation don't always work. For some rare situations, forceful action is more adaptive. Most of us have a hard time accepting that. We want to believe in the goodness of human nature. We usually want to prevent tension and conflict from building up in our relationship. We also don't want to provoke anger or hurt feelings. Shouldn't we try to keep everything calm? The answer is usually yes, but not always. Let's consider a metaphor.

Imagine that you and your family are on the high seas in a sailboat. You're at least a week away from land, and your radio has blown a circuit. You have no communication. Suddenly, you hear an awful cry from above deck. You run up to find that your 8-year-old daughter has fallen and is lying in the cockpit holding her leg. The lower leg is obviously broken because it's bent in an acute angle from the rest of the leg. You can see that it's a compound fracture because blood is beginning to soak through the pant leg. Your daughter is crying in agony. When you reach to try to see under the pant leg she screams. "Don't touch it! Please don't touch it! Oh! It hurts so much! Please. Please leave it alone!" You're a week from land without communication. What are you going to do?

Please don't touch it!

This imaginary crisis evokes a collision between two responsibilities. One is to prevent your child from suffering more acutely and the other is to protect her life and limb. It's empathy versus responsibility. If you're compulsively empathic, you might abide by her wishes and not touch the leg. However, that would probably result in a gangrenous leg and might take her life through sepsis. Most people choose the alternative. They'll protect her life and limb even though it'll cause her great pain. Some of us need to make such an intelligent choice when it comes to fixing our relationship.

There are some relationships that have fatal flaws. It's as if they have cracks in their foundations. If they're ignored, things will usually get worse. In Chapter 2, I explained how responsibility and respect form the safety foundation of a relationship. If one partner refuses to assume responsibility or is toxically disrespectful, then it's best to take action to fix the problem. This is true even though the offending partner will feel hurt or angry. If one partner refuses to deal with a fundamental fracture in the relationship, then it's best to set the bone! In order to do this kind of repair, a person has to momentarily de-prioritize emotions and focus instead on the greater responsibility. Protection of personal and relationship integrity should be a higher priority than momentary emotions. In order to fix the fracture, a person needs to tolerate the agony of seeing the partner hurt. Alternatively, one may need to tolerate the fear of the ofending partner's anger. Either way, major relationship fractures require action over emotion. Compulsive empathy is unwise in the face of oncoming danger. Timid passivity can kill a relationship that might otherwise be salvaged.

> **If one partner refuses to deal with a fundamental fracture in the relationship, then it's best to set the bone!**

Unfortunately, it's true that more people take unilateral action in their relationship for pathological reasons than for beneficial ones. Many people threaten divorce in the heat of the moment, only to retract it and apologize when they calm down. Some get violent. Others act out. These people are reacting to their own fear of shame. Remember the great no-no from the Chapter 1? These are escalations that turn out poorly.

A strategic crisis is one that's planned with forethought about the possible consequences. Instead of trying to avoid the crisis, the person allows it to build so that the issue will finally be addressed. The involved partner may need to decide whether to risk the relationship in order to improve their quality of life. It's a gamble. Here are some situations that many people find deserving of a strategic crisis.

- Physical abuse

- Ongoing infidelity

- Refusal to share access to family finances

- Refusal to respect a partner's right to decline sex

- Refusal to get help for a chronic absence of sexual desire

- Repeated violation of joint finances without the partner's consent

- Refusal to seek gainful employment when there's no agreement for the person to stay home and perform household or parental responsibilities

- Physical or sexual abuse of a child

- Refusal to get treatment for a mental or emotional illness

- Refusal to get help for chronic lying

- Refusal to get help for a continuing compulsion or addiction

The following are some examples of strategic crises in which the offended partner chose to risk their relationship by taking action, rather than remaining passive:

> Jason denied that his behavior was way out of line when he would hit and slap Brenda during their fights. After their fights, he blamed Brenda for provoking him so badly. He viewed each of them to be equally responsible for what happened during their arguments. Finally, when he choked her, she was depressed for weeks afterwards. She decided that she didn't want to continue her futile attempts to persuade him to get help. The next time he hit her, Brenda called the police and had Jason arrested. She got a restraining order, and Jason had to attend a mandatory domestic violence program. She refused to attempt any reconciliation until Jason started individual therapy after the program.

> Molly didn't think it was fair that she couldn't access the marital income through the main accounts. Dennis insisted that giving her an allowance should be sufficient. He told her that since he was the breadwinner, the money was his to manage. He complained that Molly was an unwise spender and that his allowance to her for

groceries and household needs would be sufficient if she didn't waste it as she had. Molly didn't agree to this because Dennis would use "his" money to fund his fishing trips, but she couldn't go to the beach with her girlfriends. Dennis had taken her credit cards because she had used them defiantly on a previous occasion. When Molly's requests to go to marriage counseling were refused, she finally decided on a plan. Molly took her child and went to her parents' house. She also visited a lawyer to learn about what might be involved in a divorce. From her position on the brink, Molly then extended a last chance invitation to Dennis to start marriage counseling. He finally accepted.

Dale found Kim nearly impossible to tolerate. She raged unpredictably, went into periods of miserable depression and, at other times, would fly as high as a kite. She went on episodic spending sprees that landed the couple deep in debt. Dale confronted Kim telling her that he thought she probably had a bipolar disorder and wanted her to be assessed. Kim resisted because she didn't want to be a "zombie" like her mother. Her mother had been bipolar and had required constant medication just to stay out of the hospital. When Kim started having brief sexual affairs, Dale reached his limit. He told Kim that if she would not go to a psychiatrist with him that he would be moving out within a month. Kim initially blew him off, but Dale reminded her periodically that he would be leaving if she kept ignoring him. Finally, Dale moved out when Kim was in one of her highs. She wasn't that concerned because of her frenetic lifestyle. It was three months later that Kim approached Dale and reported that she was finally on medication and wanted to go with him to marriage counseling.

To set the bone, you may have to risk ending the relationship.

What's apparent from these examples is that fostering a strategic crisis is a serious maneuver that should never be undertaken in a moment of emotion. It's best to spend several weeks considering your options before risking such a move. To set the bone, you may have to risk ending the relationship. And this challenge separates the real adults from the children. Or perhaps I should say "wounded children," because adults who have been wounded as children often can't make it over this hurdle. Core shame has a lot to do with it. Try to imagine the extreme challenge such a risk would pose for individuals who have never experienced a quality relationship. Perhaps their first image of marriage involved seeing their parents tear each other apart. Or perhaps their relationship with one of their parents involved being physically abused or sexually exploited. How can they hope for better if for years they were consistently taught that their needs were unimportant? As a general truth, I've discovered that people don't leave bad marriages because their marriages are unbearable. They leave them because they hope for a better life. That's not a mere play on words. Core shame robs a partner of their ability to hope. What's left is their ability to despise, but that doesn't push them forward to take methodical action. The human capacity to tolerate misery is astounding! People can wallow in excruciating misery their whole life if they don't think they can do better. Hope is the key.

> **People don't leave bad marriages**
> **because their marriages are unbearable.**
> **They leave them because they hope for a better life.**

Confronting Boundary Intrusions

The third type of constructive conflict is when a person confronts a partner who has intrusively invaded one's personal boundaries. It's constructive because it protects. A skillful confrontation can prevent the accumulation of shame that would otherwise occur. Chapter 8 discusses this issue in depth. The techniques described in that chapter are useful tips on how to manage this form of conflict. The When and Where Rule and micro-corrections are both very useful strategies for this. To avoid redundancy, we won't discuss what has already been presented in the previous chapter. We're only referencing it because confronting boundary intrusions is the third type of constructive conflict. You will need it in your kit if you want to keep your relationship robust.

Destructive Conflict

Destructive conflict is what many people erroneously associate as being ordinary conflict. It's a fight in which both partners use emotional attacks to bludgeon each other with shame. It's also fueled by each partner's fear of that shame. It's as if each person's unconscious says "I can't let myself feel like a worthless and unimportant victim. I *must prove* that I'm worthy of better treatment!" Then the person tries to prove that he or she is not only right and strong, but that the other partner is ridiculous and less powerful.

The precarious position of feeling your self-worth in jeopardy can have a profound effect on the nervous system. It tends to deactivate parts of your brain that are involved in metacognition. Metacognition is a process in which a person consciously monitors their thoughts and feelings. It allows a person to override impulsive behavior. This is why some readers observe themselves frequently apologizing after fits of rage. It's because they can't observe themselves during the rage itself. They can maturely view themselves afterwards but not while it's happening. They lose metacognition during their rage. Different parts of their personality are involved. Information from the person's mature world view can be offline when the person is in their rage state.

Let's define what we mean by rage. Most people assume that anger and rage are the same. I would encourage you to think of anger as being protective energy that's used to engage a challenge. From this viewpoint, you can see that anger is the energy behind constructive conflict. Anytime you refuse to accede to your partner's wishes, you're using anger. It's true that it's of such low intensity that it's hard to recognize. A parallel is that few people would recognize ultraviolet rays as one form of light.

Think of rage as being anger that's contaminated and inflated by the unconscious fear of shame. A simple formula expresses this idea.

ANGER + FEAR OF SHAME = RAGE

Fear of shame will turbocharge anger into rage. People who grew up with raging parents often don't learn these fine distinctions. They've rarely experienced the beauty of healthy assertiveness that can restore balance in a relationship. Instead, they've learned the childhood lesson to never get angry. They're desperate to be unlike their parents. It's a paradox that their shame-driven attempt to cut off anger will usually increase their own tendency to rage. By not working with their anger, growing it up and integrating it into their mature personality, they ensure that it will become a rogue self part. The state becomes cut off from the information in other mature self parts that carry wisdom and consideration for consequences. Then when these people rage, their behavior generates even more shame. When they calm down and see how they behaved like their parents, they try even harder to cut off their anger. The shame and rage reciprocally reinforce each other. This is just one of several syndromes that can convert anger into rage.

The following are three types of destructive anger that often disrupt relationships. Rage is central to each.

1. **Defensive Rage** – This is rage in reaction to someone else's anger. When the recipient of a partner's tirade is afraid of appearing weak and unimportant, she may choose to respond in a way that makes her feel strong again. Rage momentarily does the trick.

2. **Emotional Depletion** – This occurs when a person fears that he is not loved by his partner. It can also occur because the person has very poor self-esteem because of his previous conditioning by a disturbed childhood. The shame of feeling unloved can inject anger into major control fights over seemingly trivial issues. The real origin of the conflict is the unconscious pain within the individual.

3. **Neurotic Association** – This occurs when a person reacts to unconscious feelings of shame that are being triggered by her partner. The person believes that the partner is to blame but she's actually getting unconscious associations from old memories. An example would be a wife who feels abused and fears she will be hit when her partner merely shares a difference of opinion.

If you want to reduce your own rage reactions during conflict, you can come at the problem from one of two directions. You can either change the situation or you can change your emotional reactions. Managing your situation is actually a lot easier than trying to change your emotional responses. That's because your rage reactions have already become habitual and automatic. When you're enraged, the intensity of emotion is cutting off your higher consciousness. You lose your cognitive flexibility. It's much easier for you to do something about the situation long before you get too aroused. Here are some things you can do.

1. Train yourself to notice how your body responds when you're angry. Is your heart rate speeding up? Do you think it's over 100 beats per minute? Do you feel blood rushing to your head? Is your breathing starting to change? You want to notice early if this is happening *before* your rage becomes a runaway freight train.

2. Learn to use the When and Where Rule from Chapter 8. It helps you to postpone destructive conflicts in order to prepare and pace yourself. This can dramatically reduce your rage. It gives you time to organize your thoughts while you're in a calm state. An organized mind feels more prepared, safer, and is therefore less prone to rage.

3. Increase the amount of healthy nurturing in your relationship. Reread Chapter 4 for ideas on how you can do this. You can reduce the shame of emotional depletion that might be covertly fueling the rage. Many couples who've done this have found their destructive fights dramatically reduced within one or two months.

4. Refuse to discuss more than one complaint at a time. Whenever you hear your partner bring up several complaints, give him one chance to narrow it down to a specific issue. You can invite him to tell you what type of agreement he wants. If the partner stays on the level of multiple complaints, then refuse the discussion entirely. Tell him you will talk in the future when he's ready to be specific. The reason it's good to do this is because multiple complaints are impossible to digest and process constructively. They only signal the beginning of a destructive fight.

5. Learn to give your partner permission to be angry with you when she's starting to rage. This is a very powerful maneuver to reduce your own defensive rage. It helps you by giving you permission to let go. You feel less shame because you're no longer trying (and failing) to influence the partner's emotions.

6. Use the previously discussed guidelines for different types of constructive conflict. These strategies can reduce some of the triggers that provoke defensive rage. The better you become at constructive conflict, the less likely you will be triggered into rage.

Changing your actual rage response is going to be tough! You're talking about changing a conditioned emotional reaction, not your voluntary behavior. Think about altering your salivation response to the sight of a squeezed lemon. Then, additionally consider that your reaction to shame is a whole lot stronger. This is where therapy can be an option. However, don't naively assume that all therapists are equipped to help. Anger management training will usually teach you to manage triggers, situations, and overt behavior. It usually doesn't get down to the level of reconditioning the rage itself.

Eye movement desensitization and reprocessing (EMDR) is one type of therapy that is very effective at resolving core shame. When a person rages because of neurotic association to early childhood trauma, the benefits from EMDR can sometimes seem miraculous. Resolving several core traumas this way can sometimes eliminate decades of previously intractable raging. Information about EMDR is readily available on the internet. A worldwide association, EMDRIA, has a humanitarian branch that provides service to disaster victims around the globe. The EMDR treatment protocol has been well researched and is now accepted as a mainstream treatment for emotional trauma.

The best conflict skills are internal connection skills.

Conflict inoculation training is another protocol that I've developed for treating excessive rage. It's much too detailed to be presented in the current discussion. It would require a dedicated book to sufficiently outline and explain the protocol. It's similar to military training when soldiers are trained under live fire. The military does this so that trained behavior will be remembered when the soldier is in the highly arousing situation of combat. During conflict inoculation training, patients learn to put themselves in a shame state but then practice getting themselves out of it without rage. Instead of using their rage defense, they practice using their attachment system as a healthier defense. The success of this approach has led me to the conclusion that the best conflict skills are internal connection skills.

If you can connect to your higher consciousness, then your expanded awareness will be better able to handle both your rage and the situation. Of course, this assumes that you've developed a higher level of consciousness in the first place. If you're one of the unlucky souls who've never received good socialization from mentors or attentive parents, then your participation in some intimate community or therapy group would be a very good idea. Any of the twelve-step groups fall into this category. Some bible reading groups can be intimate if you break into small groups and relate biblical principles to your own life. Men's and women's support groups may also help. As a rule, healthy socialization helps you to better manage impulsive behavior. It increases your willpower to resist acting out your destructive rage.

Chapter Ten

Sharing Power and Responsibility

If you and your partner have been fighting about chores and money, then this chapter's for you. Up to now, you've probably just blamed your partner. She's just a nag. He's just lazy. You may have your unique version of blame, but it will be similar. Your partner is somehow defective.

Odds are that you *both* have had a hand in setting up the current dysfunctional system. Because that's what it is. It's a system. It's dysfunctional, but it's a system nonetheless. To understand how this is true, we'll first discuss the most common syndrome that many couples unknowingly bring upon themselves.

The Delinquent Helper Syndrome

Slavery went out of style around 1865. If you complain that you're not getting any help around the house, then that indicates that you've set up a dysfunctional system. Inherent in your words are the clues that you've done this. You're expecting that your partner's role is to *help*. What's your role? To rule? Why is it that he's expected to help you? The answer is subtle. It's because you've assumed authority over what needs to be done in the household. Your partner has abdicated his authority over this kind of planning. He's just a helper and you carry the main responsibility. You both have unconsciously collaborated to set up a system with unequal authority. You both did this because you wanted certain benefits. You wanted to nest and have a household that represents you at your best. You wanted the authority to run it exactly as you think it should be run. Your partner wanted something too. He wanted you to handle things at home so that he could focus on what represents him at his best. Perhaps it's his career. He also wanted you to be his memory. He didn't want the burden of tracking all of the domestic stuff. You could worry about that so his mind would be left unfettered. Please forgive the sex stereotyping here. The pattern will be true 90 percent of the time, but you can reverse the sexes if it's more appropriate to your situation.

Now let's look at the downside to the helper system you've created. While you get the benefit of directing that things should run the way you like, you now have a partner who doesn't feel equal ownership of the household. He's just a helper, remember? That's one step up from being a slave. Helpers don't have authority. They don't feel ownership. You can translate that into lacking motivation. Ownership fuels motivation. "Helpership" stifles it. Your partner enjoys not having to keep track of the domestic stuff. But when you tell him that you need his help, he now feels bossed around. While it's convenient that you unburden his memory, he hates it when you remind him about what needs to be done. You get to be the nag. Doesn't feel good, does it?

Ownership fuels motivation. "Helpership" stifles it.

I've invented the word "helpership" to denote something different than when empathy motivates you to help someone. That's great stuff. If you're doing it in your relationship, don't stop! However, there's a problem if you're expected to bear a continuous responsibility to help another adult. It feels awful when it's no longer voluntary. If you're in the helper role, you feel subjugated and you start resenting your partner as a controlling authority figure. Fights occur more frequently. Sound familiar?

There's a more functional alternative to the helpership system. If you negotiate responsibilities so that authority and ownership accompany them, then nobody has to be a nag or a slave. I can comfortably take a nap while my wife cleans the house. It's not because she's under-assertive. It's because both of us have negotiated ownership of different responsibilities so that there's no inequity. At another point in time, I may repair a light fixture while my wife goes out to lunch with her girlfriends. When responsibilities are distributed equitably, no one has to be resentful about not being helped. Then you can be more appreciative whenever your partner helps you on his or her own initiative.

The following procedure has helped many couples to escape the delinquent helper syndrome. It involves renegotiating all responsibilities pertaining to living together. Although it involves numerous steps, the final product is a system that feels fair. I've had many couples report that they wound up doing the same chores as before negotiations. However, they also reported that the resentment and fights had greatly diminished. In other words, the procedure doesn't just reallocate responsibilities. It also changes the way both partners think and feel about their respective roles. Less resentment is the result.

Negotiating Routine Chores

Here are the steps to renegotiate all your chores. Don't skip any step because the emotional process is even more important than the final product. You don't want to miss any of the psychological benefits by taking a shortcut.

Step 1 - Each partner lists out as many relationship chores that he or she can think of.

Who takes out the dog? Who cuts the grass? Who takes out the garbage? These are some of the routine relationship chores that should go on your list. Both partners needs to make their own list of all the routine chores regardless of who does them. If you do this step well, then your list will probably be several pages long.

It's absolutely necessary for each of you to do the work. If you rely on only one person to make up the list, then the purpose of the procedure will be defeated. The procedure is designed to have a psychological benefit by going through the complete process.

Step 2 - Both partners merge their chore lists into one master list.

It's best to use a computer spreadsheet from this step forward. You're going to merge your two lists into one and put it on the spreadsheet. You will have thought of chores your partner missed. Your partner will have thought of ones that you have missed. Then there'll be a huge overlap of chores you both listed. Merge them all together so you wind up with a master chore list on your spreadsheet.

Step 3 - Each partner takes a copy of the master list and volunteers for chores that he or she wants.

Print out two copies of the master chore list—one for each of you. Each of you will take away your copy of the master list. You will need some time to work on it in private, so you will need to schedule the next meeting for a later date .

When you privately work on your list after your meeting, you need to volunteer yourself for chores you think you should own. **<u>You never volunteer your partner!</u>** Place your initials next to the chores you'd be willing to take. Your partner will be doing the same in his or her parallel work.

Step 4 - Both partners compare the lists of volunteered chores and negotiate chore ownership.

When you meet next, you both go down each item on the master list and compare your answers. While you do this, you're working up a new draft of the master list. However, this new list will have initials next to some of the items. Where you have volunteered for a chore and your partner hasn't, then your initials get placed next to that chore on the new master list. Your partner will similarly start owning some of the chores with his or her initials entered. In the event that both of you have volunteered for the same chore, you will need to negotiate who would be the best suited to take on that particular task.. Finally, you wind up with a new master list with a scattering of chores that are owned and a scattering of chores that aren't. Print out new copies for you and your partner. Then schedule your next meeting.

Step 5 - Each partner takes a list of the unselected chores and volunteers for the ones he or she is willing to accept.

Back in your privacy corner, decide which remaining chores you're willing to "eat." You may not want them, but neither does your partner. Pick the least distasteful. Go ahead. Hold your nose and force 'em down. You will live. Put your initials next to them.

Step 6 – Both partners compare lists of additionally selected chores and negotiate again.

When you meet again, repeat the merging process that you already did in step 4. Now you have most of the items owned. However, you have a few really nasty ones left. Double rejects from both of you. They'll be tough. OK. Print out your new merged list that now has initials covering most of the items. The remaining nasties still don't have any initials. Schedule your next meeting together.

Step 7 - Each partner takes the list of remaining chores that neither one wants. Each strategizes how he or she will trade unwanted chores with the other partner.

Now you really have to put on your thinking cap. How are you going to get your partner to agree to take some of those remaining stinkies. Bullying is out! You're going to have to trade. You're going to have to think like this: If you would be willing to do this and that, would your partner be willing to do such and such? If you agree to take out the garbage, take out the recycle bin, and sweep the deck, would your partner then agree to do all the dog walking? If you agree to do the house vacuuming, would your partner agree to periodically steam clean the carpets? You need to develop these kinds of proposals to bring back to the negotiations. Don't go back empty-handed.

Step 8 - Both partners negotiate the ownership of any remaining chores until all the chores are allocated.

This is horse trading pure and simple. Both of you will need to wheel and deal. The final chores will hopefully be traded off. If not, there's another possible solution. Some couples agree to use their common funds to hire someone from outside the relationship. For example, it's not that uncommon for some couples to hire a housekeeper. Others may hire someone to cut the lawn or do house repairs. When you've found a way to handle all the chores, then schedule your next meeting.

Step 9 - Each partner writes down a specification for each chore that he or she owns.

Back to your privacy corner. It ain't over yet. Even though each of you own your responsibilities, there's still too much ambiguity left about *how* the chores will be done. When will the garbage be taken outside? How often will the dogs be walked? How high will the grass grow before it gets cut? The criteria need to be this specific so that both of you are sufficiently accountable to one another. If they're not, you will fight or nag each other about how the tasks are being done. On your chore sheet, write down your proposed spec for each of your chores (<u>only</u> yours).

Step 10 - Both partners negotiate chore specifications. They trade chores whenever an agreement about a specification can't be reached.

At your next meeting you get to negotiate specs. Go down the master list discussing each chore. If the chore being discussed is yours, then volunteer your proposed spec. Discuss where there's disagreement. If you can't reach an agreement on an item, the "last word" rule is this:

> **The partner who owns the chore has the last word in determining its specification. If the item belongs to your partner and you can't reach an agreement to change it, then your partner's proposal for a specification stands.**

There is one alternative if you still can't agree on your partner's specification for one of his or her chores. You can always offer a trade. For example, suppose your partner says he doesn't want to have to cut the grass until it's nine inches high. And suppose you just can't live with that. You could say something like this.

> "That's just unacceptable to me. I'd feel ashamed in front of our neighbors. I'd imagine they'd be expecting us to soon have our car up on cinder blocks. Look. How about this? I'd be willing to cut the grass if you take out the garbage each night and take out the recycling on Wednesdays. Now that's a good deal. How about it?"

If you can't get any deal with a trade, then your partner still has the last word about the spec. As long as the partner owns the task, the spec is what he or she decides.

Step 11 – Both partners monitor the overall equity and balance of their discretionary time. They renegotiate the balance of chores whenever discretionary time becomes unequal.

By this point, you each have your list of chores. You're doing great, but there's another consideration. Suppose that one of you has been a more forceful negotiator or perhaps has been cunning by volunteering for tasks that take very little time. You can still wind up with a unfair system. Suppose you find that all your chores require so much time that you only have two free hours during the whole week to meet with your friends. Suppose also that your husband is golfing three hours in the afternoon two days a week and then a few more hours on Saturday. What's wrong with the chore system? Clearly it's not equitable.

Fairness depends a lot on context. If you have a job that requires you to work fifty hours per week while your partner's job requires only thirty, you're not going to have an equitable division of responsibilities if you divide all chores down the middle. Fairness isn't even going to depend on how much money each of you make. If one of you claims more entitlement because of income, let me warn you in the strongest words possible. That way lies death! Subjugation won't sell. You're going to have to use another yardstick for fairness.

The best way to measure the fairness of allocated chores is to look at each person's discretionary time. Discretionary time means that the partners can choose to spend it for their own pleasure and not for any relationship responsibility. The keyword is choice. They're under no obligation to spend it any particular way other than the way they choose. The husband could just as easily decide to spend his afternoon fishing instead of playing golf. The wife could decide to go to the pool instead of meeting with her friends. There's no service that they're directly or even indirectly providing to the relationship. If we use the terminology introduced in earlier chapters, discretionary time is usually paratelic. It's spent on here and now gratification. The following list can help you get a better feeling for the difference between discretionary and nondiscretionary activities.

Discretionary	Nondiscretionary
Playing golf	Working at a job
Reading a magazine or book	Supervising children
Watching TV	Shopping for necessities
Enjoying a museum	Cooking meals for the family
Meeting with friends	Repairing the house
Taking a nap	Paying bills
Enjoying a hobby	Researching an investment
Playing a musical instrument	Going to the doctor
Socializing at a club	Cleaning and vacuuming
Dining out	Walking the dog
Swimming in a pool	Mowing the grass

Notice that supervising children is nondiscretionary. When a partner has to watch the children, she's not really free. She bears too much responsibility for the children's safety and welfare. She can't focus on her own pleasure pursuits with a carefree attitude. Harkening back to our earlier discussion in Chapter 3 about telic and paratelic states, a supervising parent is usually in a telic state. She can't really enjoy herself with total freedom. So, the bottom line is this: that the time spent as the supervising parent should not count toward a partner's discretionary time. This is a point that is grossly underappreciated by career chasers who let the partner to do most of the parenting.

When you and your partner try to balance relationship responsibilities, your yardstick is the amount of remaining discretionary time for each of you. When you both average the same amount of free time for fun and pleasure, then you know you've negotiated a fair balance. Notice that I've used the word "average" and not "daily." When you both trust that the average is fair in the long run, then resentment won't build. That's how you get to take a nap while your partner cleans the house. She trusts that her time will come.

When you both average the same amount of free time for fun and pleasure, then you know you've negotiated a fair balance of responsibilities.

One way to calculate balance is to use objective data. Both of you can carry small notepads to record your observations of your own leisure activities. By taking notes, you will be more aware of the free time you really do have. A simpler approach would be to map out a model of your average week. However, this would require that you both have a lot of trust in each other's objectivity.

If you've followed all eleven steps of this procedure, then congratulations! You've accomplished a lot. You've set the ground work for a healthy adult-to-adult ownership of chores instead of a parent to child helpership system. If you're like most couples who get this far, your fights about chores will decline. You just may be one of the couples who report that the chore distribution didn't change but the feelings did. You will probably notice that the resentment and tension are largely gone. Both of you can intuitively feel the sense of fairness that was previously missing.

Now that you have a good system, you have to maintain it. Violations will occur. Some tasks will be forgotten; others won't be performed to specification. Don't take it personally, but don't ignore it either. That's why you're going to use your healthy conflict skills to confront your partner's occasional broken agreements. Reread Chapter 8 so your skill set will be ready. It's **your** responsibility to initiate healthy conflict in order to maintain balance.

Using a Chalkboard

A lubricant is a substance between two moving surfaces that has the purpose of reducing friction and wear. Friction and wear. Isn't that what happens between two partners when one keeps asking the other to do a special chore? It's nice when chores are routine and owned. There's no need for friction unless someone breaks the agreement. But many tasks aren't routine. The dog gets sick and has to be taken to the vet. The flood light has stopped working because the fixture is bad. Someone needs to talk with the accountant about the tax ramifications of a certain purchase. These are tasks that someone has to sandwich into his or her already overburdened schedule. They're easy to postpone and easy to forget. That's when someone starts in with the reminding bit. Nagging isn't pleasant. It breeds resentment and often provokes resistance. Wouldn't it be nice to have a lubricant so you don't have to get worn out from that kind of friction?

A chalkboard can help you with this. Like a shot of graphite powder into a jammed door latch, it can reduce the wear and tear between you and your partner. This is something that you both should discuss and implement together. It works like this. Mount a chalkboard in a location that's fairly public but not overly intrusive. The hallway next to the kitchen is a great spot. Whenever one of you wants the other to do a non-routine task, first negotiate with your partner to reach an agreement. If there's an agreement, then the responsible partner writes it down on the chalkboard. When the chore has been completed, then the responsible partner erases it from the board. If the chore isn't finished after a reasonable amount of time, then the requesting partner asks the responsible partner to write down his or her anticipated completion date on the board.

This simple device pays emotional dividends for both partners. The person who made the request doesn't have to be anxious about whether the responsible partner has forgotten his or her commitment. This eliminates the need for nagging. No one has to be his or her partner's memory. However, there's an even greater benefit for the partner who's responsible for the chore. They don't have to resent their partner for exerting *personal* control over their schedule. The chalkboard is objective and impersonal in contrast to the personalized nature of being nagged. The difference is profound and relates to some research I performed for my doctoral dissertation.

In 1975 I performed a study in which I manipulated people's perceptions of why they were losing the freedom to make a certain choice. I also measured how much their attitudes shifted in opposition to someone trying to influence them. The results showed that the more people believe that someone else is personally trying to influence them, the more their attitudes will shift in the opposite direction. This phenomenon is known as "reactance" in social psychology. I also found that reactance is reduced when someone thinks that the loss of choice isn't personal. If one loses choice but didn't believe that someone is trying to influence him or her, then there's much less reactance.

The relevance of this research should be obvious. When one person nags and tries to control his or her partner's schedule, it's natural that the partner feels reactance. This can result in an outright refusal, a fight, or covert resistance with resentment. When a chalkboard is the reminding agent, the saliency of personal influence is reduced. The person with the chore also has much more flexibility in scheduling his or her task. They're not being crowded by their partner's anxious demands to get it done **"NOW!"** All this means that the simple use of a chalkboard can reduce the friction and wear between you and your partner. That's why it's a good lubricant and worthy of your consideration.

The Equality Issue

Do you and your partner agree to share power and authority equally in your relationship? Think about it. Most people give an automatic answer: "Of course!" It seems to be a non-issue. Why even ask the question? I ask this question because many people haven't really thought it through. These people believe in equality, yet they sometimes act in ways that are inconsistent with the equality principle. Here are some examples.

Leon and Vera were competent professionals. He was a physical therapist and she was a nurse practitioner. Before they met, they had been proud of their independent self-reliance. After marriage, they continued their practices and contributed equally to the household expenses. When Vera eventually became pregnant and gave birth to a daughter, she gave up most of her nursing practice in order to stay home with the child. Leon agreed to compensate Vera for her lost income by giving her an allowance. After a couple of few years, a second child came unexpectedly. Around that same time, Leon joined a more profitable business venture. His personal accounts grew healthier while Vera budgeted her discretionary spending because she had a limited allowance. She scrimped by while Leon seemed to be very comfortable. She finally prevailed on Leon to come to counseling when he scheduled a gambling trip to Vegas.

Carl and Sherry reached a crisis when Carl used joint funds to invest in his brother's restaurant. Sherry had vehemently argued against it for a variety of reasons. For several weeks, Carl tried in vain to persuade her to go with it. He finally gave up on her and cut the check anyway. When they finally came for counseling, their tempers were quite hot. After both had argued their position, I began to inquire about their beliefs. I wanted to know how they perceived the role of equality in their relationship. Both Carl and Sherry were devout in the practice of their fundamentalist religion. Carl explained that his religion dictated that he should put his wife up on a pedestal — that he should treat her as a sacred cornerstone in his life and that he should be ready to sacrifice his own life to protect her if necessary. These responses didn't answer my real question. I pressed him further. I specifically wanted to know what happens when both partners can't agree on an action. What

225

happens then? I finally got his answer to my question. He explained that his religion dictates that the husband is the shepherd of the family. If the husband and wife can't agree at the end of the day, then the shepherd has to do whatever's necessary to lead the family. The husband then has to lead.

Whenever a partner seizes the power to be a tie-breaker, equality goes out the window. All the window dressing about sacred respect won't negate that fact. When both people are aware that one partner holds the power to act unilaterally, it has a profound effect on all their negotiations. They won't be equal because ultimately their power isn't equal.

> **Whenever a partner seizes the power to be a tie-breaker, equality goes out the window.**

You both need to decide if you want equal authority and power in your relationship. It would be inappropriate for me to prescribe it. Different cultures and religions promote inequality of power between the sexes. If both partners buy into a hierarchical system, then their relationship will work more harmoniously. However, there's a problem if both partners have subtle disagreements about their parity for power. This is most evident when couples undergo a cultural shift due to globalization. Immigrants may come from a country where women are expected to obey their husbands. If the wife becomes westernized more quickly than her husband, her expectations to have equal authority will collide with his expectations of her subservience. Fireworks can result. It's very common. So it's important that partners discuss these considerations in the open. What's the expectation? If you both agree on a hierarchy and it works for you, don't let someone else tell you to do otherwise. However, if one of you expects equal power and the other really doesn't, then there will be humiliating incidents of domination. It all depends on your mutual expectations.

If you want equality in your relationship, there are two ways to implement equal power. The first way is to agree that you both can unilaterally make use of common resources. If either of you wants to buy a horse, you can just do it. If either of you wants a new car, just go buy it without negotiating with your partner. A house? A personal jet? There's no limit. This kind of system promotes competitive spending because it lacks brakes. It works fine when you have unlimited funds. For the rest of us, a different strategy is needed to implement equal authority. Let me suggest a label for this second strategy. I call it "The Two Signatures Principle" and here is how it works.

The Two Signatures Principle

Any major decision that affects common resources or children will require the agreement of both partners. If both partners don't agree on an action, then it doesn't take place.

The Two Signatures Principle is a metaphor. It's as if you both have a joint checking account where each check requires two signatures. The most important feature is that action can't take place unless both partners agree. In other words, the default to no agreement is the status quo. No action at all. Think about this. Are you willing to discipline yourself to give up something you want just so that you can maintain the rule? This is where higher consciousness is extremely useful. When you prioritize your relationship's foundation over your "desire du jour," then you're operating in a higher mental state.

There needs to be a special provision about children in the Two Signatures Principle. It's desirable to share authority in major parenting decisions. However, there are a few exceptions. One is that some decisions are time critical and your partner can't always be consulted. A medical emergency may require the available parent to make their best decision as quickly as possible. There may not be time to consult with the other partner. Another exception would be where one partner believes that the other is truly abusive and can't be trusted. This is when it's best to bring in an objective expert, possibly even the state's child protection services. Otherwise, the Two Signatures Principle requires that both parents sign off on any major action regarding a child.

Psychologically Structured Finances

"Psychologically structured finances" is admittedly a strange term. Whoever structures finances for psychological reasons? Financial planners help clients to structure their finances to reach certain life goals. No one thinks to structure their finances to emotionally benefit their relationship. But it can be done and we're going to discuss why it's a good idea.

In the early chapters of this book, we discussed a fundamental principle of intimate relationships. The passion in your relationship depends on your maintaining a delicate balance between autonomy and attachment. This means that you sometimes need to pursue your private interests. At other times, you need to prioritize connection with your partner. It follows that your decisions will fall into two categories. There are private decisions and then there are joint or common decisions. When you choose your friends, choose your hairstyle, or choose your personal hygiene products, you don't ask your partner for permission. These decisions are for you alone to make. On the other hand, certain decisions do require your partner's permission. If you want to buy a new family car, you'd better negotiate for it first. Sending your child to camp, buying new furniture for the living room, and deciding on the family vacation are all decisions requiring joint negotiations because they fall in the common domain. A good way to visualize your private and common domains is with a Venn diagram. It looks like this.

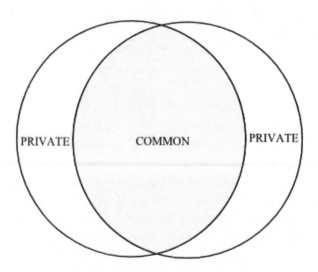

Common and private decision domains

Here are more examples of various decisions that usually belong to each domain.

Joint Decisions in the Common Domain:

Buying a new house or car
Planning the annual family vacation
Deciding whether to have another child
Choosing the color to paint the living room
Deciding whether to send a child to a different school
Deciding about surgery for a child
Deciding whether to get a pet
Financial planning for retirement and old age
Constructing the annual budget for the family
Deciding whether to let a parent live in the home
Deciding where to go for dinner together
Purchasing new expensive appliances
Setting firm rules and consequences for a rebellious adolescent
Sharing a joint hobby

Private Decisions in the Private Domain:

Choosing your own religion
Investing in your private hobby that's not shared with your partner
Going out to dinner with an old friend whom your partner doesn't like
Choosing which book you want to read
Traveling by yourself to visit parents or relatives
Getting a DVD to watch alone
Buying a new gadget that your partner thinks is unnecessary
Leaving your partner to go on a backpacking or fishing trip
Going to a concert that your partner doesn't want to attend
Buying a new bicycle when your partner doesn't like bikes
Purchasing a musical instrument and taking lessons
Contributing to a political cause that your partner doesn't prefer
Loaning a personal possession to a friend

Not all of the previously listed actions require finances, but many of them do. Now imagine this. You badly want to accept your old friend's invitation to go hear your favorite musical group. You would both share all those old memories from when you were in college together. Your partner detests the group but that's OK. You will be with your friend. You will just

229

get the money together and...Oooooops! No good! You remember how your partner has been complaining about how tight things are this month. How are you ever going to convince him or her to let you take another chunk out of the account? It won't work. There's a logical inconsistency if you have to negotiate with your partner for common funds to implement your private decisions. The boundaries are blurred between what's common and what's private. Your decision making can't really be private if you have to depend on your partner's decision about the money. You need a better system.

Your financial accounts can be structured in such a way that they can actually help your relationship. There are many benefits to designating jointly owned accounts for joint decisions and privately owned accounts for private decisions. Personal boundaries are clearer and there are fewer arguments about money. There's more discipline and more flexibility for trading accommodations with one another. In order to understand why this happens, first become familiar with the next diagram about psychologically organized accounts.

The model is divided into three fields. The center field corresponds to your common domain and the fields on the left and right correspond to both of your private domains. Each of the boxes represents an actual bank account and not just a category in a computer program. Notice how each partner's income goes right into a commonly-owned money market and gets mixed together with the other partner's funds. Notice also how each partner receives an equal amount transferred to his or her private account from the common money market.

In this model, there are predetermined monthly transfers from the common money market into a number of different accounts, each of which has been designated for a specific purpose. The amount of monthly transfer into each account should be equal to the average monthly amount for that category in your budget. You **do** have a budget, right? If not, you'd better get one unless you're in the extraordinary position of having infinite resources. The money market account serves as a buffer for any monthly fluctuations of income. If you keep a reserve in there, then automatic monthly transfers can be set up to feed each of your other accounts. This helps you to live within your budget.

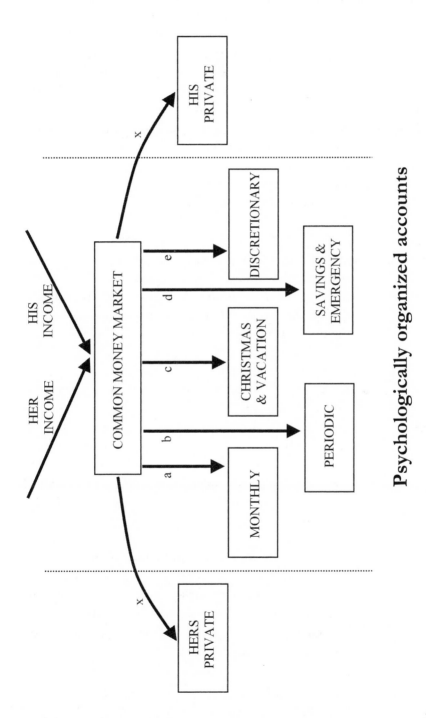

Psychologically organized accounts

The accounts in the preceding model are usually checking accounts or debit cards. Credit cards can be used, but they introduce more confusion about where you stand in each account. The monthly account is used for your rent, groceries, and other joint expenses that you can predict fairly well on a monthly basis. Periodic expenses include quarterly insurance payments, doctor's visits, and other predictable expenses that you can approximate on an annual basis. The monthly amount that you transfer to the periodic account should be equal to your annual periodic expenses divided by twelve. The joint discretionary account is for your fun and might not be a bank account. Some couples use a cash cup or even four cash cups that help them to ration their indulgences for each week.

Organizing your joint and private accounts this way will positively influence how you think and feel about your money. Check out these benefits.

- **It helps you think more realistically about your discretionary money.** Having different pots for different purposes helps you to more clearly see the limits of your discretionary funds. If you leave all funds mixed together, there's a natural tendency to think that you have more discretionary money than you really do. You'll see one large pot of money and think that you're better off than you really are. It's better to get the allocated money quickly out of sight before you get deluded. With this model, you're less likely to violate your budget. It's as if the different accounts suggest that most of your money is already spent. You're left looking at this relatively small pot of money for your discretionary spending. Your clarity of thought will be well worth the nominal bank charges for having multiple accounts.

- **It provides a powerful symbol that you both are equally important.** By immediately combining your incomes in the money market, the action tells both partners that no one will try to claim more power because of a larger income. It's a profound statement of mutual respect that's not lost on each person's unconscious.

- **It promotes clearer and healthier boundaries.** When you have your own private account, you don't have to ask permission for money to implement a private choice. If you want to go out to lunch with a friend, you don't have to beg for the money. If you want to buy a new gun or an antique doll for your collection, you can do it when you've saved enough money. Your partner's permission isn't required. It's also true that none of your private decisions will require the use of common funds. The common money is clearly earmarked only for joint interests. Apples and oranges are kept separate. The result is that you and your partner will be less tempted to unilaterally violate the common accounts.

- **It promotes flexible trading between partners.** Having separate private accounts creates better accountability if you and your partner want to lend money to each other. The transactions are cleaner. For example, John wanted to move quickly to buy a bass boat his neighbor was selling. The problem was that his private account was flat busted. Willow's private account was bloated, so John asked her for terms. What would she want in return for lending him the money? Her reply: ten percent. John immediately agreed and worked out an amortization schedule. For a number of months, John's monthly transfer of funds was diverted into Willow's private account until the debt was paid. John was able to buy the boat. Willow was happy and didn't feel used. No fuss, no arguments. Sounds hokey? Not at all! Deals like this happen when there's a good system of accountability. Financial accountability to each other promotes financial flexibility. The greater accountability provides greater safety and the trust goes up.

> **Financial accountability to each other promotes financial flexibility.**

Another benefit of having private accounts is that you can sometimes choose to help fund a joint venture. For example, you might suddenly learn of a great vacation package in the Bahamas. If you don't have enough money in your joint discretionary account, you can negotiate how much each of you will contribute toward the vacation from your private account. In this way, your private accounts can act as emergency reserves for those occasional opportunities that excite both of you.

One final point should be made before we switch to a new topic. The proposed financial structure isn't the only way of doing things. If you have a system that's working for you, you don't have to upset the applecart just because some book suggested an alternative. However, be aware that what works now in your current situation may work poorly if your situation changes. If and when that happens, you may want to remember our current discussion and restructure your finances accordingly.

Boundary Issues with In-Laws

Most people don't realize that the current western family structure is undergoing a revolutionary change. Only a century ago, nuclear families were much more embedded in an extended family system. Children often took over family farms and businesses. Many moved into their parents' residence. The deal was that grown children would acquire the family home and business but with the responsibility to care for their parents. That model of extended family has been the norm for thousands of years of human history. It's still the norm in many parts of the world, particularly in the East. In the West, all of that's changing. Globalization, vocational mobility, and government's assumption of social security has broken the nuclear family's close orbit around its family of origin. There's no longer a clear cultural norm about obligations and responsibilities between generations. This ambiguity means that there's more room for disagreement about how families *should* run.

When we refer to "culture," most people think of the norms and traditions of a geographic region. However, there's another level of culture that pertains to a person's family of origin. Each family also has its own culture. In some families, service to others is the highest virtue and self-interest may be devalued. In other families, self-interest is viewed as being legit. In some families, it's expected that the parents should be obeyed long after their children are fully grown. In other families, autonomy is highly prized, and the grown children are respected as equals. What's happening is that the breakdown of norms in the larger culture is creating a vacuum where different family cultures now collide. Nowhere is this more clear than with immigrant couples coming from eastern countries.

> **The breakdown of norms in the larger culture**
> **is creating a vacuum where**
> **different family cultures now collide.**

Ranjet and Manju had been married three years and had a newborn daughter. Both came from India, but at different ages. Manju came over as a little girl with her parents. She went to public school in California and mixed well with the other kids. Over the years, she naturally assumed western culture as her own. Ranjet was a physician. He had arrived in the United States only a few years before. They were introduced by relatives who knew each other's families back in India. After they married, the quarrels started about Ranjet's parents. Each time Ranjet's parents came to visit, they stayed a long time. Manju found them overbearing, particularly his mother. Ranjet's mother had no inhibitions about telling Manju how she should care for their newborn daughter. Manju begged Ranjet to run intereference and set some limits on his mother. Ranjet argued that his mother was just trying to be helpful and should be respected. He also asked Manju to be more polite around his parents because she was starting to leak her resentment. Manju felt jealous. It seemed to her that Ranjet's parents had more of his loyalty than she did. She also resented that her own parents weren't sent as much financial support as Ranjet's extended family back in India.

Ranjet's and Manju's conflicts were mostly the result of conflicting cultural norms. Each was trained to have a different expectation of his or her respective roles. This is the number one problem of the many eastern couples who have come to me over the years. The herky-jerky shifting of cultural expectations gives rise to friction when both partners don't shift their expectations in unison.

Cultural conflicts also occur when family cultures differ for other reasons. Nationalities and geographic regions don't have to be involved. All it takes are partners who come from very different family cultures and who expect each other to behave in old familiar ways. Unfortunately, some of the old familiar ways can be totally alien and toxic to the new partner.

Alex and Lynn were newly married but already in hot water. They quarreled about the many evenings that Alex visited his mother who lived nearby. Even though they were financially secure, Lynn objected to the occasional checks that Alex sent to his mother and his siblings. Alex was the eldest of five siblings and was used to looking after them. He described his father as a functional alcoholic who was nonthreatening, but emotionally unavailable. His parents divorced when he was twelve. His mother was a very insecure lady who was overwhelmed when her husband left. She relied on Alex for emotional support and to help the family survive. Since he was the oldest child, he often took responsibility for protecting and caring for the younger children. He remained close to his mother even when he reached adulthood. His mother had no friends and would complain about being depressed and lonely if she didn't see Alex nearly every day. To make things worse, Lynn knew that his mother was often critical of her. Therefore, Lynn didn't feel comfortable going along with Alex to his mother's house. Lynn felt desperate and Alex felt torn.

In Alex's case, codependence and enmeshment was the culture in his family of origin. He had been taught to sacrifice pleasure and to take care of others. A parent's alcoholism will often result in these types of compensatory roles. His mother's inadequacy and the needs of the younger siblings had ensnared Alex with an extraordinary sense of guilty responsibility for everyone in the afflicted family.

The main point of this discussion is that we can't afford to rely on our old assumptions about family roles. There's too much heterogeneity among mixed ethnic groups and families with their own different cultures. Norms are being shredded. We now have to negotiate expectations as we go. We can't prescribe our partner's relations with in-laws just because of our own family background. "Shoulding" on our partner doesn't work. It just leads to unnecessary heat. It's better to treat in-law issues as negotiables. Are you ready to deal?

Trading Accommodations

How often can our respective parents come to visit?

How often and for how long can we leave our nuclear family to visit our parents?

What happens to our parenting responsibilities when we visit our parents?

How much do we help our parents intervene with other siblings who need help?

How much of our marital resources do we contribute to care for disabled parents?

Do we help care for a chronically ill or dying parent in our home?

Do we accept from parents gifts that have strings and obligations attached?

What type of grandparenting authority are we willing to extend to our parents?

Do we consult with parents when we're negotiating delicate decisions with our partner?

What do we do when our parents and our partner are in conflict?

Do we get together with parents on holidays that have been traditionally shared with them?

How do we balance holidays between both sets of parents?

How much holiday and vacation time do we reserve for private intimacy with our partner?

These are just a few of the in-law issues you may need to negotiate. If each of you like your in-laws, then negotiations will probably be easy. If not, then you have a challenge. You will need to be more careful and use some of the negotiation tools we've already discussed in the previous chapter. Horse trading will be very useful if either of you doesn't like your partner's parents. You don't have to like your in-laws, but you do have to make political accommodations. Politics? In your family? Sure! As in treating a person with politeness and respect. Keeping your distastes private is not being dishonest. It's being discrete. There are many couples who do a lot of unnecessary damage by fighting over how a partner *feels* about the in-laws. Don't go there. Accept your partner's negative feelings while you negotiate with him. See what your partner wants in exchange for accommodating your need to see your parents. If you accept his feelings and trade for other accommodations, you will probably get what you need. If you use objective criteria such as alternating visits with in-laws, then the negotiations will go more smoothly. Here are some conditions that some couples might negotiate:

- Tallies are kept on the number of days that in-laws come to visit. There's an agreement to keep the tally approximately equal.

- The partner whose parents are visiting will do all the shopping, all the preparations, and all the cooking.

- Agreement to visit in-laws is contingent on an agreement to not stay in their house overnight. It's agreed to stay over in a nearby motel instead.

- Agreement to visit in-laws is contingent on not being left in the same room with them alone.

You get the idea. One thing that should **_not_** be negotiated is a partner's right to protect her boundaries. If a mother-in-law argues against the wife's parenting health care decisions, the wife needs to be free to set limits. She shouldn't be impeded by any injunction against defending her authority. Many couples get this issue confused. One partner might argue that the partner should always be "nice" and ignore the in-law's intrusions. Conversely, the offended partner might argue that the other partner should be running interference. These dynamics form an unhealthy triangle where one person tries to control the communication between two other people.

Triangles with In-Laws

Triangulated communications are one of the biggest problems involving in-laws. It's natural that you want your partner and your parents to get along. If that doesn't happen, you're probably going to feel anxious about your conflicting loyalties. Do you side with your parents or your spouse? Do you tell your partner to stop being hypersensitive? Do you tell your parents to back off and stop being so opinionated? How about neither?

The position I'm advocating is one of caution. You can choose to honestly share your opinions to anyone that asks. However, it's critically important that you don't become anyone's tool. If your parents ask you to talk to your partner for them, then it's best that you refuse. You can tell them that they have to talk directly to your partner and not through you. If your partner wants you to run interference and tell your parents to back off, you can refuse that role as well. Tell your partner to talk directly to your parents. Don't do anyone's dirty work.

The healthiest attitude is that each person is responsible for defending his or her own personal boundaries. If an in-law gives a "should" statement, it's up to the offended partner to speak up and set limits. If an in-law interrupts a partner while she's talking, then it's up to that partner to refuse to be interrupted. If a partner argues with his or her in-laws, it's up to the in-laws to make peace directly. Refuse the role of go-between like the plague. Just tell them you won't be anyone's spokesperson.

Conflicts with Step-Children

Step-children often feel resentful of a new step-parent, especially if they feel loyal to their absent parent. They may view the step-parent as being one more obstacle to their family's reconstitution. Another problem occurs when the step-child's role has been to provide emotional support to the remaining parent. Since this pseudo-spousal role is not easily surrendered, power struggles frequently occur when the step-parent tries to displace the child in the supportive role.

Step-parenting conflicts may be avoidable in some situations but unavoidable in others. For example, a child whose parent is deceased might be desperate for an alliance with a same-sexed step-parent. A similar situation occurs when the absent parent is emotionally irrelevant because of his or her abusive or uninvolved nature. Different family situations will cause children to have different reactions to a step-parent. In 1980, I started my own step-parenting experience. My wife's seven year old son Chris had witnessed the sudden death of his loving and devoted father. It was a shattering experience for both Chris and my wife. When I arrived on the scene, I felt compelled to honor Chris's memory of his father as a truly remarkable man. There was no competition for loyalty. Within a year, Chris was calling me "Dad" and I soon adopted him as my own son. He now has a child of his own, and I've progressed to the status of "Grandpa" with full benefits. I offer this story as a contrast to the frequent horror stories about step-parenting. It again underscores the point that different contexts will generate different step-parenting dynamics.

The most frequent step-parenting conflicts occur around the issue of discipline. If you're in this kind of situation, it can be uncomfortable for you as well as the child. The conflicts might appear on the surface to be about discipline, but the real issue is much deeper. Step-children will usually resent a step-parent trying to enforce discipline because they view disciplining as a parenting task. Accepting your discipline is almost like saying that you can be their parent. If they feel loyalty to their absent parent, they'll seek to defeat your discipline. And you know what? They'll win! Then your humiliating defeats will provoke you to redouble your efforts to find other ways to discipline them. It's like an arms race. The competition will eventually drag in their biological parent as a pawn. A power triangle is created when the child and your partner form their own alliance. This polarization becomes severe when you feel enraged that the child plays your mate against you. Your attempts to discipline are now contaminated with rage and resentment. Not good!

If you find yourself in this kind of polarized situation, then here's what you can do to reverse it.

1. First, you need to accept that you won't be a full parent with the authority to discipline. That's right! I'm recommending that you give up on that goal. Your unrealistic expectations are hurting both you and your family. Accept that all discipline will be enforced by your partner and not by you.

2. Negotiate a new agreement with your partner. Your part of the agreement should be that you won't directly enforce discipline. Instead, you should privately approach your partner about any discipline that needs enforcement. Notice the word "privately." Never negotiate discipline in front of the child. Get your partner to agree that he or she will be "the heavy" and will rigorously carry out any discipline upon which both of you agree.

3. Negotiate a schedule that ensures that you and your partner can regularly enjoy free time away from the child. The reason for this is because insufficient nurturance in the marital relationship can cause unconscious jealousy and resentment of the step-child. You want to ensure that this doesn't happen.

If you implement the above steps, your situation should improve to being much more comfortable. Allow as long as three to four months for the emotions to shift.

Zones of Privacy

There's a difference between defending personal boundaries versus defending relationship boundaries that you've both agreed to defend. The latter isn't about one person being his or her partner's spokesperson. It's about defending the relationship itself. Would you agree to answer a parent's questions about your partner's favorite sex positions? How about some aspect of your partner's personal history about which they feel ashamed? Do you want them to know your exact financial situation, especially if you know that they have strong opinions about how money should be invested or saved?

If you negotiate a zone of privacy, then you both have a responsibility to defend it. A critical word here is "negotiate." These zones of privacy shouldn't be assumed. One person may feel very comfortable about disclosing everything to his or her parents. In contrast, his or her partner may be super vulnerable and require a lot of privacy. This would be especially true if the parents or in-laws are intrusive. Whatever the reason, it's wise to explicitly negotiate these privacy zones. It's also a good idea to write down your agreements. Here are a few topics that couples might consider keeping private.

Religious decisions	Voting preferences
Sexual behavior	Childhood abuse memories
Negotiations about a possible move	Past history of an affair or drug abuse
Consideration of changing careers	Trying to conceive a child
Purchase of a new house	Certain health problems

While you're at it, you might as well think about the kids too. I'm sure there are a few things that you'd prefer that you both keep private from them.

Once your privacy zones are negotiated, you will have to start setting limits with your parents and in-laws. This can be very uncomfortable, especially if they've already grown accustomed to giving you directions. Changing the boundaries in enmeshed relationships is no fun. However, you do have an ace up your sleeve. It's the fact that you don't have to explain privacy. It's your right and the reason you enforce it can remain private. That means you can trump any intrusive challenge to explain yourself. Imagine the following conversation between an adult son and his parents:

"Tell us what you're going to do about (XXXXXX)."

"I'm sorry but Jana and I have decided that we're going to keep that consideration just between the two of us. We're keeping it private."

"Why do you have to be so defensive? Is there something you're planning to do that you don't feel right about?"

"Actually, our reasons for not discussing it are also private. That's what privacy means. I don't think you'd dispute our right to privacy, would you?"

"No. Of course not. I just thought that you'd have a bit more trust in your own parents, that's all."

"Dad, Mom, I'm not going to let you pry open our privacy with a guilt maneuver. It's our marriage, not yours. What we decide for our privacy is our own business, not yours. The subject is closed for discussion. Now, what else can we focus on that's agreeable to everyone?"

Does this sound a bit harsh? Sometimes that's what it takes if parents are used to having unlimited access to your life. Notice the initial disrespect that's shown by this parent who won't accept their adult son's privacy. In this kind of situation, firm resolve is required in order to change the rules. It's like "setting the bone," but with your own parents or in-laws. Hopefully, your parents and in-laws are more respectful. If so, they'll respect the privacy zones that you and your partner negotiate.

Chapter Eleven

Great Sex!

This chapter is close to the end of this book for a reason. Most of the dynamics we've discussed up to this point weigh heavily on sexual attraction and sexual satisfaction in a long-term relationship. In the very beginning of a relationship, or in a superficial relationship, sexual attraction may only require a great body, a smile, and a wink. But sexual attraction and sexual satisfaction are much more complex after a few years and especially after decades of being together. We age and our responsibilities accumulate over time. After a while, it takes more than good looks and firm body parts to create great sex.

The most important sex organ is the brain.

Perhaps it's a cliché, but it's still a truth worth stating. The most important sex organ is the brain. In this chapter, we'll discuss how to use your smarts to make sex more satisfying. But before we start I'd like to ask you an important question:

Are You a Prostitute?

If you aren't too offended to entertain this outlandish question, what criteria would you use? Is it that you don't take money for sex? Throughout history, prostitution has often involved bartering. Sometimes the payment is a goat or a chicken. Money isn't the only compensation. How about traded services? Would it still be prostitution if the compensation was a day's manual labor on the woman's residence? I think most people would say "yes." So payment doesn't have to be in physical goods. How about when sex is exchanged for financial security and social status? Would it be prostitution if a person trades sex to acquire these things or to avoid losing them? Or does it make a critical difference if the two people are married so that it appears on the surface that it's all for love?

Some women feel caught in a trap. They feel that they're expected to *supply* sex as one of their wifely duties. Some men feel an entitlement to sex in exchange for all their hard work to support the family. This exchange mentality is not really that much different from providing sex for goats or chickens. It's just more subtle. If you want to have really great sex, you need to courageously examine your true underlying motivation for having sex with your partner. If you're a man, it will probably be one or more of the following motives.

1. You want the lusty pleasure of sexual satisfaction.
2. You want the feeling of importance and power by turning a woman on.
3. You want to have some sensual fun and play with your mate.
4. You want to celebrate your love by sharing sensual joy together.

A woman's motivation can be more complex. These motives might be involved.

1. You want the lusty pleasure of sexual satisfaction.
2. You want the feeling of importance by proving you're sexually desirable.
3. You want to be a good wife by providing sex to your husband.
4. You want to reward your husband for what he does by providing him sex.

5. **You fear your partner's angry disapproval or worse if you don't supply sex.**
6. **You want to have sensual fun and play with your mate.**
7. **You want to celebrate your love by sharing sensual joy together.**

Of course the politically correct motive is the one of celebrating love. But is it so terrible or abnormal to want lusty pleasure if you can both enjoy the sexual fun? Does sex always have to carry a heavy romantic burden? Isn't it more honest to admit that our sexual experiences are usually a blend of motives, some of which involve our own satisfaction? Let's hope so. A relationship needs to involve both of you, not just your partner. Good sex is like that too. If you're not in it for your own experience as well as your partner's, then half of the relationship will be missing during sex. The following couple illustrates how some motives can distort a sexual relationship.

Gina and Ike came to counseling six months after Gina had terminated an emotional affair. It had lasted for more than a year although Gina vigorously denied that any sex had occurred. It was obvious by her secrecy that the affair had involved strong passions. For the following six months, Ike had hounded her for excessive accountability. They had fought mostly because of his prying and raging about all of the affair's details.

Both Ike and Gina were physically attractive, especially Gina with her slim figure and her long red hair. They were both around forty, had an eight-year-old son together, and had successful careers. Ike was a physician and Gina was a radiological assistant. On the surface they appeared successful, but beneath the surface they were less solid. Ike was the son of a small-town physician for whom the whole community had respect. In all this pseudo-greatness, the father rarely devoted time and attention to Ike. Ike grew up under the staggering family expectations that he would someday become prominent in the eyes of society. Covertly, he carried the old fear that he would never measure up. He used to feel that he wasn't measuring up in childhood, at least not enough to get his father's attention. His mother was amiable but less important in the family due to the father's prominence. It was a male-dominated world. His father's respect and affection was the unattainable prize. As an adult, Ike focused on showing the whole world that he was finally "enough" and deserved its attention. His large house, collection of motorcycles, dramatic hobbies, and trophy wife all attested to his worthiness. He also had an irritable temper which he sometimes flared at Gina.

Gina was raised in an enmeshed family with over-involved and authoritarian parents. Her mother was emotionally volatile and would both ridicule and rage at Gina. Her parents were on her like a vice grip. When adolescence came around, she tried to make her break. She fell in with the wrong crowd, used drugs, and most importantly discovered that she had a hot commodity to trade for attention. Gina was the most attractive girl in school. So, she made the classic trade-off: sex in exchange for attention and love. Unfortunately, many of the boys she dealt with couldn't love her, so they used her. By adulthood, she carried deep shame for how she had allowed herself to be used out of desperation. Gina was afraid of conflict. She carried deeply buried anger but didn't dare to let it out unless she was cornered. When she did display it, she would get hysterical and replicate her mother's raging imprint. Later, she would feel repulsed at her own ugly, dissociated anger and would try to stuff it some more.

Gina and Ike were very sexual at the start of their relationship. Gina was turned on by Ike's assertive potency as well as all the attention he lavished on her. Ike was attracted to Gina's stunning beauty and her sweet personality. Early on, their love-making was frequent and passionate. Then things began to change. Ike established his own clinic and shifted his attention more toward his business and colleagues. He kept his action-oriented hobbies and shared much less time with Gina, who was expected to do most of the child care. Their sex became stale and routine, almost mechanical. They didn't really talk or play before having sex. When the frequency of their sex fell off, Ike complained to Gina that she was becoming frigid. This criticism only provoked fights and made them both tense about sex. Gina redoubled her efforts to be a good wife and win back Ike's attention. She struggled to be enough in his eyes and gave him sex when she could see his frustration begin to build. Gina didn't understand what was happening. She felt numb and devoid of life. She told her friends that she didn't know who she was anymore. What she couldn't articulate was that she was trying to swap sex for love just as she had during adolescence. She was back in her old desperate trap.

Certain aspects of Gina's story are probably experienced by millions of women who have either lost their sexuality or never developed it in the first place. Gina's sexuality was poorly developed and very tenuous. All of her adolescent sexual activity had really been pre-sexual in the sense that she had traded sex for affection. Sex had merely been a tool in her failed attempt to complete her own identity. It hadn't been a true adult sexuality. It was only during the start of her marriage that Gina began to explore a more mature form of sex. Unfortunately, she was ill-equipped to protect herself from the relationship pressures that pushed her back into her old trap. Many men will reinforce this trap when they hound and criticize their wife for sex as if it's a commodity. It isn't a commodity. In most marriages, it becomes a complex and delicate emotional experience.

Intense sexual enjoyment is relatively easy to attain during the initial in-love infatuation period of a relationship. Nature takes care of that. A combination of anticipation, novelty, and neurohormones create a condition that we call "falling in love." In this state, inhibitions are suppressed and we can enjoy some of the most incredible highs of our life. Sex is usually phenomenal during this period. However, the state of being "in love" rarely lasts longer than two to three years. Boundary pressures erode our fantasies. Novelty becomes the casualty of routines. Sex can become stale. Most people don't realize that reviving great sex isn't as simple as reviving the initial "in love" state. That's because **it can't be done!** At least not with the same partner. It's hard to believe I actually said that, isn't it? But it's true. I'll say it again a different way. **You're never going to feel "in love" again in the same way as you originally did!** And your sex will have to be different, too. But don't despair. There's hope for both phenomenal love and great sex if you're willing to learn.

> ## You're never going to feel "in love" again in the same way as you originally did.

If you want great sex in your long-term relationship, you need to learn how to protect and promote it. Great sex requires a number of psychological and emotional elements. Each one can be a challenge in its own right.

Sentimental Affection

Most of this book has explained the dynamics of sentimental affection in a long-term relationship. I'm talking about the type of relationship where you're together for thirty, forty or fifty years. Sentimental love of this type requires more skill than the infatuation of being in love. It's different but it can be powerful. When you build a strong sentimental love, you can be jumping each other's bones long into old age – with passion! You can have all this, but you will have to work for it. It should be apparent that developing a great sex life depends on your creating a great sentimental bond with your partner. In that sense, this whole book has been discussing the preconditions for having great sex. If your relationship is out of balance, if there's a deficit of nurturance, or if someone isn't servicing one's own autonomy, then your sex life will probably be lousy. If you and your partner have the skills to create a loving foundation, then it's possible to have really great sex.

One qualification is worth mentioning. Even if your relationship is endowed with sentimental love, both of you will experience various moods at different times. There may be days when you or your partner can't feel affectionate because of stress or other emotions. It's not just about overall affection in the relationship. Great sex involves waiting for moments of opportunity when both of you can feel your affection at the same time.

Enjoying Your Own Sexual Pleasure

At the start of this chapter, Gina's and Ike's story illustrated how a woman can be motivated by fear to engage in sex. Fear that a husband will otherwise be angry. Fear that she's "not enough" and won't be a good wife unless she provides sex. For some women, the sexual act doesn't always involve true sexual desire. The male physiology is less capable of misrepresentation. Great sex involves both partners' expressing the pleasure-seeking parts of their personalities. Neuroscientists have referred to this part of personality as the approach system. For great sex you need to desire connection with your partner, rather than the avoidance of negative consequences. You really need to want fun and pleasure.

The capacity for hedonic enjoyment typically starts developing in childhood. We've already discussed how painful childhood experiences can create core shame and inhibit someone's capacity for pleasure. If a partner is inhibited in this way, he or she may hide in a perpetual telic state in order to avoid vulnerability. There's no hope for really good sex unless one resolves the shame that exists at his or her core. Therapy is a good option for this problem.

Sexual inhibition can be modeled by parents who are themselves inhibited about sex. Subtle messages of anxiety are picked up by a child. The avoidance of specific words for body parts may result in nervous references to "down there" or other euphemisms. References to sex as "dirty" or "filthy" can be planted into a child's unconscious mind only to inhibit their sexual development later on. That development typically accelerates in adolescence. Most adolescent boys will readily explore their sexual sensuality with masturbation and fantasy. Adolescent girls develop their sexual sensuality at a slower pace. They may learn to fantasize, masturbate, and orgasm in late adolescence or even early adulthood. About half will learn to give themselves an orgasm before they ever share it with a man. If they have this history of early sexual self-stimulation, it's very good news to any subsequent marriage counselor. If the woman was able to enjoy fantasy and masturbation before marriage, it indicates that she came into her marriage with a good relationship with her body. It also suggests that her sexual feelings probably aren't inhibited by core shame. People don't realize how important this is. Great sex requires that you have a good sensual relationship with your own body.

Great sex requires that you have a good sensual relationship with your own body.

If you haven't developed a good sensual relationship with your body, it's still not too late. But first you need to be honest with yourself about any sexual inhibitions. If you associate your own sexual pleasure to be dirty or not allowed, you may be dealing with core shame issues from your early history. If you have experienced a sexual trauma such as sexual abuse or incest, you're probably not going to have really good sex until you root out the shame with therapy. It can be done. EMDR therapy can be especially effective at resolving this type of core shame.

If you aren't repulsed by sexual exploration but just haven't done it yet, now's your time. There are a number of books that can provide exercises and fantasies for your self-exploration. You can start by exploring your general sensuality and what feels good to parts of your body other than your genitals or breasts. When you're comfortable, you can then shift to your sexual regions. Vibrators come in various shapes and sizes, and I highly recommend that you try them. If it seems a bit much at first, try the very small ones that may be less intimidating. You'll want to explore touching and focusing on various parts of your body while you simultaneously bring up fantasy images. You can accomplish two things when you practice stimulating your own body in this way. First, you can desensitize yourself to be less inhibited about sex. The second thing you can do is to train your attention. Focusing attention is an important sexual skill that influences sexual reflexes. Most women focus their attention on certain nerves and muscles to help bring about their orgasm. This skill is something that you can develop if you're willing to practice.

The bottom line is that you need to be comfortable with your own sexual pleasure if you're going to share it with someone else. If your relationship with that part of your self isn't intact, then you won't be there during sex. Your body will be there, but your mind will be somewhere else.

Enjoying Your Partner's Enjoyment

This sounds strange. "Enjoying your partner's enjoyment." What kind of process is that? Actually, it's a form of empathy, and you have some specific neurological machinery to take care of the job. We previously discussed how mirror neurons can create a model of someone else's mind in our own brain. This system is critically important if you want to have great sex. That's because great sex involves connecting more than your bodies. It involves connecting both of your minds.

> **Great sex involves connecting both of your minds.**

During foreplay and up through early intercourse, your partner's mind can be an incredible source of excitement. Their excitement and pleasure will be telegraphed in numerous ways. Heavy breathing, ecstatic facial expressions, body movements, and other nonverbal cues can combine with your partner's verbal exclamations to give you a very clear picture of what your partner is experiencing. To the degree that your head can get into your partner's head, your mutual pleasure and excitement will be magnified. When you care about what your partner is feeling, you have an additional exciting dimension to experience.

There's an interesting symmetry involving the sexual limitations of some men and women. More women than men have difficulty tuning into their own bodies. These women are more likely to be focused on pleasing their partner while ignoring their own body sensations. Conversely, more men than women have difficulty tuning into their partner's mind. These men will focus on their own sensual pleasure while ignoring the mind of their partner. Great sex requires a type of dual attention. It requires that you can enjoy your own physical sensations while you also get turned on by your partner's experience. That's what it means to be "close." You're in the picture and they are, too.

There's a natural change in sexual attention when a woman approaches orgasm. During foreplay and early intercourse, her dual attention to body and mind will work to enhance sex. However, a woman's orgasm usually requires more of her attention to help bring it about. For this reason, she will momentarily divert all of her attention to her body in the final moments before orgasm. The mental connection with her partner is re-established afterwards.

The dual attention required for great sex has a subtle but important implication. It's obvious that you need to think of your partner's sensual needs and not just your own. But what's less obvious is that you need to expose your own enjoyment if you're going to maximally excite your partner. If your own pleasure isn't in the picture, then you're actually depriving your partner of half the possible pleasure. They won't be able to empathize with your own enjoyment. Great sex requires that both of you risk sharing the hedonic parts of your selves while also caring about each other's feelings. It's mindful sex.

Respecting Your Partner's Autonomy

In Chapter 6, the point was made that enmeshment will kill sexual attraction. With certain qualifications, the opposite is also true. Autonomy enhances sexual attraction. It's like a natural aphrodisiac. If you respect your partner for being her own person with her own thoughts, you're probably going to find her to be a turn on. The one qualifier is that other elements for great sex also need to be present. You're not going to feel attracted if there's no shared affection or your partner doesn't care about your feelings. But, if all the other elements of great sex are present and you see your partner as awesomely adult, then watch out! Your passion will run hot. If you perceive your partner to have a childlike dependence, then you're going to be turned off. Healthy partners don't feel sexually attracted to children, even if they are forty years old. If this is your predicament, you might love your partner deeply. However, it will be a love without respect. That deficit will make all the difference. I see many women who care deeply for their pot-smoking husband. But the husband's childlike dependence has usually obliterated the wife's sexual attraction. It's a real bummer!

> **The emotional foreplay for great sex starts months and years ahead of time.**

Respect for autonomy can't be established at the last minute before sex. Like affection, it either develops or disintegrates over the history of a relationship. It's how you implicitly see your partner's real personality and there's no sexual technique that can change that. Because respect and affection are so intrinsic to sexual attraction, one could say that the emotional foreplay for great sex starts months and years ahead of time.

Shared Decision Making

I'd like to pose a question. Why do you think so many people fall into a sexual rut? Why do they repeat the same sexual repertoire over and over again as if they're robots? Is it because they don't know anything else, or is it something more subtle? I'd like to suggest that it's probably because making choices about sexual desire exposes them to the "Great No-No" of shame. If one of them were to ask for a new sexual favor and the other were to show disgust, the shame would cut to the core like a hot knife through butter. Shame hurts and exposing our sexual desires makes us especially vulnerable to this kind of pain. That's why many couples fall into a routine. They think that as long as they don't rock the boat and try anything new, then they'll be safe. Except that they're not really safe. They're only safe from acute shame. They're not safe from the insidious decay of a once-vibrant sexual relationship because their sex has become impersonal and monotonous.

Great sex involves both partners asking for what they want. This parallels our earlier discussion about how you can maintain passion in your relationship. If you frequently express hedonic desire, you will reinforce your identity and keep it strong. The same principle holds true with sex but on a different time scale. If you ask for what you want during sex, you can keep yourself present so that you don't depersonalize. Remaining passive can be deadly to good sex. Here are a few examples of how some partners might make requests during sex.

> "Would you touch me some more there for awhile? That feels real good."

> "How about doing it doggy style on the couch like we did before? Would you like that?"

> "My nipples are telling me that they've been feeling a bit neglected lately. They're saying they would like a little attention. Do you think you could come to their rescue?"

> "Would you be willing to wear that sexy shirt and tie that I like so much. We could pretend that we're in my office and you're the detective that I'm seducing."

> "Would you just rub me there for awhile? It teases the cat."

> "Would you slow it down just a little bit? This is so sweet I'd like it to last for awhile. I don't want to pop right away."

> "How would you feel about using the corner of the bed? You know, the position where I etc., etc."

> "Would you kiss me some more like that? I like that little thing you do with your tongue."

OK. Now we can all go and take a cold shower. Up to this point in the discussion, we've focused on how to ask for what you want during sex. That's only half of the picture. The other half involves inviting your partner to do the same. The best type of invitation is the open variety where your partner isn't confined by any suggestion. It's along the lines of: "What would you really like for me to do for you right now? What little secret pleasure could I help give you?" It's **not** along the lines of: "Wouldn't you really like to etc., etc.?" There really isn't much technique to extending an open invitation. It just involves your curiosity about what your partner wants and inviting him or her to come out of hiding. Great sex involves the most delicate of negotiations in which you both are actively involved. It's the process of expressing desire this way that ensures that your hedonic self doesn't leave the bedroom. You don't want that part of yourself to be replaced by a robot or a commodity-bartering prostitute.

There's a paradox about negotiating hedonic desires with your mate. While open negotiation can stoke passion during sex, it also leaves you more exposed to some potential pain. The negotiation process is delicate and fragile feelings are exposed. It's as if your nerves are laid bare. A clumsy rejection can really hurt. That's why good tact is essential. It protects both of you from the emotional bruising that might otherwise occur. In the next section, we'll discuss some useful guidelines for how you can better protect each other.

Protecting Feelings with Good Tact

There are two ways to protect your partner's feelings during sex. The first is to protect your partner from shame, and the second is to protect him or her from entrapment. The more that your partner trusts in your protection, the easier he or she can share passion. A smart partner always prioritizes this kind of emotional safety over any immediate gratification. Better and more frequent sex is the probable result.

I'm suggesting these three simple guidelines to protect your partner against shame.

1. **Never criticize your partner when approaching or engaging in sex.** This is a no-brainer. Your partner's hedonic system will be wide open. Any criticism is devastating when one is in this vulnerable state. Don't do it.

2. **Talk to your partner.** Ask about what your partner wants and feels. Impersonal sex is very shame-inducing. If your partner thinks that you only care about your physical pleasure, then she will feel used. Talking to your partner reassures her that you want her mind as well. That's where your partner really lives. An especially powerful technique is to use your partner's name during sex. Endearing terms such as "baby" and "darling" aren't as reassuring as her name. Your partner may wonder if she is lumped together with all the other babies and darlings in your history. There's no other endearing term that sounds as sweet to your partner as her name. It reassures her that she is held in your mind and that you're excited about that. What a turn on!

3. **When declining a sexual request from your partner, always offer her an alternative that shows that you want her.** This is a crucially important guideline to protect your partner from shameful rejection. It might look something like this:

"Hey, do you want to fool around? I'm not doing anything right now."

"Actually, I don't know if my head is in the best place for it. I'm kind of tired and I wouldn't want to let you down. But I've been wanting more connection with you lately. I was fantasizing about you earlier today. Tomorrow morning would be much better for me. Perhaps after breakfast? Could we plan for it then?"

Notice that the second partner's response is a tactful maneuver that diverts the first partner's attention to anticipating another form of connection. That's the psychology of it. You shouldn't just leave a partner's rejected request twisting slowly in the wind.

The second way you need to protect your partner's sexual feelings is to frame the situation so that she never feels trapped. You might be wondering, "Trapped by what?" The answer is subtle, yet profound. Partners often fear being trapped by obligation. And they may feel this way for good reason. If you invite her for sex and she commits himself at one point in time, she may be uncertain about how she will feel later after foreplay. It can be uncomfortable to be in a situation where she's made a commitment for intercourse, but then later she doesn't feel like following through. Even though she's not turned on, she feels trapped because she doesn't want to let you down. But then she's made a commitment that she must fulfill. It's become a responsibility. Yuk! This type of dilemma becomes more frequent as couples age, hormones decline, and life gets filled with stress. Sexual feelings become less predictable. The following guidelines are great for protecting your partner against this kind of entrapment.

1. **Make an agreement with your partner that neither of you will invite each other specifically for intercourse. All invitations will be only to explore what you each feel and want.** This guideline has the paradoxical effect of promoting better and more frequent sex. There's an agreement to avoid committing to intercourse until the very last second. This agreement eliminates the entrapment fear.

2. **Practice pleasurable alternatives to intercourse for those occasions when either one of you can't get turned on.** The keyword here is practice. It may require some training to reduce your inhibitions and enable you both to enjoy alternatives to intercourse. The more alternative choices you have, the more free you will feel to explore. You will know that if you can't get turned on, you won't frustrate your partner to death by total rejection. You'll find other ways to give your partner satisfaction besides intercourse. Nobody gets hurt.

The following illustration shows different approaches to intercourse. The second approach strategy (B) is much more tactful because it protects against entrapment.

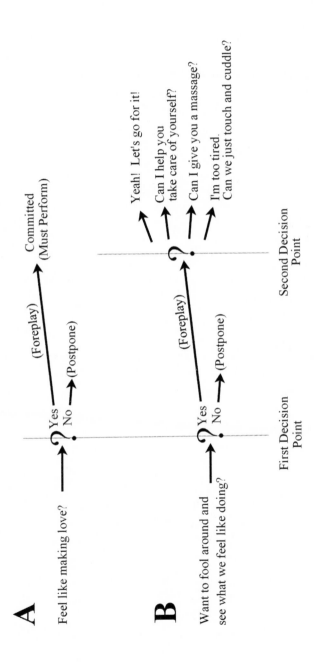

A

Feel like making love?

Yes
No (Postpone)

(Foreplay)

Committed
(Must Perform)

First Decision
Point

B

Want to fool around and
see what we feel like doing?

Yes
No (Postpone)

(Foreplay)

Yeah! Let's go for it!

Can I help you
take care of yourself?

Can I give you a massage?

I'm too tired.
Can we just touch and cuddle?

Second Decision
Point

Different strategies for approaching intercourse

The conventional invitation for intercourse is shown in Option A. One partner typically asks for an up-front commitment from his or her partner. There's no later decision point because the other partner has totally committed. It's no wonder that many partners are afraid to go down that road because they'll eventually be trapped later if they can't get turned on.

Option B is a strategy to first explore feelings and options. The point of final commitment is immediately before intercourse when both partners have more information about how they feel. If someone isn't up for intercourse, then it's understood that there are other viable options. Remember the third guideline in this section: when declining a sexual request from your partner, always offer an alternative that shows that you want him or her. That guideline applies here. It's wise to offer your partner an alternative pleasure if you decline intercourse at the last minute. Doing so protects your partner from shame.

If you're the one who is being declined, you'd best be smart about the situation. If you protest and complain, you will train your partner to fear entrapment. It will hinder your future sex life. If you show respect for your partner's delicate feelings, your future sex will be protected. This is what some therapists call "temporal integration." It's the ability to consider future consequences and make decisions for long-term benefits. Your partner's sense of safety needs to be your top priority. Many partners fail here because they focus only on their immediate gratification. Learn to think smarter than that if you want to have great sex.

Parallel masturbation can be a helpful alternative to intercourse. It's a skill that I've trained many couples to use because it reverses entrapment anxiety. In many cases, I've seen this kind of training overcome impotence because it removes a lot of anxiety. The training has some similarities to sensate focusing in sex therapy where couples practice sensual touch without having intercourse. In masturbation training, one partner caresses and erotically touches his or her partner while the other partner masturbates to climax. The two partners alternate their roles over time. An important agreement is that intercourse is ruled out for the six weeks while practice takes place. This agreement reduces so much anxiety that paradoxical effects sometimes occur. I've always been amused when a previously impotent couple comes back and sheepishly admits to having broken the rule. With one such couple, I felt exceptionally good rapport and decided to use some therapeutic play. With a very stern look on my face, I shook my finger at them and exclaimed: "You naughty, naughty children!" Everyone broke into hilarious laughter and their guilt dissipated immediately.

After six weeks of practicing parallel masturbation, couples typically feel more relaxed when approaching sex. That's because they've trained their lower brain to feel safe. They've practiced erotic touch without being trapped into intercourse. This is a conditioning process, rather than intellectual learning. It takes practice to learn this technique.

There's often a big difference between intellectual understanding and emotional safety. The latter usually requires repetitive training. I like to use a personal story to illustrate this point. When I was a young man, I decided that I would try rock climbing. The experienced guides rigged a safety line from my waist up through a carabiner attached to a tree at the top of the cliff. Then the line fed down through another carabiner that was attached to a tree at the bottom of the cliff. Two men near the tree managed the line around their waists. As I climbed, any slack in the rope would be taken in by the two men. There was no way I could fall more than a couple of feet. This was my intellectual assessment as I approached the cliff. My skills were not good, and my physique was poor for climbing. About fifty feet up, I knew that there was a ledge I could never get past. With my strength giving out, hanging from my finger tips, I couldn't feel the rope tethered behind me. I knew it was there and my intellect told me that I should be safe. However, every neuron in my lower brain screamed that **I was going to die!** I felt it in my gut. So much for intellect when dealing with conditioned emotions. A person could have a Ph.D. in zoology, but if he has negative emotional conditioning in his history, he might still be terrified by an eight-inch snake or a tiny spider.

If you've been conditioned to fear sexual entrapment, then strongly consider parallel masturbation training. You could train your lower brain to feel that you really do have a safety line behind you. You and your partner could train each other into a higher level of trust. Imagine trusting that each of you will take full responsibility for your immediate sexual gratification if your partner can't get turned on. No entrapment. It's nice. Couples who broaden their final repertoire to include parallel masturbation will usually find that they have more frequent intercourse. This is the natural consequence because they feel safer and more relaxed. Both partners are unafraid to explore foreplay because they know they won't be trapped.

Creativity

Creativity is a talent that can't be taught. There's no way that I can tell you "the seven steps" to being more sexually creative. That would be a paradox because once you're following a method, then you're no longer in a creative state of mind. Creativity needs to come from you, not from someone else. What I **can** suggest is that you think about two dimensions toward which you can direct your creativity. After that, it's up to you.

Novelty and surprise are two dimensions that really spice up sex. Both of these dimensions are neurologically related and can contribute to positive arousal. Each of us has novelty detectors in the hippocampus part of our brain. When these detectors are stimulated, then we become curious and aroused. Most of the time, this arousal feels pleasurable unless we perceive that we're in a dangerous situation. This positive arousal can make sex a lot more fun. Of course it also depends on good taste so that you and your partner don't weird out. Dropping a worm on your partner's stomach would certainly be surprising and novel, but it probably wouldn't have a positive effect. Poor taste trumps other factors. However, novelty and surprise combined with good taste can make sex exciting.

Creative novelty goes far beyond finding new sex positions. Have you ever noticed that sex is a bit more exciting in a motel room and a different feeling bed? Suggesting different locations in the house can have a similar effect. How about that huge lounge chair in the corner? Could that be put to good use? Hmmmmm. Different clothing can be a turn on too, especially if it's combined with fantasy.

The use of fantasy is one of the most effective ways to stimulate novelty, particularly if it dovetails into your partner's previous fantasies. Does he or she have a fantasy of meeting a young lover on a deserted beach? Perhaps it's an office seduction scene that he or she mentioned a while back. Play acting isn't dishonest. It's a natural way to have fun that we start at a very young age. In adulthood, we can use those skills and add the sex component to produce an endless variety of novel pleasures.

Several authors have written about how a frame of meaning can create novelty in sex. I agree, but I want to add the qualifier that not everyone can do it. People with low level of consciousness are usually too concrete to create much meaning. These people may only think about sex organs and body parts. Their limitation will doom them to eventual boredom and possibly the desperate search for novelty in porn, telephone sex or unfaithful promiscuity. If you have a higher level of consciousness, then you can use it to empathically feel your partner's joy, to appreciate the value of their hard-earned trust, to appreciate the emotional freedom that you've both created and to feel the uniqueness of the present moment in your two transient lives. If you can both feel and express things like this during sex, then there are an infinite number of ways that novelty can be generated.

Novelty doesn't just occur on a sensory level. It's determined more by how your sensory experience fits with your intuitive understanding of the situation. The latter is called context and it affects your reflexes. If you sense that your partner still resents you after a recent fight, then some of your reflexes probably won't work no matter how much you're stimulated. The contextual frame of meaning that you bring to sex will largely determine its quality. Some people say that sex without love becomes boring. That may be only partially true. It may be more accurate to say that sex without meaning will often lead a partner to desperately seek novelty on a concrete level. Whips, chains, trios, group sex, bondage, sadomasochism, animals, swinging? Really kinky sex can be a sign that someone has a hard time creating one's own frame of meaning.

> **Sex without meaning will often lead a partner to desperately seek novelty on a concrete level.**

Surprise is the other way to spice up sex by stimulating those same novelty detectors in the hippocampus. But there's a caveat. Random surprise isn't a good idea if it makes your partner feel unsafe. The best way to surprise your partner is to do something unexpectedly that you can remember that he or she has desired. When you surprise your partner like that during sex, he or she will often want to jump your bones. If you remember that your partner gets turned on by formal wear, imagine his or her excitement when you emerge from the bathroom dressed to the hilt. Perhaps it's not formal wear. Maybe it's an English accent of some actor that your partner finds hot. You could stir things up by suddenly shifting into English-speak as if you're in a movie. This kind of sudden play, remembered from your partner's fantasies, can give him or her a surprising turn on.

So what stands in the way of your creativity? You could use novelty, surprise, and remember what's in your partner's mind. But then you would have to face one more obstacle. Can you guess what it is? Let me give you a clue. How would you feel if your partner remarks that you look "silly"? What would it be like if you try something new and then your partner gives you a disgusted look? How would you feel then? Of course! You knew it all along, didn't you? You would have to face "The Great No- No" of your own shame if things don't turn out right. Maybe it's better to do what's totally safe and familiar. At least, that's what your unconscious says.

Confronting a Partner Who Avoids Sex

What happens if there's no sex at all in your relationship? Some readers no doubt think that great sex may be all very fine and good, but they'd settle on any sex at all. If this is your predicament, then listen up. You are absolutely right to expect sex with your partner. After all, that was part of the deal. It wasn't written in a contract or stated in a vow, but it was implicitly understood that you would be sexually relating. If your partner is currently avoiding sex altogether, then you have a broken contract. You need to confront the situation.

You will notice that I said that you're correct to expect sex with your partner. That statement needs a lot of qualification because you can really mess up if you interpret it incorrectly. Confronting your partner for immediate forced sex would be exceptionally obtuse. It doesn't work like that. Most sexual reflexes are involuntary and depend on emotion. The danger is that if you confront your partner to *produce* sex, then her sexual feelings will become injured and contaminated with anxiety. For all you know, that might already be the main reason why her sexual desire is blocked. Whatever the reason is for your partner's sexual avoidance, you don't want to aggravate the situation. Don't focus on her immediate sexual performance.

You need to place your focus on your partner's sexual safety and freedom. If your partner is avoiding sex, then her sexual feelings are blocked. She needs to discover what's blocking them. In fact, your partner has a responsibility to the relationship to find out. You can confront your partner about it, but she doesnt have a responsibility to produce sex without desire. Got it? It's a critical distinction; if you don't understand it then you could cause a lot of damage. You need to confront sexual avoidance by challenging your partner to methodically remove the emotional block. Notice that I used the word "methodically." I'm implying that the process will take time. She may not understand what's really going on. Perhaps core shame plays a part. Your partner might need sex therapy, assertiveness training, marriage counseling with you, or some other resource to help her do the required detective work. Maybe some of the emotional blockage is attributable to your own behavior.

> **You need to confront sexual avoidance by challenging your partner to methodically remove his or her emotional block.**

I have a recommendation if you're going to confront your partner about a sexless relationship. At the beginning of your confrontation, make sure that you *tell your partner that you don't want him or her to incur self injury by trying to force sex.* Reassure your partner that you're more concerned with what's happening to his or her sexual feelings than the concrete sexual act. It's only after you make this clear distinction that you can constructively confront your partner to do the detail work. And that means that your partner has to figure out how to find safety and freedom for his or her own sexual self.

Chapter Twelve

Mapping Your Strategy

You may have noticed by now that this book has avoided "the seven secrets" formula frequently adopted in self-help literature. A quick perusal of self-help titles gives the impression that truth always comes bundled in batches of five, seven, and ten. If it were only that simple. A less cartoonish view acknowledges that relationships are far more complex. I've never seen a book titled _Jet Engines for Dummies_. The human mind is infinitely more complex than a jet engine. The real truth of intimate relationships is messy. Good couples therapy often resembles detective work as the therapist works through a maze of interlocking dynamics. So how are average people supposed to make sense of all this confusion and improve their relationship?

The current chapter lists some recommended strategies for several common relationship problems. The list isn't all-inclusive and it can't solve the most difficult problems. After all, the title of this book refers to a first-aid kit and not deep surgery or intensive care. Simple remedies are suggested for the more simple problems. It also offers initial direction for more complex problems and that's worth a lot.

It's particularly helpful to conceptualize relationship problems as occurring on three levels of difficulty. They involve deficits in knowledge, skill, or capacity. These categories aren't necessarily exclusive, but let's not overly confound the subject. A knowledge deficit is when a person lacks the information about how the problem can be solved. They can easily learn it. Then they can voluntarily and, relatively quickly, change their behavior. For example, knowing that your partner needs regular nurturance can inspire you to immediately change your routine. Many couples have found that such a simple intervention can increase their affection and reduce fighting. The information allows a change in their voluntary behavior. This is the level at which most self-help books are written. "Follow these steps. Do this and do that." It's a strategy that works for some problems but not for others.

Skill deficits involve a greater level of difficulty. A skill involves a learned behavior shaped by training. You can't get the desired effect on your first try. You have to repeatedly practice the behavior in order to perform it correctly. Using stick shift on a car becomes easy only after a lot of practice. Implementing the When and Where Rule during a toxic conflict also requires practice. Most people can't remember the rule just from verbal instruction. When their adrenalin flows, their good judgment and memory both take a hike. However, they can train themselves to remember it if they repetitively use the rule in practice drills. Then the skills will be available to conscious memory when they need them.

Capacity deficits cause the greatest difficulty in a relationship. By referring to capacity deficits, I mean limitations that are basic and involuntary. Any improvements require much time and effort if they can be changed at all. Cognitive recovery after a stroke is one example. The stroke victim's memory may gradually improve but will still probably show residual deficits. Low intelligence, a low level of consciousness, and poor emotional regulation are all types of capacity deficits. The integrity foundation in a relationship is the capacity issue we've been discussing throughout this book.

Increasing your capacity is extremely difficult because you have to fundamentally change your brain. It's true that instructional learning and skill learning both involve new brain growth. However, that type of growth is highly specific to either verbal information or a particular behavior. Changing capacity requires pervasive changes in your brain, most of which are unconscious. For this reason, it's more accurate to say that you might be able to slowly *grow* your capacity but you can't rapidly change it to your liking. Certain kinds of experience can catalyze faster growth in capacity by accelerating the brain's ability to grow new connections.

There's no way that I can assign a simple prescription for every problem behavior that occurs in relationships. The biggest reason involves a psychological phenomenon known as equifinality. Equifinality means that different combinations of history and emotional dynamics can produce the same behavioral outcomes. For example, lying comes very naturally to a sociopath. But lying is also a common defense for someone who has conflict phobia. The psychopath is undersocialized, while the person with conflict phobia may have been trained by his parents to surrender all boundaries. The underlying emotional dynamics are different. Another example of equifinality involves women who show no sexual interest after they've married. For some women who have poor autonomy and fear conflict, normal marital friction can gradually turn them numb. Other women who never developed their sexuality before marriage might later revert to their usual non-sexuality once they feel safe in motherhood. Different pathways of personal history and emotion can lead to the same end point. This is why effective planning for change has to consider a person's context in the form of personality and social history. Their context gives important clues about which emotional dynamics need to be targeted. The problem is that there are too many contexts to put into any all-inclusive list.

In the following scenarios, some of the more common problems are described in various contexts. Where the proposed strategy involves readings, I highly recommend that both you and your partner read each section and discuss it together. The proposed strategy usually won't work if only one of you does the reading and has the responsibility to explain it to the other. Don't do that! It's a set-up for failure. You both need to take full responsibility for your strategy.

It's a good idea to plan a weekly meeting with your partner outside of the home. You can both relax in a coffee shop with a copy of this book, as well as two pads of paper. You can then take each relevant chapter from the book and discuss it section by section. Plan how you will implement any of the recommended exercises. You can also use these meetings to review your progress and make changes if your strategy needs tinkering. The trick is to be methodical and consistent. It's the biggest determinant of success. Some effective strategies require months to produce the desired outcome. Changing your capacity requires even longer, sometimes years.

Deficits in Knowledge

For these kinds of problems, change can come quickly. You need to learn how to do some things differently, but there's no skill training required. You just need to follow through with a better plan than you have in the past. Here are some common scenarios.

Problem Scenario:
You and your partner have drifted apart. You had a close relationship even following the "in love" years. However, life has become more stressful and you both struggle to take care of all your responsibilities. You almost never

have time together when you're not problem solving or doing chores. You're trading barbs or worse with increasing irritability.

Proposed Strategy:

Read Chapter 4 again. Then follow the directions for instituting a weekly together-time for intimacy. Don't settle on "date nights" in which you go out to movies or see friends. Make sure you schedule a regular weekly time for intimate talk. You can start by following the directions for intimacy exercises. Plan to have most meals together and agree to go to bed together. Your long history of closeness indicates that you're both capable of intimacy because you had more than the initial in-love infatuation. You just need to start nurturing attachment in the relationship again.

Problem Scenario:

There are many arguments about household chores. One of you frequently complains about not getting enough help. When you're both away from home, you get along and enjoy each other. Your sex life is good.

Proposed Strategy:

Read Chapter 10 again. Follow the directions for methodically negotiating responsibility and ownership for all the chores. Then negotiate an agreement with your partner that helping with chores will only be voluntary and not obligatory. In other words, there will no longer be a "helper" role. Also put up a chalk board for miscellaneous chores as described in Chapter 10. Your good sex life and your good relations away from home both suggest that your problem is narrowly focused and not some facet of a larger underlying problem.

Problem Scenario:

There are many arguments about money. One partner sometimes won't tell the other about how joint funds are being spent until the deed is done. There's a sense of defiance in the air. At least one partner doesn't own a private account for personal spending and the rest of the accounts aren't designated for specific purposes.

Proposed Strategy:

Organize your accounts after reading Chapter 10. Make sure that you each have your own private account for personal spending. Do the necessary research to construct a budget. Then organize your common accounts so that each is used only for specific kinds of purchases. Set up periodic business meetings to jointly revise your model.

Deficits in Skill

You will need to sharpen your skills in order to resolve these kinds of problems. You're usually pushing against the opposing force of well-entrenched habits and emotions. Success won't be immediate, but disciplined practice will still get you there. Here are some common scenarios.

Problem Scenario: One of you is the evader and the other is the pursuer. The evader doesn't have a history of childhood abuse that might otherwise explain the avoidance. The evader feels free, alive, and fun-loving only when away from the pursuer. In addition, the evader typically thinks more about the pursuer's desires than his or her own needs. The pursuer complains about lack of closeness, but the evader feels no attraction. He or she just feels numb and confused.

Proposed Strategy: This is probably a case of hedonic inhibition due to relationship shame. The evader hasn't done a good job of servicing his or her need for autonomy within the marriage. The best intervention strategy consists of several stages. First, the pursuer needs to explicitly agree that the evader shouldn't try to force affection. It's already being blocked. Unrealistically high expectations of emotional performance will only worsen the evader's "emotional impotence." It's more realistic to expect that it will take months of work before the evader can thaw out. Second, you both need to frequently practice boundary micro-corrections for at least six to eight weeks. (See Chapter 8) This practice will train the evader to use an active defense system that allows him or her to come back into the relationship. The third stage involves the evader practicing the hedonic strengthening exercise described in Chapter 7. It should be practiced at least twice a day for another six weeks. The hedonic exercises should start only after the micro-correction phase is finished. This multi-phase strategy follows a logical sequence: 1) readjusting expectations, 2) strengthening a new engaging defense style for the evader, and 3) strengthening the evader's core hedonic self within the marriage. This strategy requires methodical work, but it can have amazing results for those couples willing to employ it.

Problem Scenario:
You have escalating fights during which each of you tries to have the last word. They go on and on, long after any real constructive communication has ended. However, when one of you finally chooses to leave the conflict,

the other follows. You have never openly discussed each other's right to privacy.

Proposed Strategy:

It's important that both of you can separate and allow each other privacy to self-stabilize. Read Chapter 8 again, particularly the section about "The When and Where Rule". It's very important that you practice the recommended exercises. This will give you the skill to postpone conflict when you're overly aroused and have difficulty remembering the rule. You should also learn the principles of effective negotiation. You can train by reviewing previous fights with your partner. Then you both can discuss what you might have done differently if you had used the principles. This type of post hoc review will instill the principles more deeply into your memory.

Problem Scenario:

One of you doesn't enjoy intimate conversation. The other partner is frustrated and wants to feel closer. There's still good will, sex is good, and you both enjoy having fun together. The person who avoids intimacy has no family history of trauma or abandonment.

Proposed Strategy:

This is a case that can be helped by training. The good will, playful affiliation, and absence of trauma all suggest that there's not a more serious capacity problem like hedonic inhibition. It's more likely that the person has not been trained for intimacy. If the person comes from a family that was concrete and avoided intimate talk, then he or she probably never developed a good theory of mind. A theory of mind is the implicit understanding of how feelings and thoughts operate in a person. A good theory of mind allows a partner to feel competent at intimacy. One doesn't have to fear being emotionally inadequate. Group therapy is great for training this kind of competence. It needs to be a process group that's relatively unstructured and focuses on emotions and interactions among group members. I've seen many couples dramatically improve their intimacy by one of the partners participating in this kind of group. The time scale for improvement will usually be more than a year.

Deficits in Capacity

These kinds of problems are the toughest nuts to crack. A huge obstacle is that few people really want to admit to having a weakness. It's shameful. Who wants to admit that they're immature and have a low level of consciousness? Who feels proud about being overwhelmed by anxiety when they face disapproval? It's no fun to admit that you're afraid to have fun. It's hard to be honest about these things. But if you both can't be honest about what's really happening, you will be dead in the water.

Problems with capacity sometimes require years to improve. For this kind of change, you need a good catalyst. A catalyst is something that you add to a change process to speed it up. When you grow your capacity, you actually catalyze neuronal growth in your brain. Certain kinds of social environments can turn on the genes that cause this faster growth. Therapy is one example of a catalytic environment. Personal growth speeds up in certain kinds of individual and group psychotherapy. Intimate communities in 12-step groups are also catalytic. There's a hard science beneath the effectiveness of these self-help groups.

Here are some common scenarios involving someone's poor capacity.

Problem Scenario:
You have escalating fights where each of you tries to have the last word. They go on and on, long after any real constructive communication has ended. If one of you tries to leave the conflict, the other follows in hot pursuit. The pursuit is relentless to the point of opening locked doors or even forcing entry. You have had unproductive discussions about the right to privacy. One partner refuses to accept the principle of privacy from the other and insists that it's his right to not be put off.

Proposed Strategy:
This scenario is not just about skill deficits. The egocentric perspective and violence by the pursuing partner indicates emotional problems. First go to couples counseling. It needs to be established that the right to privacy is paramount. If you or your partner still can't tolerate the other's retreat from conflict, then that indicates a serious deficit in that person's capacity for self-soothing. Therap dy would be in order, particularly if it involves mindfulness training. Dialectic behavior therapy would be especially effective. It can change how the brain regulates anxiety.

Problem Scenario:

Your partner frequently breaks agreements and then lies about it. He or she regularly uses a drug, perhaps marijuana or cocaine, and blames you for nagging about the transgressions.

Proposed Strategy:

There's no one way to respond to this, but you need to realize that your partner's personality is probably regressed because of drugs. You might have to "set the bone" with a separation or even consider divorce. Your partner needs treatment from a professional and/or a self-help program such as Narcotics Anonymous if he or she can't stop or keeps relapsing. It will take close to a year for the brain's metabolism to rebuild to normalcy. It will take an even longer catalysis in a recovery program for one's level of consciousness and emotional stability to grow. Figure a few years in recovery until one is stable. Meanwhile, get into a self-help group for yourself. Groups like Al-Anon, Nar-Anon, and S-Anon can greatly reduce the unconscious shame that you will inevitably absorb by being in this kind of a relationship.

Problem Scenario:

One of you has a history of hiding sneaky behavior. You (or your partner) also hate conflict and will do almost anything to avoid it. You may have also had an affair that's been recently discovered. You show real remorse and guilt each time you're discovered in one of your transgressions. However, it's only a matter of time before the next betrayal occurs. Your history might involve one or more parents who were authoritarian, exhibited violent tempers, or were extremely critical. It's also possible that you may have had parents who completely avoided anger and conflict

Proposed Strategy:

The person probably isn't a psychopath, but he or she probably does have a relatively low level of consciousness combined with a fear of conflict. One's level of consciousness can be raised by participating in a process therapy group for over a year. This can improve one's self control so that he or she doesn't always act out his or her impulses. The partner will also need some assertiveness training to better integrate his or her anger. In my own practice, I use a conflict inoculation protocol to desensitize the person to facing disapproval.

Problem Scenario:

One of you prefers to work all the time. It might involve a job or it could be parenting. Either way, the person historically avoids allocating time for fun and relaxation. This individual may have been raised in an alcoholic family or some other family configuration with unstable parents. He or she may have been saddled with responsibility for siblings or a compromised parent. Now in adulthood, this individual's current relationship is running down. The other partner feels hurt because she or he is never pursued for enjoyment. Small quarrels occur about trivial issues.

Proposed Strategy:
This scenario superficially appears to be a problem about needing more nurturance between partners. That's certainly involved, but the root of the problem runs a lot deeper. The telltale symptom is the partner's historical avoidance of fun. Suspect core shame and hedonic inhibition. This person will probably show discomfort with the "I Want ...Will You" test. It's critical that the person comes out of denial about his or her inhibition. Ego-state psychotherapy will probably be the most effective intervention. It can help counter-condition the person's core shame about experiencing pleasure. The person could also benefit by reading Chapter 7 and regularly performing the hedonic strengthening exercise during daily meditation periods. He or she will probably work on this issue for many years.

This previous list is obviously limited. It's only a subset of an infinite number of scenarios. It illustrates how devising a good strategy requires that you face what's really going on. As much as you may want to do that, "The Great No-No" might stand in your way. It can be shameful to admit that you have deficits. Many men can't do it. Women generally have an easier time with it. Knowledge deficits are the least difficult to face. They can be fixed with some quick study. But how about admitting that you lack a particular skill or even some emotional capacity? It takes courage to face those kinds of deficits. Do you have it? I'm asking because the future of your marriage might depend on it.

Chapter Thirteen

Conclusion

It should be apparent from our discussion that we human beings are extremely complex, and our intimate relationships are even more so. Relationship problems occur with varying levels of difficulty that correspond to different levels in our nervous system. Paradox rules us at the deepest level. Instead of our personalities being one consistent system, each of us carries different self parts that conflict, negotiate and compromise with one another. Most of us want to be intimate, to feel emotionally connected with another. Conversely, we also want to be independent and self-sufficient. This conflict and tension is at the core of what it means to be human. To emphasize either need too much can tilt a person into a dehumanizing disequilibrium. If one only seeks a sense of closeness, one loses a sense of oneself as being loveable. If one is totally independent of others, he or she might need to be put behind bars for being a psychopath.

One of the biggest myths about relationships is that most break-ups occur because partners can't get close enough or because they can't communicate. This makes about as much sense as saying that most people die because their brains stop working. The coincidence is accurate, the causality is not. The paradox is that most failures in intimacy occur because partners are not sufficiently separate. By "separate" I do not mean giving each other the cold shoulder or ignoring each other. I'm referring to keeping one's identity separate, valid, valuable, and whole, without requiring the other partner to provide the missing pieces. If you feel unlovable and are too ashamed to admit it even to yourself, then you're likely to claw at your partner to restore your sense of worth. You will probably try to obligate your partner as if he or she were a parent, while at the same time trying to change that parent. "If you loved me…" is a classic guilting maneuver in this fashion. Such intrusiveness, arising from enmeshed personal identities, is far more responsible for break-ups than mere communication problems. In fact, most communication problems in intimacy derive from problems with autonomy.

While enmeshment is one of the most serious threats to intimacy, a total emphasis on independence is stunting. If there are no occasions when you can lean on the other person, you will miss a lot of the good stuff: the back rubs at night, the shared sorrow that helps reassure that you're "OK," and other affirming reminders that you really are worth being cared for by another. Yes, it *is* important to learn to do it yourself. But it's also important to be able to choose when to let another do it for you. The key word here is "choice." Without choice, you will lose the balancing skills required to maintain a healthy, intimate relationship.

Balancing is a good metaphor for relationships. Paradoxically, each of us wants to move in opposing directions. We want to be independent, yet we want to merge. We want to rely on ourselves, yet we want to be nurtured and affirmed by others. This balancing act needs a lot of skill. Just as the high-wire acrobat must keep his mass in motion to approximate balance, we also must stay in motion by constantly choosing our priorities among opposing needs. If we freeze into rigid roles, our intimacy is lost to the nets below. If our shame and inhibition eclipse either our need for separateness or our need for dependence, we lurch into disequilibrium. We must prevail over "The Great No-No" if we want to remain free to love. And so, we must keep on choosing, never quite settled, never permanently satisfied with the status of things. We can never finally resolve our paradox. But if we accept it and dare to keep choosing, if we have the courage to keep ourselves growing this way, then we can probably negotiate the tightrope of intimacy.

Addendum: Message to a Daughter

This book has focused on how partners can revitalize their existing relationships. However, some of the discussion is relevant to how one can go about selecting a mate. If a new partner demonstrates fractured integrity so that future relationship problems are predictable, then it might make sense to reject such a poor gamble. The relevance of this logic was demonstrated when my daughter Heather was twenty years old. She came to me several days after her painful breakup with a second boyfriend in as many years. Heather looked straight into my eyes to underscore the earnestness of what she was about to say.

"Dad?" She said. "Will you teach me to not trust?"

At first I was nonplussed. It seemed a terrible request. Skepticism and cynicism aren't my favorite attributes. But then I got an idea. Perhaps I could interpret her question to be less absolute. Then I might be able to give her a helpful answer. I asked for a few days to think about her question and she agreed. Several days later, I invited her to go out to our favorite Italian restaurant. After our dinner, I handed her a list of five guidelines to help sharpen her caution when selecting her future partner. Since then, a number of my clients have asked me for similar advice. I've given them the same guidelines that I gave her. If you're contemplating a new relationship, they might be useful to you as well.

1. **Quickly leave a new relationship if the person tells even a few convenient lies.** The biggest challenge is to resist your natural desire to minimize the lying. If you don't, it may be the biggest mistake of your life. There's a high probability that the person will betray you in the future because he has insufficient integrity to preserve a secure relationship.

2. **Don't get married unless you and the other person have had three good fights.** Until you see him get angry with you, you really haven't seen his shadow side. If he doesn't risk conflict, he will gradually distance himself out of the relationship. You want a relationship with someone who isn't conflict phobic.

3. **Team up with someone who can balance pleasure and responsibility.** He needs to be comfortable being "healthily selfish." He needs to love himself as well as you. If he can't, you will eventually wind up being deprived along with him.

4. **Prioritize character over passion. Select a partner who will "pay the price" for the sake of his integrity.** You want someone who will struggle to be honest and consistent even when it costs him discomfort. Don't rely on what the person says. Notice what he does when he thinks he's unobserved. Don't be seduced just because he is nice to you. There are many nice people who will show strong feelings for you but who will later betray you because they don't have much character.

5. **Don't stay with someone who insists you don't have the right to retreat into your own privacy.** Privacy is an absolute right. If a new partner insists that you shouldn't "abandon" him when you want to be alone, then he's not accepting responsibility to stabilize himself like an adult. Adults don't "abandon" other adults. We don't have that type of responsibility for each other. We do have the responsibility to not abandon our children. If a partner insists that you shouldn't "abandon" him, then he really wants a parented relationship and not an adult-to-adult relationship.

Glossary

Affiliation - The sharing of an experience together while both parties are interacting with the outside world. It differs from intimacy in that deeply personal information is not disclosed. Examples: chatting at a cocktail party, going to the movies together, exploring a new environment together or playing tennis together.

Attachment - The instinctively satisfying experience of feeling that your personal identity is valued by another. Attachment is the sense of being connected to another.

Attachment mechanism - The instinctive neurological reflex system that drives attachment. This system is shaped by early interactions with caregivers. The resulting attachment styles are secure, ambivalent, avoidant, or disorganized. The attachment mechanism, with its embedded style, is later reactivated and used in adult life to attach to others.

Autonomy - In common usage, autonomy is the ability of a person to operate independently without having to depend on others. However, this author is reframing the term to mean psychological autonomy. Psychological autonomy is an individual's dependence on one's own frame of meaning instead of the perceived approval of others. Throughout this book, the author is referring to true psychological autonomy.

Boundary - The sense of deservingness that something is your prerogative or rightful possession. In common usage, this term is often confused with the act of asserting one's rights. This author recommends defining a boundary as an intuitive feeling of deservingness, not the external assertive act itself.

Boundary intrusion - The unilateral violation of one of your boundaries. Examples: Interrupting your sentence while you're speaking, intimately touching you without permission, telling you what you are feeling without asking you, or giving you a "should" statement about a personal choice.

Catalyze - Commonly, to catalyze is to speed up a process by adding a special ingredient. The author uses this term to describe how certain dimensions to experience that can accelerate neurological growth in the brain. (e.g. Novelty catalyzes strength of memory and social interaction catalyzes the development of conscience.)

Compulsive empathy - The internal mandate to unconditionally focus on another person's feelings. The compulsive aspect refers to lack of choice. A term coined by this author, compulsive empathy means that there's no consideration of other responsibilities or concerns that might be considered more important than the other person's feelings.

Context - A psychophysiological term that refers to your implicit understanding of the current situation. It includes unconscious expectations about what will probably happen next in the situation.

Contract - An agreement with obligations between two people. It can be negotiated explicitly but it can also be created implicitly by repetitive routine (e.g. Both partners expect to meet every night at 6:00 to eat dinner.)

Coordinative inhibition - The fact that different motivational reflex systems will inhibit each other. This is a psychophysiological term derived from Soviet neuroscientists. It suggests that the reflexes wrestle each other for dominance, limiting each other in the process.

Core shame - The inhibition and a sense of un-deservingness that can become installed due to attachment wounds in early childhood. Core shame, a term coined by this author, is in contrast to relationship shame that can result from repetitive subtle insults during the course of an adult relationship.

Counteraction - A psychological defense that occurs when a person tries to prove that he's the opposite of what he fears. Example: a person fears being weak as he was when abused as a child. Consequently, the individual become a bully.

Counteractive abuse - (see above) The abusive bullying that can be unconsciously motivated by counteraction, as used originally by this author.

Depersonalization - The sense of losing one's identity or self. In psychological literature, it usually refers to a momentary psychological reaction to a specific situation. However, this author proposes that a more chronic type of depersonalization can occur in a relationship. (See relationship depersonalization)

Disenmeshment - The shifting of one's attention away from trying to manipulate a partner's thoughts, feelings, or behavior. This term was coined by this author.

Dissociation - A psychological defense in which some aspect of experience is "split" away from awareness. Example: the feeling of being in one's body can be split away so that a trauma can be experienced as if it's happening to someone else and is observed from afar. Aspects of memory can be dissociated so that a person knows something when in one emotional state but doesn't know it when they're in another state.

Dopamine - An important neurotransmitter in brain synapses. Dopamine releasing circuits are heavily involved when we initiate action or movement.

Enmeshment - The adopting of an enduring role of trying to manage the emotions of another.

Equifinality - The principle that a given behavior can be brought about by different experiential and emotional dynamics. Different childhood experiences and different emotional patterns can sometimes result in the same behavioral problems.

Fight - flight system - A known reflex system in the brain that readies a person to deal with a threat. It involves the release of powerful neurohormones and increased arousal via the sympathetic nervous system.

Hedonic - Involving the pursuit of pleasure and enjoyment.

Hedonic inhibition - The unconscious restriction of a person's pleasure seeking system by their covert inhibitory system, a term invented by the current author.

Heterocentric - A mature perspective that considers multiple dimensions and values other people. A person with a heterocentric perspective is not self-absorbed.

Higher consciousness - A positive state of mind in which a person has access to one's most mature wisdom and can think creatively.

Implicit memory - Memory that can't be consciously recalled but which can still generate emotions and trigger reflexes. Conscious or explicit memory is indexed by the hippocampus part of the brain while implicit memory is not.

Inhibitory system - A reflex system that retards certain behaviors that might otherwise be destructive. For example, a mother's stern admonition "NO!" can inhibit a small child about to run across a busy street. After sufficient training, the child may show hesitation when coming to a street corner. However, over-training or misdirected training may result in someone who inhibits certain needs for the rest of their life.

Integrity - The ability to base one's actions on an internally consistent framework of principles. However, this author is also including the ability to maintain one's separate identity, not just manage consistent behavior. Therefore, personal integrity involves attaching to one's own personal values and also maintaining one's sense of separate self.

Intimacy - A personal sharing between two people about what is experienced to be most important in their lives. They communicate their frame of meaning for their own experiences.

Introjection - The process whereby a child learns to replicate an attitude or behavior modeled by a parent. Recent studies strongly support the existence of mirror neurons in the child's brain that can replicate activation patterns in the brain of the parent being observed. It is an unconscious intuitive process that can absorb whole patterns of information called schemas. (See mirror neurons)

Level of consciousness - The level of sophistication and maturity in a person's implicit frame of meaning about what is important. It develops over a person's lifetime, can fluctuate somewhat from situation to situation, and can also be measured.

Limit - An individual's refusal to allow another to take advantage of him. Example: To say "No!" As used by this author, it is useful to distinguish between setting external limits versus feeling internal boundaries. The latter is an internal felt sense.

Metacognition - A type of cognitive process that involves very flexible decision making. Metacognition allows a person to override conditioned reflexes and habitual behavior. It involves a person observing one's own cognitions and then voluntarily modifying them. Imaging research of the brain has shown metacognition to involve activation of the upper anterior cingulate cortex and certain parts of the prefrontal cortex.

Micro-correction - A person's immediate response to a boundary intrusion by another in order to repair the damage. Coined by this author, Micro-correction is characterized by limited emotional intensity and, where possible, a request to "re-do" the interaction in a constructive way.

Mirror neurons - Neurons that activate in an observer while perceiving another person engaged in a behavior. The mirror neurons in the observer replicate some of the areas of brain activity of the person being observed. Because of these mirror neurons, the observer can empathically sense what the other person is experiencing.

Nurturance - The providing of pleasing care to another.

Paratelic - The state of being in-the-moment, not worried about the past or future. It involves enjoying the current experience for its own sake and for no other reason.

Reactance - In social psychology, the tendency for people shift their attitudes when they lose freedom. For example, coercion will often induce a person to have a more favorable attitude toward the choice that was denied. Similarly, a heavy-handed attempt to influence a person will often cause their attitude to shift in the exact opposite direction.

Reaction formation - A habitual defense of behaving a certain way so as to prove that one is NOT what one fears. For example, someone rages for fear that they will be otherwise victimized like they were as a child.

Relationship depersonalization - The frequent experience of "losing oneself" in a relationship (example: "I don't know who I am anymore"). Coined by the author, it refers to a more chronic and subtle sense of depersonalization than the acute depersonalization states described by psychiatric patients.

Relationship shame - Covert inhibition that gradually accumulates from repetitive subtle insults over the course of a relationship. Also coined by this author, relationship shame is in contrast to core shame that may be installed during a person's childhood.

Resource - In therapy, a memory that generates a sense of empowerment to a patient. The memory can be thought of as activating more advanced parts of a patient's personality. The current author proposes that such resource memories can activate important dopamine circuits in the brain leading to higher level of consciousness.

Shame - The humiliating feeling that one is not the way one should be. Some psychologists define shame as an unpleasant emotional reaction that is generated when a need is in the process of being expressed but is suddenly disrupted. The author of this work proposes that shame is the mere conscious "tip" of a much larger inhibitory system that operates to prevent certain behaviors and even reflexes. It might be described that unconscious inhibition prevents the person from thinking about engaging in a taboo behavior so that they won't have to later feel conscious shame.

Spirituality - The current author refers to "spirituality" as being essentially the same as high level of consciousness. It pertains to feeling connected to various dimensions of the world beyond one's insular self. It also pertains to feeling attached to abstract principles such as truth, beauty, generosity, creation, contribution, etc. It is not limited to mere beliefs about God or organized religion.

Telic - In reversal theory, a term describing a state in which one's attention is not focused on enjoying present experience but instead on reaching some future goal. Most work involves a telic state. Spontaneous play does not.

Temporal Integration - A person's ability to consider consequences that extend well into the future. A person with temporal integration doesn't merely react to a situation for immediate gratification or immediate relief but has foresight and behaves accordingly.

Transference - In psychoanalysis, feelings that are unconsciously generated from past memories. A current relationship may bear some resemblance to an old relationship. The resemblance may thereby trigger unconscious associations that generate powerful emotions. The person often doesn't understand the origin of their powerful feelings because they're only looking at the current relationship.

About the Author

Bryce Kaye received his B.A. in psychology from Columbia University and his M.A. and Ph.D. in psychology and personality from the University of Illinois. His earliest research was on the subject of reactance to the elimination of freedom, consistent with his career-long interest in human boundary interactions. After receiving his doctorate, he directed an outpatient alcoholism treatment program. In that position, he authored and was the principal investigator for a federal research project on how different personalities interact with alcoholism treatment. In 1984, Dr. Kaye began his private practice in Cary, North Carolina where he treated marital problems, depression, anxiety, trauma, dissociation and compulsive disorders. Over the years, he has evolved treatment methods based on principles derived from psychophysiological research.

At the time that this book is being written, Dr. Kaye owns two psychological practices. One is located in Cary, North Carolina and the other is located in the small river town of Oriental, North Carolina. In Oriental he lives on his pilothouse sailboat with his wife Helen and their two Yorkshire terriers. When he is not writing or seeing clients, he and Helen spend their time cruising the sounds and outer banks of North Carolina.